‘So Strange a Monster as a Jesuiste’

'So Strange a Monster as a Jesuiste'

The Society of Jesus in Sixteenth-Century Scotland

MICHAEL J. YELLOWLEES

To Morag, Kate and Kirsty

First published 2003
by House of Lochar

A CIP catalogue record for this book
is available from the British Library.

ISBN 1 899863 88 5

Typeset in Monotye Plantin by XL Publishing Services, Tiverton
Printed in Great Britain
by Bell & Bain Ltd, Glasgow
for House of Lochar
Isle of Colonsay, Argyll PA61 7YR

Contents

Plates

(between pages 116 and 117)

Acknowledgments

Any book inevitably involves collaboration and there are a number of people I would like to thank for their assistance. In particular, Father Thomas McCoog, SJ, the Archivist of the British Province of the Society of Jesus at Mount Street in London for his comments on the draft manuscript, for providing transcripts of entries in the Novices Register and for a preview of his published *Innes Review* article. Thanks also to Professor Michael Lynch of Edinburgh University for his advice over the past 20 years, and to Father Joseph de Cock, SJ, at the Archivum Romanum Societatis Iesu in Rome, Fathers Jack Mahoney and John Moffatt, SJ, at the Sacred Heart in Edinburgh, Dennis Deas, former head of Classics at Dalkeith High School and Conchi Saenz of Edinburgh University for their various contributions. My thanks also to Kevin Byrne and Georgina Hobhouse at House of Lochar on Colonsay for helping bring this project to fruition. Finally, as the book is essentially a synoptic overview of printed primary and secondary material I have in part relied on other historians' interpretations of events. Any misinterpretation of their work is my mistake for which I apologise to those concerned.

Abbreviations

Sources not cited here will be abbreviated in the endnotes in the following form – J.W. O'Malley, SJ, *The First Jesuits* (Cambridge, Massachusetts, 1995) [O'Malley, *The First Jesuits*]. Unless stated otherwise page numbers have been referred to.

ABSI	Archive of the British Province of the Society of Jesus, London
AHSI	Archivum Historicum Societatis Iesu
ARSI	Archivum Romanum Societatis Iesu
CRS	The Catholic Record Society
CSP Dom.	*Calender of State Papers, Domestic Series of the Reigns of Edward VI, Mary and Elizabeth* edd. R. Lemon and others (London, 1856–72)
CSP Foreign	*Calender of State Papers, Foreign Series of the Reign of Elizabeth*, edd. J. Stevenson and others (Nendeln, Liechtenstein, 1966)
CSP Rome	*Calender of State Papers relating to English Affairs, preserved principally at Rome*, ed. J.M.Rigg (London, 1916–26)
CSP Scot.	*Calender of State Papers relating to Scotland and Mary, Queen of Scots, 1547–1603*, edd. J. Bain and others (Edinburgh, 1898–1969)
CSP Spanish	*Calender of Letters and Papers preserved principally in the Archives of Simancas*, ed. A.S.M. Hume (London, 1892–9)
DHGE	*Dìctionnaire d'Histoire et de Géographie Ecclésiastique* (Paris, 1912–90)
DNB	*Dictionary of National Biography*, edd. L. Stephen and S. Lee (London, 1908–12)
HMC	Reports of the Royal Commission on Historical Manuscripts (London, 1870–)
IR	The Innes Review
MHSI	Monumenta Historica Societatis Iesu
Angliae	*Monumenta Angliae*, edd. T. M. McCoog, SJ, and L. Lukács, SJ, 3 vols., MHSI, 142, 143, 144 (Rome, 1992–2000)

RMS	*Registrum Magni Sigilli Regum Scotorum*, *The Register of the Great Seal of Scotland* edd. J.M. Thomson and others (Edinburgh, 1984)
RPC	*The Register of the Privy Council of Scotland*, edd. J.H. Burton and others (Edinburgh, 1877–)
RSS	*Registrum Secreti Sigilli Regum Scotorum*, edd. M. Livingstone and others (Edinburgh, 1908–)
SHR	The Scottish Historical Review
SHS	The Scottish History Society
SRO	The Scottish Record Office, Edinburgh

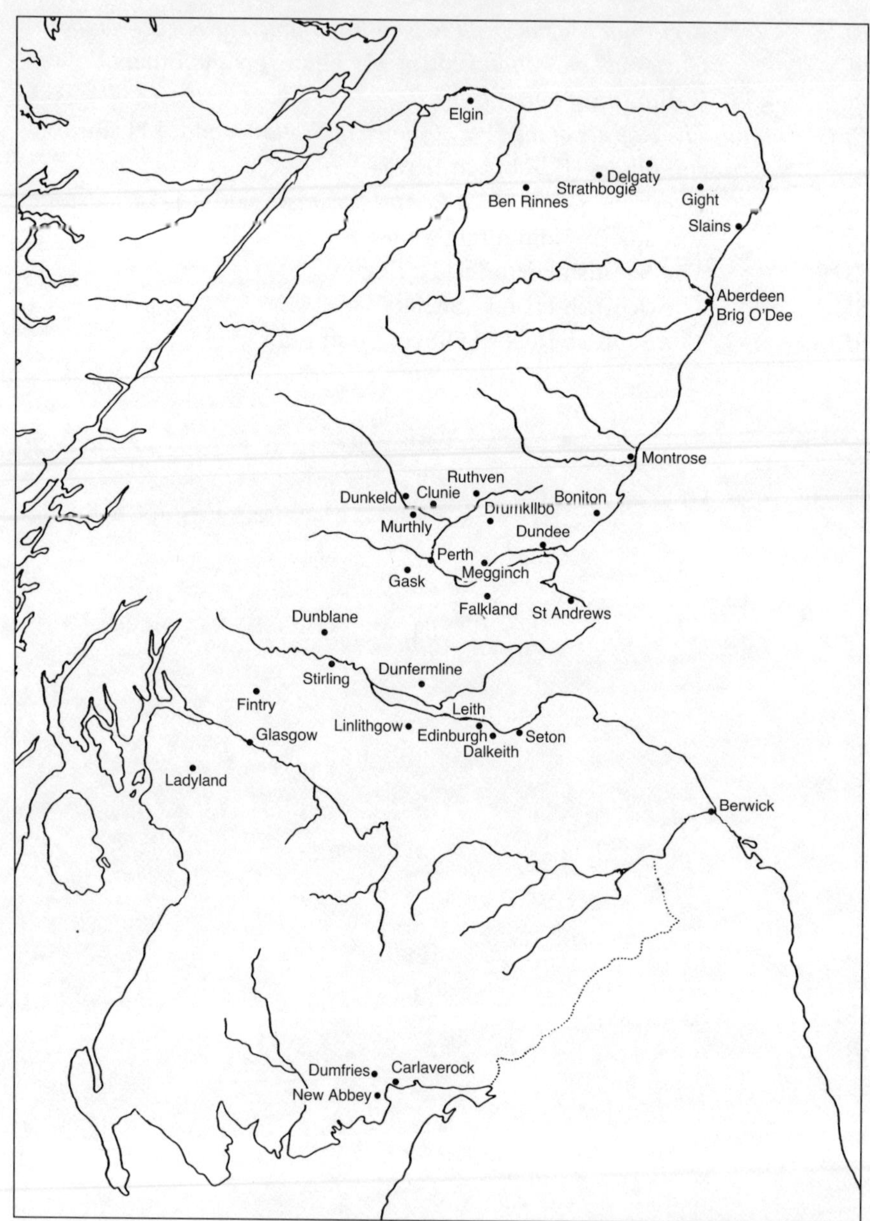

Places in Scotland associated with the early Jesuit Missions

Places in Europe associated with the early Jesuit Missions to Scotland

Introduction

Devils and Dissemblers, Saints and Savants

The English Jesuit, Francis Edwards, has suggested that a Jesuit is not the most appropriate person to comment on the the Society of Jesus. While he may be well qualified to provide an insight into Jesuit thinking and practices he may find it hard to be impartial, and may inevitably be drawn into the propaganda war waged by the Society and its opponents since the Reformation. Anti-Jesuit propaganda and the Society's response to it have been dealt with at some length in numerous works, including J.C.H. Aveling's, *The Jesuits*, Thomas Campbell's, *The Jesuits 1534–1921*, and Jean Lacouture's, *Jesuits:A Multibiography.* Aveling, a former Anglican priest turned Benedictine monk, who was converted to Catholicism by the Jesuits, gives a candid analysis of the Society and how it has been perceived by supporters and critics over the past five centuries. Campbell, whose work contains a number of factual errors amongst his comments on the Scottish Mission, gives an example of early anti-Jesuit propaganda from a Protestant history of Germany, which describes how the Jesuits apparently 'made use of mysterious and magical devices and performed a variety of weird antics and contortions in subterraneous caverns, from which they emerged haggard and worn as if they had been struggling with the demons of hell'. Lacouture refers to a 'Black Legend', which he describes as being based on 'fantasies anchored most tenuously in reality', and to the stereotypical caricature of a Jesuit: 'thin, sallow and smooth-skinned, tonsured to the bone.... Devious in manner, modest in demeanour, but sly and vain of his appearance, he went his way, from confessional to bedchamber, stage left, stage right a stiletto concealed between the pages of his prayerbook or between soutane and velvet hairshirt, all *ad majorem Dei gloriam*'. Scottish anti-Jesuit literature has included Hector MacPherson's, *The Jesuits in History,* published in 1914, in which he predicted the downfall of British society if the Jesuits were allowed to 'carry on unmolested their work of iniquity'. The old fashioned prejudices of hard-line Protestants such as MacPherson had generally died out by the start of the Second World War, though in Edinburgh during the mid-1930s John Cormack's Protestant Action Party was a prominent force in local government.[1]

In the past objectivity has rarely been evident in the works of scholars on either side of the religious divide, and Jesuit historians, were no exception. It is only recently that critical Jesuit history has been written by the likes of John O'Malley, SJ, and Thomas McCoog, SJ. The latter, in his recent history of the early British missions, refers to Hugh Trevor-Roper's two principles of Jesuit history: the principle of 'distorting background' in which compromising details are conveniently omitted and of 'unequal scholarship' in which the 'scrupulous straining at small historical gnats' diverts attention from 'the silent digestion of large and inconvenient camels'.[2] Being neither a Jesuit, nor a Catholic, hopefully does not disqualify anyone from attempting to write a history of the Society, but may in some ways be an advantage. In the absence of any expertise on theological and doctrinal issues these have generally been avoided, and instead more emphasis placed on the historical and political aspects of the early missions.

Surprisingly, considering the voluminous amount of Jesuit literature produced over the centuries, there is no single volume history of the Society in Scotland covering any period since its foundation. Scottish Jesuit history has in the main been restricted to hagiographical works on the early seventeenth-century martyr, John Ogilvie, in which the confessional predilections of the authors are all too obvious, and some more recent articles in the *Innes Review* on the early missions and a number of other individual Jesuits. Father McCoog in his recent history of the sixteenth century British missions expressed the view that despite his book there was still no concise history of the early Scottish missions. Further research by him recently published in the *Innes Review* will, in his words, 'serve as a guide to future scholars who wander into the chartless seas of sixteenth-century Scottish Jesuit history'. Likewise, this short account cannot claim to be comprehensive, but will hopefully provide some guidance for wandering scholars.[3] Father McCoog's research, based on primary sources in the Jesuit archives in Rome, and this study, drawn mainly from printed primary and secondary material, suggest that there is ample scope for more detailed study. The secondary material includes a number of accounts which form part of more general histories of the period or the introductions to volumes of primary material. These are a good starting point in trying to understand the Society's role in what has been referred to, perhaps euphemistically, as the Scottish Counter-Reformation.[4]

It is clear that the terms 'Counter-Reformation' and 'Catholic Reformation' are interpreted differently by historians of differing persuasions. In a recent study Father O'Malley has asked the question: 'What's in a name?': a great deal apparently. He suggests that a more inclusive category, which he refers to as 'Early Modern Catholicism', should be used alongside the more traditional terminology. The traditional term, Counter-Reformation, has usually suggested an aggressive and delayed reaction to the Protestant Reformation; however, another recent study by Michael Mullett, *The Catholic Reformation*, adopts the same approach as O'Malley and argues that the Councils of Trent (1545–63) continued the work of earlier reforming councils beginning with the council at Florence in 1438. In a Scottish context Jenny Wormald in *Court, Kirk and Community, 1470–1625*, also argues that the Counter-Reformation, in the form of Archbishop Hamilton's reforming councils of 1549 to 1559, predates the Protestant Reformation of 1560, while John Hungerford Pollen, SJ, in *The Counter-Reformation in Scotland*, seems in no doubt that the Catholic response to the Reformation was post-Reformation, and that it was Jesuit-inspired. The Catholic response and the role of the Society were also addressed by Donald MacLean, the professor of church history at the Free Church College in Edinburgh during the inter-war years, in his book *The Counter-Reformation in Scotland, 1560–1930*. While the book is of interest it must be treated with a certain amount of caution as it was clearly written for a Protestant readership.[5]

The absence of a history of the Society is suprising, but may be attributable to its relatively low profile in modern Scotland. Nevertheless, references to the Society crop up with surprising frequency, whether in the press, where the misdemeanours of the occasional errant Jesuit have been exposed, or at the box office where the Society has enjoyed rather more favourable exposure. Two films, based on modern novels, *Black Robe* and *The Mission*, set in North and South America respectively, have received a certain amount of critical acclaim, as did Father Ernest Ferlita's 1968 play, *The Ballad of John Ogilvie*. As well as numerous academic works there have also been a number of 'popular' studies of the Society, dealing with its history and its rôle in modern society.[6] This interest in the activities of the Society may be partly attributable to the increased public appetite for all kinds of hermetic literature, so effectively satired in Umberto Eco's novel, *Foucault's Pendulum*, in which the Society is portrayed as a secretive organisation, like the Knights Templar or the Freemasons.[7]

Contrary to what Pollen and other Jesuit historians, who have applied

Trevor-Roper's principle of 'distorting background', would have one believe the main players in the early stages of the post-1560 Counter-Reformation were not Jesuits, but monastic and secular clergy, such as Abbot Quentin Kennedy of Crossraguel, Archbishop John Hamilton of St Andrews and Bishop Robert Crichton of Dunkeld. Crichton's continued adherence to Catholicism and his encouragement of recusant activity in the immediate aftermath of the Reformation contributed to a number of his kinsmen leaving Scotland to join the Society. Research to date has suggested that there were relatively few Scottish Jesuits during the second half of the sixteenth century. However, Father McCoog's trawl through the Jesuit archives has revealed that there were considerably more than previously thought. There were in fact about fifty Scottish Jesuits during this period, some of whom are already relatively well known through their involvement in the Scottish Mission. Others do not appear in any of the accounts of the Society's activities in Scotland and spent their whole careers working on the continent, while others died or were dismissed from the Society before completing their training.

With hindsight it is easy to dismiss the early Scottish Mission as irrelevant, but there is no doubt that it had a profound effect on Scottish affairs at the time, especially during the 1580s and the 1590s, when to contemporaries the political and religious fate of the country appeared to still hang in the balance. The Kirk's reaction is an indication of the stature of the early Scottish Jesuits and of the wider reputation of the Society, though in truth it was also a reflection of the reformers' paranoia. The threat of the Jesuits, perceived or otherwise, is well illustrated in the poem, *The Winter Night* by James Anderson, the post-Reformation minister of Bendochy and Collace in north-eastern Perthshire, in which he spoke of their industry and tenacity:

> and to perform their enterprise
> They leave not off with once or twice
> But up again they mint to rise
> The Truth to stop and stay[8]

Anderson may well have known a number of the early Scottish recruits who were drawn from the area around Dunkeld where he spent the early part of his religious career as a monk of the Cistercian abbey of Coupar Angus and subsequently as a reformed church minister.[9] James Brodrick, SJ, in his classic, but partisan, account of the Society during this period, *The Progress of the Jesuits 1559–79*, states that each of these young Scottish recruits 'subsequently earned his modest niche in the temple of Catholic fame'. As well as serving on the Scottish Mission, a number of the Scottish Jesuits rose to positions of prominence within the Society or were appointed as advisers to the royal families of Scotland, France, Spain and Austria. In Scotland they exerted considerable influence over Queen Anne and to a lesser extent over her husband, James VI, whose dealings with them were largely governed by political expediency, and in particular his determination to succeed to the English throne on the death of Elizabeth. There was also a more mundane, though equally important, side to their work, the education of young boys, including the sons of the Scottish nobility and gentry. Although successful in this rôle, a number of them, including William Crichton, were clearly frustrated by college life and became involved in secular affairs which were not part of the Jesuit 'way of proceeding'. In many ways the exploits of the likes of William Crichton, Robert Abercrombie and William Murdoch are worthy of comparison with some of their more distinguished English contemporaries.[10] Crichton has, in fact, been likened to the celebrated English Jesuit, Robert Persons, who played a prominent role in the affairs of the Scottish exiles. Both were men who got their hands dirty and were touched with the sins of the world.[11] The history of the Scottish Jesuits is a story of great courage and persistence, but also one about ordinary men and their shortcomings; men who got their hands dirty.

* * *

To understand what motivated these young men to leave Scotland in the late 1550s and early 1560s to join a religious order which none of their countrymen had previously entered some general explanation of the nature of the Society may be helpful. It was not, and is still not, a monastic order, but an order of religious clerics. Jerome Nadal, the Spanish born Jesuit visitor in the early years of the Society, stated that 'we are not monks ... the world is our house'. The status of a religious order according to canon law is that of an institution following a common rule and governed by superiors whose authority is approved by the church, but which enjoys a high degree of autonomy. The members of such an institution bind themselves to it by vows of poverty, chastity and obedience. The Society is 'religious' in that its members pronounce vows and 'clerical' as many of its members are priests. It is a peculiarity of the Society, imitated in a number of other orders, that its members are not required to wear a habit or perform any choral office. The Jesuit dress code is determined by whatever is worn by priests within the area where they are working.[12] The Society's founder and first superior general, Ignatius Loyola, a Spanish nobleman and soldier turned teacher and spiritual leader, was responsible for a number of innovations which distinguished the order from others. As well as the rejection of common choral duties, i.e. the recitation or chanting in common of the liturgical hours, matins, lauds and vespers, the Society also introduced a special fourth vow of obedience to the pope, extended the period of probation for novices, centralised authority in the hands of a general and provincial superiors and instituted various other grades of membership.[13] The grades of membership, and in particular the novitiateship, are dealt with in more detail in Chapter 3. The fourth vow was the result of Loyola's belief that the surest authority for finding the will of God was through that person in the church with the most universal responsibility, a feature which, coupled with the Society's exemption from local episcopal control, created a special relationship with the Papacy unknown in earlier orders. This special status was often resented by other clerics and civic authorities, and in 1575 James Tyrie and a number of his colleagues at Clermont College were called before the professors of the University of Paris to clarify the nature of their order and their rôle at the college. The professors were apparently not satisfied with the explanation they were given and the parties remained at loggerheads for many years to come while the Catholic and Huguenot parties wrestled for control of the city.[14]

As well as obedience to the pope great emphasis was also placed on obedience throughout the whole structure of the Society as a means of creating what a number of commentators, including A. Lynn Martin, in *The Jesuit Mind: The Mentality of an Elite in Early Modern France*, have referred to as an 'apostolic community of love'.[15] In the *Constitutions* of the Society, this idea is expressed in the context of the unity of head and members: 'Since this union is produced in great part by the bond of obedience, this virtue should always be maintained in its vigor'.[16] One of the first Scottish recruits, Edmund Hay, subsequently rector at Paris and provincial of France, referred to an obedience so pure that its 'purity may bring us great consolation'.[17] Despite this emphasis on obedience the Dutchman, Nicholas de Gouda, an early member of the Society and the papal nuncio to Scotland in 1562, believed that there was 'nothing inconsistent with simple obedience in pointing out to a superior certain particulars and the exceptional circumstances of the subject matter. A superior, though he be in the place of God, cannot see all things, but God, who does see all, disposes of them sweetly by means of superiors'.[18] However, the emphasis on obedience presents an ideal rather than describes a reality, and there are many examples of this ideal not being attained. Juan de Polanco's *Chronicon Societatis Jesu*, an account of the Society from 1537 to 1556, puts paid to the myth of unquestioning obedience, and instead shows that many fathers were not prepared to be dictated to. The exemplary Jesuit was, and still is, a man who accepted that he was a member of a spiritual elite, had a strong spiritual and academic foundation, was able to teach and to preach and knew how to deal with people.[19]

The Jesuits' ministry involved preaching and catechising and there are numerous references in their correspondence to the notion of fishing for souls or gathering harvests in vineyards, which in the case of Scotland were often barren. Their style or 'way of proceeding' can be best understood against the background of the foundational documents of the Society, Loyola's *Spiritual Exercises*, the *Formula Instituti* and the *Constitutions*.[20] The *Spiritual Exercises* are a manual for spiritual advisers to lead their charges through a series of meditations and contemplations, which would be expected to lead to inner conversion, discernment regarding significant life choices and a consolation to provide the basis of lifelong commitment to Jesus: a vehicle to 'help the individual tap his inner resources for the motivation that lifelong commitment entailed'.[21] The *Formula Instituti* was the general outline of the fundamentals of the Society prepared for Pope Paul III (1534–49), which established the structure and authority of the order. The *Constitutions* laid down in more concrete form the principles by which the Society was to achieve its aims. Although the *Formula* described members of the Society as soldiers of God the military allusions have been exaggerated and comparisons with the medieval military orders of the Crusades are inappropriate. Loyola himself used the military metaphor more in the spirit of the Knights of the Round Table rather than of the Roman legionary.[22]

While the original ideals of Loyola and the first fathers are still relevant to the modern Jesuit, the ever-shrinking Society under the leadership of contrasting generals, has had to evolve to move into the Twenty first century. While it continues to play a prominent role in traditional areas, such as education and mission work, it has also become involved in modern developments, including mass communications and atomic research. One need only surf the world-wide web to see how Jesuit organisations have embraced internet technology. At the Thirty fourth General Congregation of the Society in January 1995 it was decided that one of the immediate aims of the Society should be the elaboration of the *Constitutions* and the redefinition of its identity and mission. In this statement of the Society's aims the influence of the general, Father Peter-Hans Kolvenbach, and his predecessor, Pedro Arrupe, and also the representatives of the Indian and African regions, are apparent. Although the Society has evolved and adapted, Karl Rahner, the influential German Jesuit, attributed the continuing success of the Society to its 'disinterested service' in various pastoral, ecclesiastical and socio-political spheres. Such disinterested service was described by Peter Canisius, the first Dutch Jesuit and a close friend of Nicholas de Gouda, in the following terms: 'It is a matter of complete indifference to me whether he [the general] orders me to remain here forever or sends me to Sicily, to India or to any other place. Moreover if I am sent to Sicily I simply say that I shall be delighted to fulfil any duty, as gardener, student or professor of any branch of learning whatsoever, even though it be unknown to me'. In Scotland this disinterested service continues in the fields of education and pastoral care with approximately thirty Jesuits serving as parish priests or teachers in Edinburgh, Glasgow and the Highlands and Islands.[23]

Chapter 1

The First Jesuit Mission to Ireland and Scotland

Despite early post-Reformation reports of the sighting in Edinburgh of 'so strange a monster as a Jesuiste' the existence of the Society was known of in Scotland prior to 1560, by which time there were two Scottish Jesuits, Robert Methven and Thomas Rouye.[1] Even before its official foundation as a canonically established order in 1540 by the papal bull, *Regimini militantis Ecclesiae*, information about the Society had filtered back to Scotland through various channels, probably curial officials in Rome and students in Paris, of whom there were significant numbers from the time of the unofficial foundation of the Society at Montmatre in 1534.[2]

The first Jesuits to visit Scotland arrived in 1541 *en route* to Ireland on a papal fact finding mission, organised in response to the increasing number of appeals to Rome from the Irish nobility and clergy condemning the religious settlement imposed on them by Henry VIII. One of the first appeals sent in 1534 by the vice-deputy of Ireland, Thomas Fitzgerald, 10th Earl of Kildare, had provoked little response from Pope Paul III, who could do little to prevent the Irish parliaments of the mid-1530s crushing the opposition of the spiritual peers, repealing his authority, quashing appeals to Rome and declaring Henry head of the Irish church.[3] After the failure of Kildare's rising in 1534–5, suppressed by his successor as vice-deputy, Sir William Skeffington, there were further appeals to Rome by Bishop Rory O'Donnell of Derry and Conn Bacach O'Neill, 1st Earl of Tyrone dated 31 December 1538 and 31 October 1540 respectively.[4] O'Neill's rather presumptuous pledge of loyalty on behalf of the Irish people was well received by Paul, who, in response to a further appeal from Robert Wauchope, was already organising an Irish mission by two nuncios, Jean Codure, a French Jesuit from Provence and one of Loyola's original companions, and Francesco Marsupino, a secular priest and doctor of canon and civil law from Arezzo, near Florence.[5]

Robert Wauchope, was a priest of St Andrews and a kinsman of

Cardinal David Beaton, the primate of Scotland, and although a Scot was the temporary archbishop of Armagh in north east Ireland. He has been described, rather appropriately by John Durkan, one of the leading Scottish historians of the past few decades, as 'an outstanding example of Scottish academic excellence, one of a number of ecclesiastics who gave distinguished service in the universities and in the Church abroad: a type Scotland continued to produce throughout the Counter-Reformation period. His work for reform made him in some ways the most noteworthy Scottish churchman of his time'.[6] This excellence was achieved despite being disabled by almost total blindness. Wauchope was a former prebendary of Ruffel, near Dunkeld, to which he was collated on the resignation of his elderly relative, David Wauchope.[7] As a canon of Dunkeld he became a friend of the precentor and future bishop, Robert Crichton. Wauchope was later a candidate for the vacant see of Dunkeld to which James Hamilton, 2nd Earl of Arran, procured the appointment of his brother, John Hamilton, ahead of both Wauchope and Crichton. After a long and acrimonious legal battle the latter eventually succeeded to the see in 1554.[8] Wauchope spent much of the 1520s and 1530s in Paris enjoying the patronage of James Beaton, Archbishop of Glasgow, and teaching at the University, where he was a contemporary of two notable Scottish academics, Hector Boece and William Manderston. He also spent some time in Rome before visiting Scotland in 1534, and it was on his subsequent return to Paris that he began to take an interest in the activities of the newly founded Society.[9]

In July 1539 Wauchope was unexpectedly appointed to the archbishopric of Armagh following Archbishop George Cromer's delation to Rome for heresy, or, more accurately, for conforming to the royal supremacy. The appointment was a temporary one until Cromer cleared himself of the charge, resigned or died, and may have been influenced by the English cardinal, Reginald Pole, one of Wauchope's former pupils, and by Cardinal Marcello Cervini of Santa Croce, who later became Pope Marcellus II (1555). The appointment may also have been a papal attempt to win favour with James V, who had been secretly supporting the Irish rebels since the early 1530s.[10] As well as expressing concern at the Henrician religious settlement and the plight of the Irish people Wauchope was also keen to take the opportunity to gather information about his distant charge. His unwillingness to acknowledge Henry's supremacy over the Irish church and his involvement in other papal business, coupled with his poor eyesight, meant that he had few opportunities to visit Ireland. Although it has been suggested that he never reached Armagh it would appear that he conducted a visitation in 1550, confirmation of which can be found in the report of two French envoys he met at Culmer Fort on Lough Foyle. His short campaign of Catholic revival seems to have received little support from the Irish clergy, including the royal appointee to Armagh, George Dowdall, who despite his reluctance to acknowledge Wauchope defected to Rome in the following year. At the time of his death in November 1551 Wauchope was making arrangements for a further visitation.[11]

It was indicative of the Society's growing stature that this was the first mission by one of its fathers outwith Italy. Following Marsupino's withdrawal the mission became a purely Jesuit affair and on 13 March 1540 papal faculties were issued to Codure and his new companion, Alfonso Salmerón, from Toledo in central Spain.[12] This further commitment clearly put a great strain on the Society's resources, and a few days later in a letter of introduction written on behalf of another Spanish Jesuit, Francis Xavier, Loyola apologised to his nephew Beltrán de Loyola, for being unable to write more fully as he was preoccupied with administrative matters: 'owing to the great urgency and haste with which we have been asked to send some of our men to the Indies, others to Ireland, and others to every part of Italy, it is not possible for me to write in full'.[13] In August Loyola again referred to the preparations for the Irish mission, which due to a lack of resources was delayed until the following year.[14] Redated faculties were issued to Codure and Salmerón on 24 February 1541; the delay since the issue of the original faculties being partly due to problems arising from Wauchope's other controversial appointment to the Premonstratensian abbey of Dryburgh in the Scottish borders. Although instances of papal intervention in Scottish appointments had declined Paul was keen to secure his nominee's appointment to the abbacy. Wauchope was duly appointed on 8 November 1539, the day after James had nominated his own candidate, Thomas Erskine. Protests from James in the spring of 1540 led to the reversal of this decision and Erskine's appointment in May 1541, although Wauchope continued to pursue his claim until 1544.[15]

A further delay ensued when Codure fell ill and another replacement had to be found. In fact, he never recovered and died later that summer.[16] He was replaced by another Jesuit, Paschase Broët from Picardy in northern France, who had joined the Society in 1536 along with the man he was replacing. Codure's death was a significant setback for the mission as he had been the pope's personal choice. It had been hoped that the easy going Codure would be able to control Salmerón's quick temper and haughtiness. Nevertheless, Broët was a more than adequate replacement, which was confirmed by Loyola in a letter to the Portuguese Jesuit, Simon Rodrigues, written on the eve of a later mission to Ethiopia:

> Master Salmerón is young and is still almost as boyish and beardless as you knew him ... Master Paschase [Broët] alone seems to me to have in full every requisite gift. First he is so good that we consider him in our company as an angel; secondly in addition to the learning he possesses, he is much experienced in the reform of bishoprics and convents; and, as he went to Ireland as a nuncio, none of the Society knows so much about these affairs for he is very active and very diligent ... Besides he is in person very comely and strong, and his age is little more or less than forty.[17]

On 15 May faculties were re-issued to the nuncios and confirmation sent to the Irish nobles and clergy that two Jesuits were being sent to assist them. The faculties were again renewed on 15 July, though the eventual departure of the party was further delayed until 10 September when it finally left Rome under the nominal control of Francisco Zapata, a young Spanish nobleman and aspirant to the Society. Salmerón and Broët had originally planned to finance their journey by begging, but funds were provided by Zapata, who presumably hoped that these would guarantee his subsequent entry into the Society.[18] As well as the faculties authorising the nuncios to carry out their various spiritual functions, preaching, celebrating mass and hearing confessions, they were also issued with three sets of instructions drawn up by Loyola in September 1541, including *Del modo de negociar y conversar in Domino*, 'How to deal with others in Our Lord', in which he advised the nuncios how to conduct themselves in any negotiations:

> In dealing with people and above all with equals or inferiors, speak little but listen long and willingly according to their rank. Let greetings and farewells be merry and courteous. If you speak with persons of influence consider first (to win their affection and snare them in your toils for the greater service to God) what their character is, and adopt yours to it... If a man be passionate and lively of speech, speak in the same manner avoiding grave or melancholy expressions. With those who are by nature circumspect, reticent or slow of speech, model your delivery accordingly, for this is what pleases them. With

> those who are sad or tempted, you will be affable, showing great joy to struggle against their low spirits... be all things to all men.... If for the Glory of God and the good of souls it is necessary to risk your lives you must be willing to do so, but without rashness, without tempting God.

The other instructions dealt with more mundane matters, such as the day to day conduct of the members of the party, travel and accommodation.[19]

The nuncios' itinerary included visits to the representatives of some of the main parties associated with Papal, Scottish and French attempts to destabilise the situation in Ireland. They travelled via Viterbo, to the north of Rome, where they met with Cardinal Pole, the governor of the Papal States and one of the original sponsors of the mission, who warned them of the dangers facing them. At Lyons they met with Cardinal Beaton, who after receiving a papal brief advised against the mission proceeding. He emphasised to them Henry's firm hold on the country and the uncivilised nature of the Irish: 'the wildest people in the world, barbarous and incapable of any discipline'.[20] Undaunted they proceeded on to Paris where they met with Charles Guise, Cardinal of Lorraine, whose sister, Mary of Guise, was queen of Scotland. Due to bad weather the passage from France to Scotland took longer than usual and their ship was forced to seek shelter at Canfor, in Flanders, and in two English ports, where they tied up for ten or twelve days. Their foreign appearances, their dress being 'a bit in the Roman style', and their inability to speak English aroused a certain amount of suspicion, but no-one was sufficiently interested to challenge their explanation that they were Spanish travellers.[21]

On 31 December or the following day, the party reached Edinburgh where the nuncios hoped to gather more detailed information on the situation in Ireland.[22] Much of the news coming out of Ireland was extremely pessimistic, and warnings similar to those given by Cardinal Beaton were received from Gavin Dunbar, Archbishop of Glasgow, Farquhar Farquharson, Bishop of the Isles, and Jean de Morvillier, the French ambassador in Scotland. Within a few days of arriving the nuncios were granted an audience with James, details of which were sent to Loyola on 2 February 1542.[23] Salmerón reported that the papal briefs had been delivered to the king, who promised them letters of introduction and a guide for the onward journey to Ireland. During the audience, which Zapata did not attend due to the pain from his frost bitten feet, the nuncios also delivered a letter from the Cardinal of Lorraine to his sister, the queen. According to Salmerón she showed a particular interest in the activities of the Society, including Loyola's *Spiritual Exercises,* about which she was well informed 'from three or four Scotsmen whom we [the Jesuits] had known in Rome, who had talked about our life and profession'.[24] Her informants probably included curial officials, such as John Thornton and John Greenlaw, Wauchope's chaplain, or well-travelled clerics, such as Robert Crichton, who spent a great deal of time in Rome during the 1530s and 1540s negotiating his provision to the precentorship and subsequently the bishopric of Dunkeld.[25] The nuncios left Holyrood Palace greatly encouraged by their reception, though their optimism was misplaced as they were to discover on their return from Ireland.

Following the audience in Edinburgh, Broët visited Glasgow where he had been advised there were a number of Irish merchants and students. Having failed to make contact with any of them he travelled south to the port of Irvine on the Ayrshire coast to make arrangements for the crossing to Ireland. He finally managed to meet three Irish priests *en route* to Rome, who confirmed that the resistance to Henry had collapsed during the course of the previous winter when most of the leading Irish nobles, including O'Neill and Manus O'Donnell of Tyrconnell, had submitted to the newly appointed deputy, Anthony St Leger.[26] Forewarned, but undeterred, the nuncios donned their kilts and proceeded with their mission. As James had promised they were provided with a guide, Rory Farquharson, the brother of the bishop of the Isles, and letters of introduction to the Irish nobles.[27] They left behind a number of admirers and potential recruits, including John Greenlaw, who had 'rendered us countless services in seeking out quarters for us, and in looking after us generally, and in knowing our language, since those we know are of little use to this country. He is so devoted to the service of God you would think he had found his retreat yesterday, and talks of nothing else but the Exercises'. Although he may have aspired to join the Society there is no evidence of Greenlaw ever doing so, and in fact there were to be no Scottish recruits for almost twenty years.[28]

The party arrived in Ireland, probably near Derry on Lough Foyle, on 23 February and stayed over Lent until 28 March. Details of the mission are fairly sketchy, but from the information that is available it would appear that the nuncios achieved little. In general the Irish people appear to have reluctantly accepted the Henrician religious settlement, while the climate of goodwill created by St Leger made the Irish nobles wary of meeting with the nuncios. Francis Thompson, the

Victorian biographer of Ignatius Loyola, in a somewhat melodramatic account of the mission wrote that the nuncios 'found the Irish terrified at their coming: they had to sleep under a fresh roof every night, lest they should draw discovery and punishment on those who sheltered them, and it was only by slow degrees that the cowed people took heart of grace. But the new Jesuit fervour presently warmed and animated the abandoned people: the priesthood, hunted down and decimated, in particular found courage and hope from their ministrations and exhortations'.[29] According to Broët the aim of the mission had been 'to bend our efforts to the establishment of peace among the chiefs and lords of Ireland, so that in their unity they might the more vigorously resist the king, protect themselves, and even take the offensive, if need be for the faith and the strengthening of obedience to the Apostolic See... But our eyes were opened to the fact that the disease of internal strife in this country is a hopeless thing and, in our judgment, irremediable because of age-old hatred as well as because of a savage and barbarous way of life, worse than bestial and hardly to be believed unless seen'.[30] In fact none of the leading Irish nobles were prepared to meet the nuncios and O'Neill, despite his earlier appeal to the pope, and O'Donnell went as far as to promise to betray them to the authorities if they attempted to make contact. They also had little success with the Irish bishops, twenty two of whom had already submitted to Henry.[31] The few who were prepared to oppose him, such as Arthur O'Friel, Archbishop of Tuam, and Thady Reynolds, Bishop of Kildare, were driven from their sees and forced into hiding. Many papal nominees to Irish sees were forced to submit their bulls of appointment for ratification by the crown or to accept suffragan or assistant status under royal appointees. Under such circumstances, and with a price on their heads, it is no surprise that the nuncios spent much of their visit in hiding. Loyola reported that the nuncios 'suffered not a little for the Lord', and Salmerón, with a touch of sarcasm, remarked: 'God be praised that the time of our stay in Ireland was not without its share of the cross... it was Lent and the right time for penance'.[32] While on an equally miserable mission to Poland in 1555 Salmerón recalled his trip to Ireland: 'Ever since we arrived in Poland, we have run into such conditions for sleeping and eating that I am convinced they are every bit as bad as those experienced in Ireland. The man who passes through this kingdom but once has gone through purgatory, has done penance for all his sins, and in addition has also gained a plenary indulgence. That is how tough it is'.[33] Many in Rome were sceptical about the mission, and in anticipation of the nuncios' swift return special faculties were confirmed for use in Scotland. Likewise their supporters in Scotland were pessimistic about the prospects of success and were surprised that the nuncios returned at all, having assumed that they would not meet them again until the Resurrection.

The return visit to Scotland was much briefer and the nuncios stopped off in Edinburgh for just a few days. Instructions, together with the new faculties, had been sent from Rome ordering them to prolong their stay in Scotland, but these did not arrive in time to delay their departure from Edinburgh, sometime after 9 April 1542.[34] In any case these fresh instructions were superseded by events. James's initial enthusiasm appears to have waned slightly and he did little to encourage the nuncios to stay. It was later suggested that 'owing to the new ideas spreading from England, he [Salmerón] was unable to do anything effective. So rejected, as it were, by the heat of Pluto's rage, he returned to Italy'.[35] James was certainly under pressure from Henry to encourage the spread of Protestantism and to ensure that Scotland did not become a base for English Catholics and other dissidents. The tension between the two kings developed into open conflict when James failed to attend a conference organised by Henry at York in September 1542, and his subsequent failure to unite his nobles culminated in the heavy defeat of the Scottish army at Solway Moss in November.

Somewhat unfairly James was blamed for the failure of the Irish mission and was accused of failing to give it his wholehearted support. Having found a suitable scapegoat the nuncios returned to the continent only to run into further trouble. It had originally been planned that they would return home through England, but their rather naïve proposal to seek an audience with Henry was abandoned and they returned to Italy via France. William Paget, the English ambassador in France kept Henry fully informed of the nuncios' whereabouts, and with some amusement reported the details of their arrest in Lyons on charges of spying:

> There hath lately bin in yor Majesty's land of Ireland two Freres Spainardes sent thither by the Bishop of Rome to practise with O'Donnell against your Majesty. They passed through Scotland with letters of commendation to the King of the Scots. With them was sent for that purpose the Bishop of the Isle's brother, that is Farquhard Farquhardson, which Bishop lyeth at Icolm Kille, between Scotland and Ireland. The two Spainardes and the Bishop's brother be arrived within these two days in the town on their return

> from Ireland, where, as they say, they have done no good, because the Scottish King kept not his promise. And this confession have these two Freres made to the Lieutenant of this town so here they were arrested for spies...

The nuncios were soon released following the intervention of Cardinals Niccolò Gaddi and François de Tournon and allowed to continue their journey to Rome.[36] Salmerón and Broët returned to their duties within the Society, while Zapata completed his studies in Paris and returned to the Jesuit novitiate in Rome. He subsequently fell out with Loyola and was refused entry to the Society for his criticism of Jerome Nadal, the Society's visitor.[37]

Francis Thompson has suggested that the mission was a source of inspiration for Irish Catholicism: 'The mission was seemingly a failure; but who shall say what part it may not have played in heartening the Irish to that stubborn resistance which preserved the Irish Catholicism for after-ages?'. Despite the limited success of this and subsequent missions during the sixteenth century there is little doubt that the presence of the Society contributed to what Colm Lennon has referred to as 'the ideology of Irish Catholic Nationalism', which emerged during the following century.[38] However, any accounts of Jesuit successes prior to the mid 1590s when James Archer was sent to South Leinster were largely exaggerated.[39] The increase in activity towards the end of the century and the resulting successes were partly attributable to the assistantship of a Scottish Jesuit, James Tyrie, although his period in office was followed by a spell of inactivity under the former Belgian provincial, George Duras. During the early part of the seventeenth century the Irish mission regained much of its earlier momentum and while it went from strength to strength the Scottish mission went into temporary decline. The unwillingness of the Irish superior to assist his Scottish colleagues meant they had to rely on assistance from the Franciscans, who were particularly active in the Western Isles.[40]

Chapter 2

Nicholas de Gouda's Mission of 1562

Despite the nuncios' cool reception from James V on the return leg of their Irish mission and the steady advance of Protestantism during the 1540s and 1550s relations between Scotland and the Papacy were closer than they had been for many years. However, this closer relationship did not lead to any greater understanding, and it was still the case that 'great ignorance about Scottish affairs prevailed in Rome: what was known concerned almost entirely court circles and certain parts of the lowlands; about the rest of Scotland ignorance was absolute'.[1] Relations might have been closer still had Pope Marcellus II (1555), who as a cardinal had always shown an interest in British affairs, survived in office for more than three weeks. His successor, Paul IV (1555–9) quarrelled with Mary I of England and in doing so helped pave the way for a Protestant victory under her sister, Elizabeth. Pius IV (1559–65), who reversed his predecessor's foreign policy and aligned the Papacy with Spain rather than France, believed that little could be done to reverse the situation in Scotland. He was also labouring under the misbelief that the Council of Trent, first convened in 1543 to deal with various aspects of clerical discipline and doctrine, would be able to halt the spread of Protestantism. As late as May 1560 papal instructions issued to Sebastian Gualtieri, Bishop of Viterbo and the nuncio for France, advised him that Scotland 'is not declared schismatic'. Just three months later the Reformation Parliament abolished the pope's authority and introduced the reformed Confession of Faith. Papal interest in Scottish affairs was given fresh impetus by Mary's return to Scotland in August of the following year. As a mark of his approval Pius sent her the papal honour, the Golden Rose, and in the following spring pleaded with her to send representatives to the final session of the Council of Trent. Her inability or unwillingness to do so was explained in a letter to Pius, which was read out at the Council on 10 May 1563; she also made further representations through her uncle, the Cardinal of Lorraine. By this stage Pius was much better informed about the young queen's religious and political intentions following Nicholas de Gouda's mission in the summer of the previous year.[2]

Nicholas Floris or Florissens, who adopted the name of his home town of Gouda in Flanders, was one of the earliest recruits to the Society, and only the second Dutchman to join; the first being his close friend Peter Canisius, with whom he worked for many years in various parts of Europe. The two developed a very close friendship of which Canisius wrote: 'Our Lord has united us in spirit even if in this life we must be separated in the body. May He bring us together in our blessed fatherland, where it will be plain to see how truly we are brothers'. Canisius was later to assist with the preparations for de Gouda's mission to Scotland.[3] De Gouda was born around 1515 or 1517, and despite a humble upbringing was, between 1534 and 1537, a distinguished student in the Arts faculty at Louvain University.[4] After graduation the 'Pearl of Louvain' became the curate at Bergen-op-Zoom to the north of Antwerp in North Brabant, where he was also the spiritual director of the Marquise, Jacqueline de Croy.[5] In 1545, having undertaken his Spiritual Exercises, de Gouda entered the Society at Louvain, much to the dismay of the Marquise, who begged him to return to his parish. After completing his novitiate he returned to Bergen-op-Zoom for a short time, but was soon summoned to Rome by Loyola to continue his studies. Despite de Croy's repeated appeals there was little prospect of de Gouda returning to his former parish on a permanent basis. The Society's lack of resources and manpower meant that there was a continual movement of personnel and this small parish was no longer suitable for a man of his considerable talents. Following preparations for an aborted mission to Poland de Gouda was sent to Venice to establish a new college, and while there on 25 July 1550 he pronounced his vows of profession.[6] Apart from Loyola and his first nine companions de Gouda was only the eighth recruit thereafter to make his profession. When it became clear that the college in Venice was struggling de Gouda was transferred to Ingolstadt in Bavaria, where it was reported he had 'begun his schools and given general satisfaction. He made a great name for himself in public disputation showing that he was adept in philosophy as well as theology'.[7] After a spell in Vienna with Canisius they were both transferred to Ratisbon (Regensburg) in Bavaria, where Canisius was involved in the proceedings of the Reichstag.[8] They continued working together at the Diet of Worms in 1557 where de Gouda played an important rôle as an *adjunctus* or advisory theologian.[9] Despite poor health he was involved in a series of rigorous debates with a number of leading Protestant reformers, including Philip Mélanchthon, Johannes Brenz and Johannes Pistorius. Not suprisingly his duties at the Diet did have an adverse affect on his health and there was a fear he might never be fit enough again for public lecturing.[10] Nevertheless, he appeared to make a quick recovery and in the following year set out for Rome with Canisius to attend the First General Congregation of the Society. His recovery was short lived and *en route* to Rome he fell ill and was sent back to Bergen-op-Zoom to recuperate. Although plagued by ill-health he achieved a number of further minor successes, including the compilation of a report to the Bishop of Liège in Cologne on the standard of his clergy, before being sent to Scotland.[11]

Despite these successes it was felt by many that de Gouda was not a suitable choice of nuncio for the mission to Scotland. However, Salmerón, the acting general in the absence of Diego Laínez, who was in France attending the Colloquy of Poissy, was under pressure from Pius IV to find a suitable candidate. The Society's resources were so stretched that no one else was available to undertake the mission, and when advising de Gouda of his appointment Salmerón was at pains to stress that there were less than three hundred Jesuit fathers in Rome, all of whom were otherwise engaged. As a veteran of the first Jesuit mission twenty years earlier Salmerón was fully aware of the dangers involved and must have known that de Gouda might not be up to the task. In his defence he may have been unaware that de Gouda was still poorly as he had been advised by Adriann Adriaenssens, the rector of Louvain, that the Dutchman had started preaching again.[12] On 3 December 1561 Pius wrote to Mary offering assistance and advising that a papal brief was to be conveyed to her by de Gouda, 'a man whom we very highly esteem'.[13] A fortnight later formal briefs were issued instructing him to make the necessary preparations.[14] Financial assistance to the tune of two hundred scudi was to be made available, together with the services of a lay brother to accompany him on the mission, which it was thought would last two or three months. At the same time Salmerón wrote to Everard Mercurian, the Belgian provincial for Lower Germany, instructing him to make the necessary arrangements for the mission, and enclosing the papal brief to be delivered by de Gouda. Salmerón was keen to make sure that a suitable travelling companion was found as he admitted that no one in Rome had much knowledge of Scotland. The only two Scottish recruits at this time, Robert Methven and Thomas Rouye, had been sent to Padua and Vienna respectively and were presumably not consulted. In case the grant of two hundred scudi never reached the nuncio bills of exchange were also provided and further funds were to be sent from Rome to Cologne. Salmerón stressed that de Gouda's mission was to take priority over any other current business, and Mercurian's subsequent failure to ensure this earned him a sharp reprimand.[15]

Despite the preparations being relatively well advanced concern was still being expressed in a number of quarters about de Gouda's appointment, not only on account of his failing health, but also his inability to speak French. Laínez expressed amazement at the appointment and made his views on the matter very clear. As well as de Gouda's poor health and his linguistic shortcomings it was also felt that he was politically naïve, being 'a person wholly given to spiritual matters and not the man to find out accurately the state of the country'.[16] It was suggested that de Gouda should be accompanied by Ponce Cogordan, the Society's hard-nosed procurator, who was an excellent linguist. Unfortunately Cogordan was also rather elderly and in poor health, and therefore an equally inappropriate choice.[17] A more suitable candidate might have been Mercurian himself, who as well as being younger and more politically astute, could speak French. However, in some respects de Gouda, despite his shortcomings, was not such a poor choice. There was little likelihood of him being viewed as a political appointment, and as a student of Louvain and curate of Bergen-op-Zoom he would have come into contact with Scottish students and merchants from whom he may have gleaned some understanding of the country and the people. As a result of Bergen-op-Zoom's trading links with Scotland the town's church had an altar dedicated to Saint Ninian, which was patronised by the Scottish community until the middle of the sixteenth century.[18]

In late March de Gouda received a letter from Mercurian instructing him to go to Louvain, where he would be given a further letter from Salmerón, the papal brief and a letter from Marcantonio, Cardinal Da Mula, instructing him to go to Scotland. It is clear from correspondence at the time that Mercurian was still having problems with the organisation of the mission, and, as had been predicted by Giovanni Francesco, Cardinal Commendone, Bishop of Zante and the papal nuncio in Germany, was struggling to find a ship prepared to sail north before Easter. By May the preparations had ground to a halt and Salmerón wrote to Mercurian and de Gouda to express his frustration. He had been waiting for news of the success of the mission and was annoyed instead to hear of the delayed departure. He complained to Mercurian that this 'caused us no little vexation and astonishment at the negligence' shown.[19] Mercurian's excuse that he had been waiting over two months for instructions was not well received. As correspondence continually went astray he was told he should have sent further letters to Rome. Salmerón also expressed his dissatisfaction to de Gouda and instructed him that if the situation in Scotland was too dangerous and he was unable to meet the queen he should simply prepare a short report for the pope. Salmerón was, nevertheless, confident that the nuncio would be able to obtain access to her. Mercurian and de Gouda were told to speed up the arrangements, which Salmerón expected to be completed within a month. Suitably chastised, Mercurian and de Gouda got on with the preparations, the latter turning to his old friend Canisius for advice and assistance. Canisius also provided hospitality at Augsburg for a number of the Scottish party while *en route* to Louvain.[20] In early June de Gouda was able to confirm that the preparations were complete, and shortly afterwards the party, accompanied part of the way by Mercurian, set off for Zeeland to embark for Scotland. Even at this late stage there were rumblings of discontent. De Gouda, still smarting from his reprimand, complained that the preparations would have been completed earlier if Mercurian had received speedier responses to his letters to Rome.[21] Despite his imminent departure there were still lingering doubts about his appointment, but Francis Borgia's confirmation of the papal brief appointing Mercurian in place de Gouda was received too late to be implemented. The accompanying letter from Pius to Mercurian, his 'beloved son', in which the pope accepted that de Gouda's ill-health had delayed the mission, was clearly an attempt to placate the irate provincial.[22]

After a further delay in Zeeland, due to the lack of ships sailing north, the party finally received news that berths were available on a ship already making its way down the River Scheldt to join the Scottish fleet. The passage appears to have been stormy, but otherwise uneventful, and the party arrived at the port of Leith to the north of Edinburgh on 18 June, eight days after embarking. De Gouda was accompanied by Jean Rivat, a little known French Jesuit, and a young Scotsman, Edmund Hay. Another young Scot, William Crichton, was already in Scotland sorting out his personal affairs before joining the Society. Fifty years after the mission Crichton wrote his *Memoirs on the Mission of Father de Gouda in 1562* for Father Sacchini's *Historia Societatis Jesu*, in which he claimed that he and Hay had already been admitted to the Society prior to de Gouda's departure. Contemporary letters by de Gouda and Adriaenssens state that the two young men had merely resolved to join the Society, which was corroborated by a further letter by de Gouda written in December 1562 in the aftermath of the mission, stating that Hay and Crichton were on their way to Rome to join the Society. It would appear therefore that prior to the mission the young mens' applications to join the Society had been accepted with a view to them commencing their studies on their return from Scotland.[23]

It is clear that both the young Scots had impressed the Society, and Adriaenssens in a letter written shortly after de Gouda's was full of praise. Hay was described as a Scottish priest and 'a trustworthy, learned person, twenty eight years of age, son of a confessor [of the faith]. He and another distinguished young gentleman, also the son of a confessor, had resolved to go to Rome next September, if God so disposed, and to join the Society. While both of these cousins are well educated, the former [Edmund Hay] is unusually eloquent, prudent and amiable and has a noble bearing. The latter [William Crichton] left for Scotland a short while ago to put his affairs there in order. I am much delighted to think that Father de Gouda will have such friends in Scotland. Both of them have acquaintances in the queen's court and have spoken with her and others'.[24] Hay was not originally selected for the mission, but had approached de Gouda in Louvain, where the nuncio had been summoned for a meeting with Mercurian. Although his colleagues may have been concerned about the outcome of the mission de Gouda's confidence was boosted by 'a wonderful increase in my strength, beyond what I or any other expected', partly brought on by the arrival of Hay, whom he likened to the 'angel Raphael'. It is clear that the involvement of Hay and Crichton was crucial to the success of the mission.[25]

Hay is variously described as a priest or a friar, but it is not clear when he took holy orders. He left St Andrews University in the mid 1550s and was probably ordained during the intervening period. As well as returning to Scotland to assist de Gouda and wind up his private affairs he also had an ulterior motive. Henry Foley, SJ, the meticulous chronicler of the English province of the Society, quoting a Jesuit account of Hay's recruitment of James Tyrie of Drumkilbo describes how Tyrie had from an early age resolved to join a religious order dedicated to reconverting Scotland to Catholicism.[26] A local priest, perhaps his kinsman Sir James Tyrie, the vicar of Megginch, encouraged him to apply himself to his studies; advice which he appears to have heeded as by the 'beginning of defectione [he] was a young man verie weil lettired, and learned'.[27] Father Tyrie's later career is dealt with in more detail in subsequent chapters, but it is worth noting at this stage that, unlike most of his contemporaries, he never returned to Scotland. Crichton may have spent some time in Rome acting as a procurator at the papal court on behalf of a number of Scottish litigants, including a kinsman Alexander Crichton, later dean of Dunkeld. In November 1561 he was in Louvain and in the following year was in Rome assisting with the preparations for the mission.[28]

On disembarking at Leith de Gouda and his companions were taken to the house of a kinswoman of Edmund Hay, where, on the same day, they were met by Crichton and Stephen Wilson, a royal servant who, according to Crichton, recognised de Gouda from a previous meeting in Louvain. Wilson was well travelled on the continent and may possibly have been a graduate of Louvain University. He was also a former treasurer of Dunkeld and an accumulator of benefices, who attracted controversy throughout his long career.[29] Shortly after arriving de Gouda sent a message to Mary via Wilson requesting an audience. He had to wait a month for a reply, but was able to spend this time recuperating from a number of minor injuries sustained during the course of the passage. Most of the time had to be spent in hiding as his arrival in Scotland was soon common knowledge. Wilson, whom de Gouda referred to as 'Crichton's imprudent friend', was partly to blame, having disclosed details of the nuncio's arrival to friends, who were presumably equally indiscreet. Information may also have been passed on by the crew of their ship, but on the whole they seem to have been generally disinterested in the identity of their passengers.[30]

As with other Jesuit missions to Britain details were quickly passed to the English authorities by their agents in Edinburgh and Rome. In Scotland news of de Gouda's arrival spread quickly. In the days leading up to the fourth General Assembly of the Kirk in late June and early July public resentment against the nuncio increased, inflamed to a certain extent by the news of the Massacre of Vassy and the renewal of the Wars of Religion in France. De Gouda noted that his arrival was 'bruiked all over the kingdom throwing the heretics and the congregation into confusion and indignation' and that he himself was denounced as an 'emissary of Satan, and a nuncio of Baal and Beelzebub'.[31] John Knox, who was amongst those alarmed by his arrival, warned that the recovery of Catholicism posed a serious threat to the stability of the country as 'yf the Papists think to triumphe whair thai may, and to what thai list, whair thair is not a partie able to resist thame, that some will think, the godlie mon begyn whair thai left'.[32] In some respects his fears were not unfounded, given the lack of popular support for the Kirk and its failure to establish a truly national church during the early stages of the Reformation.

In response to the Protestant reaction to his arrival de Gouda was removed for his own safety to the Hay family seat at Megginch, near Dundee, where he remained in hiding for almost two months. English intelligence reported that he had passed through Dundee accompanied by a Scottish friar 'that had lefte his frocke in Lovane'. This was presumably Hay, but it is by no means clear as Crichton in his *Memoirs* states that Hay returned to Megginch due to threats against him and entrusted de Gouda to his care. De Gouda's account is slightly different: 'he [Hay] remained with me all the time I was there [in Scotland]'.[33] In late July Thomas Randolph, the English ambassador in Edinburgh, reported to Cecil that de Gouda was still lying low: 'he keapte himself quiet for a tyme, as thoughe ether lyttle accompte had byne made of hym, or that the wonder of any so strange a monster as a Jesuiste to be seen in Scotland myght be blowne over'. English intelligence also confirmed that de Gouda was a guest of Peter Hay at Megginch, but until the audience with Mary had actually taken place the English appear to have remained unaware of the purpose of the mission. Strangely, in another report of May 1565 by Randolph to Cecil concerning a later mission by William Chisholm, Bishop of Dunblane, the ambassador seems to have forgotten his earlier comments and advised that Chisholm had 'brought from Louvain a holy man of the Jesuit's order, the first that ever in Scotland durst show his face'.[34]

When Hay finally managed to arrange an audience with Mary, following her return to Edinburgh after summering in Dunfermline and Stirling, de Gouda was accompanied to the capital by an armed escort. The queen had proposed sending George, 5th Lord Seton to accompany him, but it may have been decided that he was too prominent a chaperone and that his absence from court would have attracted unneccessary attention. De Gouda was secretly escorted across the Firth of Forth by William Livingston, the laird of Kilsyth, a friend of Mary, who was later involved in the murder of her Italian secretary, David Riccio.[35] He was then escorted to Edinburgh where he was met at the city wall and guided across adjoining fields and then along the wall to the house of the queen's almoner, Archibald Crawford, parson of Eaglesham and vicar of Kilmarnock.[36] On Friday 24 July de Gouda was smuggled into the palace while the queen's Protestant servants were attending midweek sermons. Despite this diversion it was still thought necessary for a number of other royal servants to keep a look out, and it has been suggested that one of the four Maries, the queen's ladies in waiting, kept watch outside her chamber along with Hay and

Rivat. De Gouda initially met with Mary alone, but when it became clear that her Latin and his French were inadequate Hay and Rivat were asked to join them to act as interpreters. The rest of the audience was conducted in Scots between Mary and Hay, who translated for the two foreigners.[37]

The three main issues discussed were Mary's response to the papal brief, the delivery of further briefs to the Scottish bishops and the preservation of Catholicism in Scotland. In response to the papal brief Mary asked de Gouda to assure Pius of her loyalty to Rome and to explain to him the pressure she was under from her Protestant advisers and clergy. In his report de Gouda was naïvely uncritical of Mary and totally sympathetic to her plight, whereas a more astute observer might have been able to distinguish between her political pragmatism and personal attachment to Catholicism. De Gouda had no misgivings about her assurances of loyalty and appears to have been unaware of her rôle in the establishment of the Kirk, including her acceptance of the financial system known as the Thirds of Benefices, whereby the crown was given one third of the revenues of all church benefices to pay the stipends of the clergy and augment its own finances.[38] Cecil on the other hand was fully aware of Mary's vested interest in the Reformation, though he was incorrect in believing that she was 'no more devout towards Rome than for the contentation of her uncles'.[39] The delicate political balance which Mary was forced to maintain meant that many of her actions appear inconsistent with a strong attachment to Catholicism.[40]

Mary doubted that the Scottish bishops would agree to send a representative to the Council of Trent, but despite her pessimism it would be incorrect to suggest that they would have been unable to get permission to travel abroad. James Beaton, Archbishop of Glasgow, had been in Paris since July 1560, while in 1563 Henry Sinclair, Bishop of Ross and Lord President of the Court of Session, was permitted to go abroad on health grounds. He died in Paris a few years later following a lithotomy. De Gouda seems to have failed to appreciate that their problem was not obtaining permission to leave Scotland but their position on returning. To help de Gouda Mary agreed to have the papal briefs issued to the bishops rather than summoning them to Edinburgh or having the nuncio deliver them in person. She also agreed to organise a meeting with her Protestant half-brother, Lord James Stewart, which not surprisingly never took place.[41]

The audience with Mary appears to have come to a premature end when Lord James and the queen's Protestant retainers returned from church. De Gouda was whisked away, although he was spotted by Thomas Randolph, who reported to Cecil: 'As I myself stondinge that daye with the L. of Lidington [Lethington] sawe so straynge a visage that he semed to be the self same man that before I did here subscribed'. Although de Gouda had been spotted Randolph assured Cecil that the queen was discreet and able to keep her own counsel. His letter also suggests that he was confident that she would not prejudice her political position by trying to strengthen links with Rome. As the audience had ended prematurely a further meeting may have been arranged, though de Gouda gives no account of this, and it is only implied in his report that there was a second audience. After the first audience Mary's secretary was sent to de Gouda to deal with two outstanding points: firstly how to strengthen her attachment to the Catholic faith and secondly clarification of the pope's attitude towards her. The queen's secretary had a further meeting with de Gouda at which he confirmed that Mary would have the papal briefs delivered to the bishops, in response to which the nuncio asked that she confirm this in writing in her reply to Pius. Having confirmed she was prepared to do this Mary 'gave' de Gouda her letter to the pope to read unsealed, hence the suggestion of a second audience. The letter was checked by Hay and Rivat before being signed and sealed by Mary. What is not clear is whether this business was conducted at a further audience or whether the letter was conveyed backwards and forwards by the queen's secretary, though de Gouda's report suggests the former.[42]

Although Mary arranged for the distribution of the papal briefs de Gouda was still keen to contact the bishops personally. Predictably the majority were unwilling to communicate with him, and despite the fact that he had identified only two as heretics their response to the papal briefs was lukewarm. Henry Sinclair, as well as being unwilling to attend the Council of Trent, was reluctant to compromise his judicial position, despite being summoned by Mary to meet de Gouda. He advised the queen that under no circumstances would he meet him as by doing so he would expose himself and his family to great danger. No response was received to further pleas by de Gouda, sent via Adam Forman, the Carthusian prior of Perth, who was in Edinburgh at the time petitioning Mary for the restoration of part of the goods of his monastery. William Chisholm, senior, Bishop of Dunblane since 1526, had indicated that he would be prepared to meet de Gouda in Dunblane, but subsequently refused to do so when the nuncio arrived on his doorstep. De Gouda was more impressed by Chisholm's nephew, William Chisholm junior, who as co-adjutator of Dunblane since 1561 was to succeed his uncle as bishop.[43] He was 'a man of mark both in public speech and in private exhortation', and although keen to join the Society was never accepted as it was felt his talents could be used more profitably elsewhere. Polanco in a letter to Adriaenssens expressed the view that 'the Church of God has so much need in our days of good pastors like him, that it does not seem as though it would be pleasing to the Divine Majesty that he should hide himself in religion, like a 'light placed under a bushel'. However strongly the love of poverty and humility may influence him, he should also remember that he is wedded to his Church, and that such a spiritual marriage cannot be dissolved unless there be some great impediments which do not allow him to do his office'. Polanco, or the general, then wrote to Chisholm advising him that his entry to the Society was dependent upon the pope, to whom he should write explaining why he was unable to exercise his episcopal function. Despite being refused entry Chisholm was to remain a supporter of the Society and on a number of occasions called upon the services of its members.[44] After his return to Flanders de Gouda received a reply from William Gordon, Bishop of Aberdeen, the uncle of a future Jesuit, James Gordon, who complained of persecution by the Protestants. Despite his powerful Catholic kinsmen, Gordon, like the majority of his colleagues, did little to further the interests of the Catholic church. The fact that he remained in office until 1577, by which stage most of the other pre-Reformation bishops were dead, in exile or had been removed from office, is perhaps an indication of where his loyalties lay.

Robert Crichton of Dunkeld was the only bishop prepared to meet the nuncio, and sometime between the end of July and early September de Gouda was taken from Megginch to Dunkeld. Crichton was the youngest son of Sir Patrick Crichton of Cranston Riddel and the nephew of George Crichton, Bishop of Dunkeld from 1516 to 1544. After graduating from St Andrews he was appointed provost of St Giles in Edinburgh and in 1530 became precentor of Dunkeld under his uncle. He spent a considerable amount of time in Rome furthering his claim to the bishopric and was well known at the papal court, where he was a personal acquaintance of Pius his 'great friend and protector… when he was pursuing his business in Rome'.[45] Pius, as Giovanni Angelo Medici, was bishop of Ragusa and subsequently a cardinal during the 1540s when Crichton had been in Rome. Crichton's protracted legal battle with John Hamilton, Abbot of Paisley, was finally settled when Hamilton was appointed to St Andrews. Hamilton's bastard brother, Arran put forward another candidate, Donald

Campbell, Abbot of Coupar Angus, and the dispute rumbled on until 1554, during which time Crichton continued to lobby the College of Cardinals in Rome and Mary of Guise's brother, the Cardinal of Lorraine. Despite complaints by the Estates of Scotland to the pope and the College about Crichton's conduct he was finally appointed to the bishopric and made his first appearance in parliament in 1554. Some doubt has been expressed about Crichton's continued Catholicism, and although he attended the Reformation Parliament in 1560 he was no supporter of Protestant reform. During the course of the parliament his cathedral was sacked by two local Protestants, the lairds of Kinvaid and Arntilly, on the orders of the Lords of the Congregation.[46] According to Thomas Randolph, Crichton remained 'as obstinat as ignorant' and refused to listen to John Knox, whom he dismissed as an 'olde condemned heriticke'.[47] Crichton, who was one of the less disreputable bishops of the period, was sarcastically referred to by Knox as one of the 'chief pillars of the Papistical Kirk'.[48] Although he refused to sign the Confession of Faith, he was reluctant to prejudice his position by rejecting it outright; Randolph reported that 'as he would not utterly condemn it so was he loath to give his consent hitherto'. Along with his former rival John Hamilton of St Andrews and William Chisholm, senior, of Dunblane, 'they did liberally profes, that they wold aggre to all thing myght stand with Godes Word, and consent to abolish all abuses crept in in the Churche not agreable with the Scriptures'. In August 1560 he survived an attempt to stay his living and in the following year joined Mary's household on her return to Scotland. However, he was very unpopular in Edinburgh where he was scared to show his face in public 'for fear of afterclaps'.[49]

Although Crichton enjoyed the support of the local Catholic magnate, John Stewart, 4th Earl of Atholl, the meeting with de Gouda was held under strict security at the bishop's palace on an island on Loch Clunie to the east of Dunkeld, described in Alexander Myln's *Lives of the Bishops* as 'the key to the see'.[50] His household at Clunie included a significant number of Catholic clergymen and laymen, who together with a number of the leading figures in the chapter and the majority of the chaplains of the choir, were involved in recusant activity throughout the 1560s.[51] Crichton's concern is indicative of the tenuousness of his position, which, despite constant pressure from the Kirk and Lord James Stewart, he managed to maintain until 1571, when he was convicted of treason, deprived of his bishopric and forfeited. In his account of the meeting de Gouda reported that:

> Among all the bishops, the last named [Robert Crichton] was the only one who dared to admit me to speak to him, and this only on the condition that I should pass myself off as a certain banker's clerk, come to request payment of a debt. This was to prevent even his servants finding out who I was, yet he now resides in a certain island, at a considerable distance from others. He entertained me at dinner, but on condition that we talked of nothing except money matters all dinner time. Your reverence will be at no loss to gather from these particulars how little could be done for the cause of religion by negotiation with these good men. So much then for the bishops.[52]

Despite being written many years after the event Crichton's recollection of events is similar, though he does add a number of further details:

> But amongst all the bishops there was none who dared give him [de Gouda] audience excepting only one, of the name of Crichton, Bishop of Dunkeld, who had retired to a residence of his on an island in a lake. Father Crichton went there to persuade him to receive the apostolic nuncio, but could not obtain more than leave to bring him as the clerk of an Italian banker, to whom the bishop owed money, and so he did. When the father gave him the brief in his chamber, the poor bishop shed so many tears, and Father de Gouda no less, at the thought of the miserable state of religion in the kingdom of Scotland, that for a while they could not say a word to one another. The father consoled the unhappy bishop, who wrote an answer to the Pope.[53]

De Gouda's view that the collapse of Catholicism was principally due to the failings of the hierarchy is slightly harsh given that there was also evidence of episcopal reforms having been carried out in accordance with the edicts of the Council of Trent. There is little doubt that the continuing pluralism and nepotism of the Scottish clerical dynasties such as the Crichtons, Chisholms and Beatons, undermined the effectiveness of these reforms and the reputation of the Catholic church. Ironically it was these same dynastic clerical families who were the most loyal to Rome, though a cynic might suggest that self interest was an important factor. De Gouda was also concerned that the queen's advisers were mostly Protestants, the inevitable consequence of many Catholic nobles choosing not to attend court. In their absence the likes of Lord James Stewart and William Maitland of Lethington were able to wield considerable influence. In an attempt to bolster their confidence papal briefs were sent to a number of unnamed Catholic nobles, two of whom were probably Seton and Atholl. The latter, along with his kinsman Robert Crichton, certainly received briefs in 1564.[54]

On the state of the religious houses de Gouda reported that; 'The monasteries are nearly all dissolved; some completely destroyed, churches and altars are overthrown; all things holy profaned; the images of Christ and of the saints are broken and cast down'.[55] His evidence was drawn from a number of first hand accounts and from his visit to Dunblane where he was able to witness the destruction for himself. Bishop Crichton would have made him aware of the looting of Dunkeld Cathedral by the lairds of Arntilly and Kinvaid who were instructed 'to tak down the haill images thereof and bring furth to the kyrk-zayrd and burn thaym oppinly. And siclyk cast down the altaris and purge the kyrk of all kynds of monuments of idolatrye'.[56] He also met with Adam Forman, the Carthusian prior of Perth, who, following the looting of his priory, had 'retired with his bretheren to Errol', near Megginch.[57] The Cistercian abbey of Coupar Angus was likewise subject to the 'insults of many lay magnates and their inferiors', who were also responsible for the pilfering of other religious institutions within the area.[58] While de Gouda's assessment of the state of the religious houses may have been based on fairly limited evidence, the basis of his argument has been confirmed by modern research: 'The evidence for the looting and purging of churches during 1559 and in subsequent years is beyond doubt, and the evidence, during the ensuing decades, for the widespread dismantling of monastic, collegiate, and even parish churches, which had also been made redundant in whole or in part, is also indisputable'. While the case against the reformers is strong there is also ample evidence to suggest that many churches had been allowed to fall into a state of disrepair. The last provincial council in 1559 had decreed that all ruinous churches be repaired or rebuilt, while a contemporary tract, *The Lamentatioun of Lady Scotland*, spoke of churches filled with 'Fedders, Fylth, and Doung'.[59]

De Gouda was also highly critical of the Protestant clergy, dismissing them as 'apostate monks or laymen of low rank... quite unlearned, being tailors, shoemakers, tanners, or the like'.[60] This observation was clearly inaccurate as it has been shown that in all parts of the country the Kirk relied heavily on large numbers of pre-Reformation clergymen to serve in its churches. A number, such as David Fergusson, minister of Dunfermline and Rosyth, a self educated skinner, and Andrew Simpson, minister of Cargill and a former schoolmaster in Perth, were originally laymen, but many more were former canons, monks, friars or priests, often serving in religious houses in or near to the parishes in which they subsequently ministered. Despite his moderating influence particular criticism was reserved for John Winram, the sub-prior of St Andrews, who was appointed superintendent of Fife with responsibility for visiting churches and examining the clergy. De Gouda was especially critical of his breach of the vow of celibacy and his marriage to a merry widow at the ripe old age of seventy.[61]

Alphons Bellesheim in his *History of the Catholic Church of Scotland* described de Gouda's report as 'the narrative of a clear-sighted eye-witness, and as throwing a new and valuable light upon the condition of the faithful Scottish Catholics groaning under the intolerable yoke of the Congregation'. The able, but inexperienced, Edmund Hay agreed with de Gouda's evaluation of the situation, which he believed accurately reflected 'the miseries with which Scotland is afflicted (the particulars of which he has collected with great diligence, and recorded with great accuracy), as well as the causes which produced these evils, and the best way of remedying them'. However, although honest and well intentioned, de Gouda's report displays a great deal of naïvety and over-simplification. A number of his suggested solutions were unrealistic, and a more astute diplomat would have quickly realised that there was little prospect of Mary's advisers sanctioning a Catholic marraige or a Spanish alliance.[62]

Despite his pessimistic report to Laínez de Gouda's mission was not a complete failure. When he left Scotland on 3 September, apparently disguised as a sailor, he was accompanied by William Crichton, Ninian Winzet, the Catholic controversialist, and René Benoist, Mary's chaplain. It was hoped that Winzet would join the Society, but despite being offered the opportunity he showed little interest in following his companions to Rome. De Gouda was hopeful he would be offered a place at the German College in Rome even though he could not afford to fund his own education.[63] Despite these plans for his future Winzet was still in Flanders in September of the following year, where he published his *Buke of Four Scoir Thre Questiouns* and a translation of Lirinesis' *Antiquity and Truth of the Catholic Faith*.[64] He subsequently studied at Paris University, funded by a pension from Mary, and at Douai, along with two future Scottish Jesuits, George and John Durie. After Mary's flight to England he was part of her household until it was reduced in size on the orders of the authorities, at which stage he joined Bishop John Leslie of Ross in London before retiring to France. Following his graduation from Douai he was appointed abbot of the reconstituted Scots monastery of St James at Ratisbon where he remained until his death in 1592. Hay returned to Flanders soon after de Gouda with Robert Abercrombie, William Murdoch, James Tyrie and John Hay. One account suggests that James Gordon, fifth son of George, 4th Earl of Huntly, was also 'won' to the order by Hay and Crichton, but it is unclear whether he left Scotland with either group, or later in the year following his family's defeat by Lord James Stewart at the Battle of Corrichie, near Aberdeen, on 28 October 1562. The fact that he is not mentioned in either account of the mission suggests he made his own way to Louvain.[65]

On arriving in Flanders on 13 September de Gouda hurried from Antwerp to Louvain to report to Mercurian, but had to travel on to Cologne and then to Mainz before he finally tracked him down. Mercurian and Jerome Nadal assured the tired and dejected nuncio that he had acquitted himself well and ordered him to return to Louvain to recuperate. De Gouda was reluctant to do so and felt he should go to Rome in person to report to the pope, though he did concede that his younger companions, Hay and Crichton, could perform this task equally well.[66] The two young men, together with a number of travelling companions, made their way to Rome, via Trent, where they met with Laínez, who was acting as a papal theologian at the Council. Their onward journey was facilitated by letters patent from Polanco, which ensured hospitality at Jesuit houses *en route*. The Scottish mission really marked the peak of de Gouda's career, although he did achieve some further minor successes as a preacher in Rotterdam, Delft and Gouda. At Louvain he organised a theology course for secular clergy, which appears to have been well received: 'sa science aussi bien que sa vertu, sa chaude éloquence et son experiénce des âmes, son tact et son affabilité lui gagnaient le couer et l'espirit de ses élèves'. However, his health continued to deteriorate and he died of tuberculosis in November 1565.[67]

The young Scots who arrived in Flanders were well known to each other. John Durkan in his accounts of the early Jesuit missions in the *Innes Review* and *Scottish Tradition* refers to a Perthshire connection involving a number of the new recruits and suggests that at least one of them emerged from what could be termed as 'the Crichton circle'. In fact the majority of the young men were connected in some other way, and at least four of those involved can be shown to have had links with Robert Crichton.[68] Most lived in the diocese of Dunkeld in parishes lying within a twenty mile radius of the cathedral and came from a similar social background. Although a number are described in Jesuit reports as being of noble birth the majority of them were gentry, with only James Gordon coming from a first ranking noble family. In a later dispute between Crichton and John Cecil, an English secular priest and double agent, Cecil mocked Crichton's attempts to prove his pedigree: 'the highlandmen and borderers of which gauge I rather take you to be, M. William, than to have for your chief that noble and worthy gentleman, the L. of Sanker [Sanquair], as you would have the world believe abroad, to whom (as I am credibly informed) you are as near a kin as Paul's steeple to Charing Cross, but so well are you mortified after so many years spent in so sacred a religion, that being a bitter branch of a sour and unsavoury crab, you would by collusion be engrafted in the stock of the most pleasant pippin in the west of Scotland'.[69] Family ties were also to play an important rôle in the recruitment of later generations of Jesuits. John Ogilvie, executed in 1615, was the nephew of George and William Elphinstone, who were both members of the Society in the late sixteenth century.[70]

* * *

William Crichton (c.1535–1617) was the son of Patrick Crichton of Camnay and a cousin of Bishop Crichton.[71] He was described as being of 'average health', although this is not supported by later evidence which suggests that he suffered from bouts of illness. In a report by Adriaenssens to Salmerón he was described as the 'son of a confessor of the faith', though it does not mention that his family was in fact a cadet of the Crichtons of Ruthven, who were supporters of the Reformation. He may have spent some time in the service of Bishop Crichton, though he should not be confused with the William Crichton who was the sub-dean of the cathedral until his death in 1565. His cousin, Edmund Hay (c.1534–91), was the son of Margaret Crichton of Ruthven and Peter Hay of Megginch, a staunch Catholic and a remote kinsman of the Catholic earls of Errol.[72] Jesuit records indicate he was born in Albany, the area to the north of the Forth, either in Perth or Megginch.[73] Hay's protégée James Tyrie (c.1543–97) was the son of David Tyrie of Drumkilbo and a first cousin of the infamous Patrick, Master of Gray, his father having married a sister of Patrick, 5th Lord Gray. A number of his kinsmen, including John Tyrie, the vicar of Cramond, served as parish clergy in the diocese of Dunkeld. Tyrie's interest in the Society was not shared by all his family, and his brother David, who married a Fotheringham and became a Protestant, was later to bring the activities of his brother to the attention of John Knox.[74] James Tyrie has also been described as a kinsman of William

Crichton, although the exact nature of their relationship is unclear.[75] Tyrie's grandmother, Elizabeth Abercrombie, was a relation of Robert Abercrombie (1536–1613), the son of Alexander Abercrombie of Murthly.[76] In a later General Assembly report Robert was described as the 'fader bruthir' of the current laird, who had succeeded his father in 1581. In the *Dictionnaire d'Histoire et de Géographie Ecclésiastique* Abercrombie is described as Edmund Hay's nephew, though this relationship is not referred to in other sources. In a report written by him in the aftermath of a mission in 1581 Robert states that he sailed up the Tay Estuary and landed at a spot close to his grandfather's castle and his father's house. His grandfather's castle may have been the Hay seat at Megginch, while his father's house was presumably at Murthly, a considerable distance upstream. Robert was also related to Richard Abercrombie, the last abbot of Inchcolm, and to his successor, the commendator, James Stewart of Beath, and as a result spent part of his youth at court.[77] As well as being related to the Stewarts on his mother's side Robert was also a kinsman of the Hays of Park and Delgaty, including John Hay, another recruit to the Society. Robert was subsequently treasurer of Dunkeld from 1561 until his departure in 1562, but for a number of years thereafter continued to profit from the revenues of a number of benefices, including the parsonage of Buttergill and the vicarages of Dunkeld, Little Dunkeld and Dowally. In 1559 he had failed to confess his faith before the St Andrews kirk session, and despite a subsequent legal challenge retained Buttergill until 1587. In the Division and Assumption of the See of Dunkeld made in 1564 Abercrombie was still named as the treasurer, though the office was by this stage the subject of a court action between himself and Stephen Wilson, the former incumbent. Abercrombie was finally deposed from the treasurership in 1573, but during his absence his affairs were managed by his brother Andrew, a Dominican friar, who was one of Mary's Catholic preachers and another member of Crichton's Catholic circle.[78] This Andrew Abercrombie should not be confused with the man of the same name who was the son of John Abercrombie, an advocate, and was sub-chanter of Dunkeld from 1565 to 1591.[79] The family's links with the cathedral were obviously close and their father, Alexander, a prominent local Catholic, was Robert Crichton's procurator.[80] As well as being related in some way to the various branches of the Hay family the Abercrombies were also kinsmen of the earls of Huntly, but again the exact nature of the relationship is unclear. James Gordon of Huntly (1541–1620) was the fifth son of George, 4th Earl of Huntly and an uncle of the 6th earl who was to play such a prominent role in the Catholic party in the 1580s and 1590s. John Hay of Delgaty (1547–1608) was a native of Aberdeenshire, though it would appear he also had associations with Dalgety in Fife. The similarity between the place names has caused confusion in some accounts. However, Hay's report of his mission of 1578–9 makes it clear that he was from Aberdeenshire and refers to him travelling north from Dundee to stay with members of his family, including his brother William, the laird of Delgaty. He also refers to another brother, Edmund, an advocate who should not be confused with the Jesuit of the same name. Hay was an academic of some note and was described by the Jesuit biographer, George Oliver, as a man of 'commanding abilities, primitive fervour, apostolic zeal and infantine docility'. His volatility and his unwillingness to follow instructions subsequently led to him being withdrawn from the Scottish Mission.[81] William Murdoch's (1539–1616) origins arc unclear and little is known of him except that he was a native of Dunkeld and at the time of the Reformation was in the service of Robert Crichton.[82] A clue to Murdoch's background may be provided by his later use of the alias Stevenson, perhaps on account of some earlier association with the family of that name, which held a number of benefices in Dunkeld.[83] In early seventeenth-century correspondence Murdoch signed himself 'Steinsonius' and referred to his foster parents, who were perhaps of the same name.

One man connected with de Gouda's mission who would never have been admitted to the Society was Stephen Wilson or Culross from Glendevon. Wilson was a former chorister of Dunblane and treasurer of Orkney and had been Robert Abercrombie's predecessor as treasurer of Dunkeld. His subsequent attempts to regain the treasurership of Dunkeld were unsuccessful and it passed to a Protestant incumbent, Duncan McNair.[84] During the late 1550s and 1560s Wilson acted as a royal messenger, and along with James Thornton, another unsuccessful litigant for a Dunkeld prebend, was vilified by Knox as a servant of the 'Roman harlot'.[85] Wilson, despite the initially lax recruitment procedure, was never allowed to join the Society, and would apparently not have been admitted even with papal dispensation. He achieved great notoriety in Mary's service, being accused of having 'the whole practice with the Louvainians' and of being the 'rankest Papist in Scotland'.[86] Despite this he managed to accumulate a large number of pensions and benefices during the course of his lifetime.[87]

As well as family connections the majority of the young recruits had a common academic background. Abercrombie, Crichton, Edmund

Hay, Gordon and Tyrie were all students at St Andrews between 1551 and 1557–8, the first three being contemporaries in 1551. Abercrombie and Gordon were graduates of St Mary's College, while the others graduated from St Salvator's.[88] Orthodoxy had been maintained at St Salvator's by a number of provosts, including the East Lothian theologian and historian, John Major, and William Cranston, the vicar of Tibbermore, in the diocese of Dunkeld.[89] Robert Crichton and Cranston were known to each other from the late 1530s through their connections with Paris University.[90] Following the Reformation Cranston fled to France and was joined in exile by Edmund Hay, a former regent of St Salvator's, and Thomas Smeaton of Gask, who joined the Society, but subsequently converted to Protestantism.[91] The understanding and support shown by Edmund Hay towards Smeaton at the time of his conversion shows the importance of these ties which often proved strong enough to bridge the religious divide. On account of earlier academic achievement the progress of Jesuit recruits through the various stages of their formation was often accelerated. While Crichton and Edmund Hay were sent straight to Rome to begin their novitiates, Abercrombie, Gordon, Tyrie, Murdoch and John Hay were required to undertake further studies at Louvain.

Following de Gouda's mission there is little evidence of further contact between Bishop Crichton and the Society. His main concern appears to have been self-preservation though there is ample evidence of regular celebrations of the mass in Dunkeld and Edinburgh before and after his removal in 1571. In a report written in 1580 by Robert Abercrombie on the state of Catholicism in Scotland he singled out his former master as the country's only remaining Catholic bishop.[92] Nevertheless, it has been suggested that Crichton's continued commitment to Rome was exaggerated. Bellesheim was critical of him for not being more energetic in his opposition, while other critics point to his reappointment as bishop of Dunkeld in 1584 and his subsequent burial in St Giles Cathedral as evidence of his conversion to, or at least his tacit acceptance of, Protestantism.[93] However, his reappointment should be looked at in the context of James's plans to re-establish episcopacy and there is nothing to suggest that Crichton became a Protestant. Furthermore, as a former provost of St Giles he was entitled to be buried there. Although at the time of his death in late March 1585 he was still being referred to as an 'old doting papist' and 'an excommunicated and professed papist', he does not appear to have played any part in the Jesuit missions of the 1580s.[94]

Chapter 3

Nests of Rats and Tombs for Jesuits

On reaching the continent the young Scottish recruits were assigned to Jesuit colleges in Louvain and Rome. Their exact movements in this early period are rather unclear, but it is known that they visited Trent to meet Laínez and to witness the Council in action. William Crichton in his account of de Gouda's mission reported that Tyrie, Abercrombie, Murdoch and John Hay remained in Flanders, while he and Edmund Hay were sent to Rome.[1] Gordon, who seems to have made his own way from Scotland, also studied for a spell at Louvain. In October 1562 de Gouda advised Laínez that Edmund Hay, and presumably Crichton, were due to arrive in Mainz and would then continue on to Rome.[2] A month later Polanco confirmed to Francis Borgia, Salmerón's successor as vicar-general in Rome, that the Scottish party had visited Trent and that of the six or seven young men who had arrived in Flanders three were to continue to Rome; Edmund Hay, William Crichton and George Hay, who it was suspected would not join the Society.[3] George Hay entered the German College in December, but there is no record of him ever becoming a Jesuit. Also travelling with them was Richard Creagh, who soon after was appointed Archbishop of Armagh, and with whom Crichton was imprisoned in the Tower of London in the mid 1580s.[4]

As the 1560s and 1570s were a period of flux within the Society it is impossible to make many general comments on the careers of the young Scottish recruits. However, it is clear that the requirements of the Society and the backgrounds of the recruits had a bearing on their progress within it. It is also clear that as students and as priests they were required to move between colleges and houses throughout Europe. Within a year of leaving Scotland most of the new recruits had joined the Society. Edmund Hay and Crichton entered in early or late December shortly after arriving in Rome, while Abercrombie, Murdoch and Tyrie followed in August 1563, and were joined a month later by Gordon. Academic experience generally determined the length of a new recruit's formation, and while some, such as Edmund Hay, were ordained within a few years, others took much longer to complete their studies. Murdoch was not ordained until about 1571, while Walter Hay, Edmund's brother, was never ordained and remained a lay brother until his death in 1584. Others, such as Crichton's nephew, James, who had a history of poor health and ill-discipline, were weeded out before completing their studies, while some such as Stephen Wilson, never got a foot in the door: 'The Scots Carmelite may be helped in all that appertains to God's service, but do not mention entrance to the Society. We should not take him even with the Pope's dispensation'. On a visit to Rome Wilson's couthiness seems to have offended his more sophisticated Italian hosts. A number, including Peter Livius, who entered the Society in February 1562 and took his vows a few months later, and Thomas Gordon, James Gordon's brother, appear briefly in the records of the Society and then disappear. In the absence of further information it must be assumed that they died or left the Society.

Despite the procedures outlined in Loyola's *Constitutions* recruitment and promotion through the various grades within the Society was initially haphazard, and towards the end of his life Loyola admitted that he had been too lax in his acceptance of novices. He could also be somewhat arbitrary in disciplining members, often dismissing them for fairly trivial offences. Figures for Italy for the period from 1540 to 1565 show that 35% of those recruited left the Society or were dismissed, of whom 22% left or were dismissed as novices, while 29% left after ten years service. The information gathered by Father McCoog regarding Scottish recruits for the period up to 1603 suggests slightly different trends. Of the fifty or so who entered the Society five were dismissed, of whom only one, George Durie, was dismissed after ten years service. Perhaps more significantly eight died within ten years of joining, from which one might deduce that the continental climate did not suit the Scottish constitution. Of those who were not struck down permanently a number were plagued by ill-health, including John Hay, who had to return to Scotland for a period, and William Crichton, who regularly took short breaks to recuperate. When William Murdoch was arrested and interrogated by the Scottish authorities in 1607 he tried to claim that he had returned to Scotland for health reasons, though the accounts of his activities would suggest that he enjoyed good health. Too much should not be read into these figures since they include statistics from later in the century when the selection procedure was more structured. However, they do indicate that the Scottish recruits generally displayed the commitment required by the Society, the most notable exceptions being Thomas Smeaton, a future moderator of the General Assembly of the Kirk, and George Durie.[5]

Prior to entering the Society as novices aspirants spent a brief probationary period familiarising themselves with the order. It was also used by the Society to observe the new recruits and to check that they met the usual minimum requirements for entry into any religious order; the usual impediments to entry being heresy, homicide, membership of another order, marriage or servitude and mental deficiency. The novitiate was the first formal stage within the structure of the Society and generally involved two years' training within a college under the supervision of a novice-master. Seniority did not excuse anyone from these supervisory duties and Robert Abercrombie's novice-master was the general, Diego Laínez. Although the procedure to be followed was laid down in the *Constitutions* there were initially considerable differences in interpretation and both Edmund Hay and William Crichton undertook abbreviated novitiates. Even though the novitiate became more standardised the Society had great difficulty in overseeing all the houses and during the 1560s Jerome Nadal, in the course of his many visitations, came across numerous lapses and discrepancies.

At the outset of the novitiate the novices signed an inventory, known as the Minister's Book, containing details of their personal effects, which were returned if they did not complete the initial two year period. Robert Methven , who was the first Scot to enter the Society in 1558, brought with him works by Cicero and Petrarch. Edmund Hay and William Crichton also had extensive collections, while Robert Abercrombie's entry refers to catechisms in Latin and Italian by Canisius. The novices's time was spent in prayer, doing housework and studying, interspersed with a number of tasks designed to test their commitment. At some stage during the novitiateship, generally during the course of the first year, the novices would spend approximately four weeks in total seclusion completing Loyola's *Spiritual Exercises*. Approximately a week was spent contemplating each of four themes or experiences: the consideration of sin, the life and role of the Redeemer, the love and mystery of the Lord's Passion and the Resurrection and Ascension. On the basis of Jerome Nadal's *Responsa* it is clear that not all novices made their Exercises, and of those who did, not all completed them in four weeks. The *Responsa*, which were developed by Nadal as part of the *Interrogationes* conducted during the course of his visitations, were answers to a questionnaire seeking details of the respondent's career, including personal information, academic achievements and progress within the Society. The novices were also assigned to teaching duties and, on the centralisation of the novitiate in Rome, were required to work in the poorer parishes in the city and as servants in the hospital of the Archconfraternity of the Holy Trinity. The final task was a pilgrimage for a month to a distant shrine without food or money. In undertaking this pilgrimage and in many other aspects of the Society's works great stress was placed on a Jesuit's ability to beg for alms, at which William Crichton, in his later capacity as rector of Lyons, was to prove highly adept.[6]

Following the centralisation of the novitiate in Rome the novices were initially housed in the Gésu or in a Jesuit house, and later in a large residence close to the San Andrea al Quirinale bequeathed to the Society in 1566 by the Duchess of Tagliacozza. When Edmund Hay and William Crichton began their novitiates in December 1562 there were some 150 students boarding at the Roman College, along with a further 600 quartered elsewhere in Rome. Within fifteen years this number had swelled to several thousand by which stage the novitiate system was flourishing under Fabio de Fabiis, who had been a novice along with St Stanislaus Kostka, who died during his novitiate, Claudio Acquaviva, a future general, and two Scots, John Hay and Thomas Smeaton.[7]

After the initial two-year period the novices pronounced simple vows of poverty, chastity and obedience and were received into the Society to begin their studies for the priesthood at the Roman or German Colleges founded by Loyola in Rome in 1551 and 1552 respectively. The time when novices pronounced their simple vows could vary and for some it was only a few days after their admission. The three earliest recruits to the Society, Robert Methven, Thomas Rouye and Peter Livius all took their vows within a few months of admission. For approximately nine years the young scholastics studied a curriculum of literature, maths, science, philosophy and theology, including a lengthy period of teaching under the supervision of a more experienced father. At some stage following ordination to the priesthood a further year, the tertianship, was devoted to asceticism and a period of retreat. There were two classes of priests, the professed of solemn vows, who studied philosophy and theology, and the spiritual coadjutors who pronounced simple vows and were only required to undertake a secondary education generally comprising all or a combination of grammar, humane letters and cases of conscience. The professed were qualified to hold any office within the Society and to participate in the General Congregations, and although entry to the highest offices within the Society was not available to spiritual coadjutors they could engage in most activities, including serving as college rectors. It should be emphasised that the procedures set out in the *Constitutions* were simply guidelines and if it suited the requirements of the Society advancement through the various stages could be accelerated.[8]

On account of their previous academic experience William Crichton and Edmund Hay were excused the majority of their novitiates and entered the Society within a few months of arriving in Rome, and little more than a year after intimating their intention to join. Their scholastic periods were also considerably curtailed, as within a few years both had been appointed as rectors of Jesuit colleges. Before joining the Society William Crichton had already studied at St Andrews, Paris, Rome, Leipzig and Louvain. As a Jesuit he later studied philosophy and theology, the latter under the eminent Spanish Jesuit, Francesco Toledo. On account of their academic experience and subsequent good progress within the Society Hay and Crichton were admitted to the profession in 1568.[9] However, they were exceptional and the careers of the majority of the young Scots proceeded along more conventional lines. Most were required to undertake the full syllabus at each stage of their formation, and William Murdoch in particular appears to have spent a number of years completing his studies. Unfortunately the early records relating to these first Scottish novices are relatively scant. The only extant Scottish *Responsa* is that of William Seton, who was perhaps a travelling companion of Thomas Smeaton in 1566. There is no record of Seton having joined the Society and one must assume that he was weeded out during the early stages of the somewhat haphazard selection process. With the more formal establishment of the novitiate during the following decades records became more comprehensive, and by the 1590s there were very full records of each novice entering the Society kept by, amongst others, William Crichton during his various spells as rector of the Scots College. The entry in the register in 1596 for John Ogilvie, records, amongst other information, that he was 'received out of Calvinism'.[10]

* * *

This is perhaps an appropriate stage to make a few general comments about the Jesuit colleges and in particular the peripatetic Scots College. Most of the first generation of Scottish recruits spent a large part of the 1560s and 1570s in colleges throughout Europe, initially as students and subsequently as teachers and rectors. The colleges were regarded as central to the struggle against Protestantism and their staffing took priority over many other apostolic functions. They were also seen as a means of enhancing the standing of the Society, attracting future recruits and influencing the sons of the upper classes. In 1553 Paschase Broët, the French provincial and a veteran of the Irish Mission in 1542, suggested to Loyola that the colleges provided the opportunity 'for those who complain and oppose us to be quiet and for many others to do us favours'.[11] Modern commentators have looked on them as offering a powerful combination of a classical humanist education and the morally disciplined religion of the Catholic Reformation. However, those appointed to teach in them were often less enthusiastic. Oliver Mannaerts, a future French provincial, referred to the colleges in France as 'nests of rats and tombs for Jesuits' and in the early years of the college system there was a great deal of concern expressed about the academic and moral standards of many of the Jesuit teachers.[12] All the staff at Tournon were thought to be incompetent, while in Paris there was a general perception that there were only one or two good professors in the Society, the rest were stupid and ignorant.[13] The college at Innsbruck, where Edmund Hay spent some time, was described as an 'absolute Babylon' due to the mismanagement of the rector, Johannes Dyrsius. The Jesuit college at Louvain, which had been tolerated by the university since 1542, was considered by Nadal to be in need of reform. He recommended that the rector, Adriaenssens, should be replaced, though in fairness to him there is no doubt that the college suffered from being compared with the university, which was 'a shrine and citadel of wisdom, either as to the number of its students, the fame of its doctors, or the wealth and convenience of its instruments of learning'.[14] The comparison was perhaps slightly unfair as this comment was made in a report attacking the high level of drunkenness at the university.

Despite the shortcomings of many of the colleges and their staff the Society remained committed to its educational strategy and by the end of the 1560s standards appeared to be improving. The number of colleges also continued to increase as a result of the establishment of new ones and the acquisition of existing ones. The University of Tournon, near Valence on the Rhone, was transferred to the Society in 1561 by Cardinal François de Tournon, who had assisted Salmerón and Broët on the return leg of their Irish mission. Edmund Hay was one of those in favour of a proposal that the Society should assume control of the old college at Guyenne in Bordeaux to take advantage of its large catchment area. The college had almost 5000 students and was situated in an area 'à grand besoin d'hommes hônetes, soit pour instruire le peuple du haut de la chaire, soit pour élèver la jeunesse dans la piété, les bonnes moeurs et les lettres'.[15] In the aftermath of his mission to Scotland in 1566, Hay reported to Polanco that the Jesuit colleges even enjoyed a good reputation in Britain and tentative arrangements were made for the establishment of a college in Scotland. One modern commentator has attributed this rise in standards to the introduction of younger rectors, such as Hay and Crichton.[16]

The plans for a Scots College came to fruition in the late 1570s and early 1580s. The exact date of the foundation of the college was the subject of some debate which was resolved by Hubert Chadwick, SJ.[17] In an article in the *English Historical Review* Chadwick dismissed the suggestion that the college was founded by James Cheyne of Arnage at Pont-à-Mousson in 1576, or a few years later in 1581, and argued that the original foundation was in Paris in 1580, when a college was endowed by Mary, Archbishop Beaton and Bishop Leslie of Ross to train priests to work in Scotland.[18] He based this on a letter from Leslie to William Allen written on 14 October 1579 in which he requested a copy of the rules and constitution of the English College at Rheims to use as a model for the establishment of a Scottish equivalent in Paris.[19] Further evidence of its foundation around this time is to be found in letters from Beaton and Leslie to Gregory XIII (1572–85) requesting financial assistance. On the basis of this correspondence it would appear that the college was founded in February 1580 under the presidency of Cheyne and in the spring of the following year was transferred to Pont-à-Mousson, where it was attached to the pensionat of the Jesuit college, which itself was part of the university founded there in 1574. The new college was partly financed by a papal pension of 600 crowns granted in terms of an apostolic letter of 1581, which was to subsist for fifteen years. In 1584 the pension was increased on condition that Irish students were admitted to the college, and by the end of the year there were thirty six Scottish and seven Irish students. In the following year an outbreak of the plague forced to college to temporarily relocate to Trier in Germany. Mary's execution in 1587 brought an end to her royal patronage and the resulting financial hardship was only relieved by a loan from the Jesuit college. Relations between the Scots and Irish were strained and the withdrawal of the royal grant provided a convenient opportunity for the Irish to be removed.

In August 1590 the college was forced to close due to lack of funds, but reopened at Douai in April 1593 with William Crichton as rector and James Tyrie, a former rector of the college at Pont-à-Mousson, as his assistant. Within a few months of settling at Douai the college was again on the move this time back to Louvain, where Crichton purchased accommodation for the forty students. The following year control of the college was formally entrusted to the Society and the Society's practice of placing intern students under non-Jesuit officials was adopted. This policy was initially unsuccessful and in 1595 after two ineffectual appointments Cheyne was put in charge of the interns.[20] The college also struggled financially and because of a lack of funds Crichton was forced to beg for assistance. Despite these problems the college enjoyed a period of stability at Louvain and remained there for thirteen years, initially under Crichton and subsequently under another Scottish Jesuit, George Christie of Dysart. A request to the pope for a further pension was turned down, and instead Clement VIII (1592–1605), following petitions from Leslie, Tyrie and other supporters, decided that a Scots college should also be established in Rome so that 'well fitted youths and adolescents of Scotland might become familiar with good traditions, true piety and sound doctrine'. On 5th December 1600 he granted the papal bull *In Supremo Militantis Ecclesiae* conferring on the college all the privileges enjoyed by the other foreign colleges in Rome. It was also endowed with the revenues of an abbey in the kingdom of Naples and a monthly pension from the Dataria. The Society took control of the college in 1615, the first Scottish rector being Patrick Anderson, a nephew of Bishop Leslie.[21] The relocation of the existing college continued to generate considerable debate, with Crichton favouring and Christie opposing a return to Douai. Father Verannenan, the rector at Louvain, made it clear that he did not want the college to remain there. Acquaviva instructed that the matter be settled locally, and so while Christie was absent, perhaps in Scotland, the college returned to Douai, where it was to remain for a further 150 years.[22]

As well as some controversy over the exact movements of the college during this period considerable doubt has also been expressed about its effectiveness and the Scottish exiles' commitment to it. Meyer in his seminal work *England and the Catholic Church under Queen Elizabeth* was particularly critical, claiming that the 'Lamentations over the small results from this [the Scots College at Rome] and the other Scottish seminaries constantly made themselves heard, while the not infrequent outbursts of insubordination among the alumni, and their unwillingness to pledge themselves by oath to receive Holy Orders and devote themselves to missionary work in Scotland, clearly proves that in the land of John Knox it was far rarer to find enthusiasm for the catholic church among the rising generation than in England, whence numbers of young men came to fill the continental seminaries to overflowing'. When asked by the Bishop of St Omer why there were so many English seminaries and no Scottish ones Crichton claimed that 'the English were more persistent and went begging far and wide, while the Scots were of a more reserved and aristocratic temperament unsullied by this vulgar trait'. The lack of interest prompted an appeal, *The Antiquity of the Christian Religion among the Scots*, written in 1594 and attributed, probably incorrectly, to James Tyrie. It called on Scottish Catholics and others throughout Europe to support the Scots College, recently transferred from Pont-à-Mousson to Douai, and was a reflection of the growing optimism within the Catholic community following the Earl of Huntly's victory over the royal army at Glenlivet:

> Sick of their former rashness and folly, they daily return in all humbleness to the bosom of the Catholic church, from which, in the madness of their impiety, they cut themselves adrift, so that in a short time the Catholic religion has been greatly increased by numerous additions. But it is a matter worthy of the greatest grief, that when there is so plenteous a harvest to be stored in God's granary the labourers are so few, for although a seminary was built by Gregory XIII of blessed memory at Pont-à-Mousson in Lorraine for the Scottish nation, and moved by Clement VIII now in possession of Peter's Chair, by reason of his anxiety over the war which is disturbing Lorraine, to Douai in Flanders, yet such scanty numbers does it contain that it is not adequate for educating all the promising young men who daily flock abroad in the hope that being perfected in devotion and literature they may help in the welfare of their country. Unless they are assisted by the liberality and generosity of the pious, the propagation of God's name and the welfare of the souls in the kingdom of Scotland will be much retarded.

The appeal suggested that the problem was a lack of resources rather than recruits. Patrick Anderson, prior to his appointment as rector of the Scots College in Rome in 1615, reported that there were over one hundred youths in Scotland waiting to train abroad. Despite Meyer's comments, the report of 1594 and *The Records of the Scots Colleges* indicate a steady, if modest, flow of Scottish students to the colleges at Douai, Madrid, Valladolid and Ratisbon.[23]

* * *

As the early careers of the first Scottish recruits were so diverse it is simpler to deal with each father individually and then return to the overview in the early 1580s when the Scottish Mission was formally established. Little is known about the first three Scottish recruits, Robert Methven, Thomas Rouye and Peter Livius, who entered the Society in 1558, 1560 and 1562 respectively. Methven and Rouye were dead by 1562, while Livius disappears from the records shortly after entering. He studied at the Roman College, but appears not to have graduated and one must therefore assume that he died or was dismissed.

After a short stay in Louvain Crichton and Edmund Hay set off for Rome where they both entered the Society on 5 December 1562. While they were *en route* Polanco wrote to the vicar-general, Francis Borgia, with details of the new recruits. Crichton 'though very young is nevertheless a Master in Arts and well versed in languages'.[24] Despite his youthfulness Crichton's progress through the ranks of the Society was swift and in 1565 he was appointed as rector of the college at Rodez in southern France. The appointment was revoked and instead he was sent to Lyons, where he was to remain until 1583, except for a spell at Avignon between 1570 and 1573. Crichton was personally chosen by Edmond Auger, the provincial of Acquitaine, who had attended the Second General Congregation of the Society in Rome in June 1565 and returned to France accompanied by the young Scotsman. Although still relatively inexperienced Crichton professed his solemn vows at Lyons on 28 August 1568, and in 1575 was appointed vice provincial of Acquitaine under Mercurian.[25]

Thanks to the voluminous amount of correspondence passing between the provinces and the Society in Rome it is possible to build up quite a detailed picture of Crichton. Throughout his time in Lyons he maintained an active interest in Scottish affairs and extended a welcome to the numerous Scottish visitors who passed through the city, including William Chisholm, who for a number of years shuttled between Scotland and Rome acting on behalf of Mary and Pius V. Information received from Chisholm and other visitors was forwarded to the Society in Rome, though there were occasions when Crichton's interpretation of events proved to be misleading. In a report written in April 1566 he advised Borgia that Henry Stewart, Lord Darnley, had been attending Mass and that the queen's chapel was regularly filled with Catholic worshippers. Within a few months he had reassessed his view and concluded that the 'Catholics live licentious lives and are therefore cold'.[26] He was also accused of showing an unhealthy interest in secular affairs – an accusation which was to lead to numerous run-ins with the Society and the civic authorities in Lyons. His interest was not curbed by numerous reprimands from his superiors or the decree of the Fifth General Congregation of the Society in 1593, introduced at the instance of James Tyrie, prohibiting involvement in secular affairs. Ironically Crichton and Edmund Hay were amongst a group of fathers who in the 1570s expressed their disapproval of the political activities of a number of their colleagues, including Auger.

The steady stream of visitors to Lyons helped to relieve the tediousness of college life. Unlike some of his colleagues Crichton was keen to be actively involved in the Scottish Mission and on a number of occasions asked to be relieved of the rectorship of the college. His attempts to avoid being re-appointed for a second term of office at Lyons led to a long running dispute with the incumbent rector, Ignatius Balsamo. Despite his attempts to highlight his colleague's talents and his own short-comings Crichton was unable to prevent his re-appointment. However, once re-appointed Crichton dropped the pretence of flattering his colleague and the animosity between the two rumbled on for a number of years. Balsamo was especially critical of Crichton's interest in politics: 'Our recreation is so secular that it is difficult to believe… The Father Rector… is the first to propose discussions on the affairs of wars, of this kingdom, and of that province, and we almost never speak of things appropriate to us'. As his dispute with Balsamo suggests Crichton was a fairly cantankerous character. Although sympathetic towards sinners from outwith the Society he could be very intolerant of those within it. He was highly critical of colleagues who used 'excessively harsh, dishonest and harmful' words against a variety of sinners, including heretics, politicians, soldiers and women! Barthélemy Guerauld was also criticised for having lost the 'teeth of his conscience' and for being inconsistent in confession, while a fellow rector Giovanni Battista Atanasio of Chambéry was castigated for his limited preaching skills and for having 'neither the mind to study nor the memory to remember'. Amongst Crichton's other shortcomings was his inability to speak fluent French, and in fact his grasp of the language was so poor he often preferred to use Latin. Even by the mid 1570s after ten years in France the locals in Lyons had problems understanding him. Furthermore many of them did not like his forthright manner and during his term as rector he enjoyed mixed relations with the civic authorities and the business community. Although Crichton may have been a fairly abrasive character he did at least have the good grace to acknowledge his own shortcomings, and many years later when defending the reputation of a Scottish colleague, John Myrton, he conceded that 'few are comprised totally of talents'.[27]

For all his faults Crichton was a committed member of the Society and despite finding teaching duties mundane he carried them out diligently. His letters show a concern for all aspects of college life and for the interests of his pupils. They also demonstrate a continual struggle with the college finances and, in the early years, a desperate shortage of teachers. With only two teachers for 180 pupils Crichton was understandably frustrated by the lack of progress shown by the 'barefooted brats'. By 1576 the college roll had risen to 500, although this was still considered relatively small when compared with other Jesuit colleges. The problem of low numbers could have been resolved if the college had been prepared to accept boarders, but this proposal was dismissed on account of the high cost. Balancing the books was always a problem and there were often insufficient funds to buy every day provisions. In 1574 Crichton spent over three times the college's annual income, which in itself was barely sufficient to cover the cost of the wine. His unwillingness to take in boarders led to conflict with the college's patrons, who refused to accept that it might close due to rising costs.[28] On top of all these problems Crichton did not enjoy good health, although he did live on to the ripe old age of eighty two, despite spending a number of years in prison in England. He often spent a few days in Tournon recuperating, and although his constitution may have been more robust than he suggested, it would appear that he did suffer from a number of ailments, including vertigo.[29]

Edmund Hay's first appointment following his brief novitiate was to the college at Innsbruck where his assistance was highly valued by Canisius, the Austrian provincial. In late August 1564 the Society decided to post him to Paris to work under the French provincial, Oliver Mannaerts, with a view to helping out with the increasing number of Scottish students.[30] Canisius was reluctant to let him go: 'I do not want to hinder the common good, but this change will do considerable harm to Innsbruck College, of which he is, I might say, the principal pillar. He is highly esteemed by the educated classes here and listened to with great pleasure and applause'. Hay was also popular with the Imperial Court, particularly with Emperor Ferdinand's five daughters, and in order not to offend the Imperial family his transfer was delayed until September when the court was absent from the city.[31] While Hay was *en route* from Vienna to Paris Polanco forwarded his letter of appointment as rector of Clermont College to Mannaerts.[32]

There was a certain logic to the posting as Hay was one of a number of Scots to whom letters of naturalisation had been given on Mary's marriage to the French dauphin. He also spoke reasonable French, albeit with a broad Scottish accent. As well as his duties as rector Hay's presence in Paris was required to bolster the reputation of the Society, which was under attack from a number of quarters, including the bishop, the *parlement* and the university authorities. As the Society had only recently been granted legal status in France Hay was reluctant to introduce changes too quickly and in the summer of 1565 he advised Polanco that he was still not yet in a position to 'fish freely'.[33]

Hay, like Crichton, was an important source of information on Scottish affairs and the activities of the Scottish exiles. Unlike his cousin, he was more wary of becoming overly involved in secular matters and often apologised to Borgia for the political content of his letters: 'Of these things I write, though such is not our Society's custom'. Although Hay is generally portrayed as being less politically orientated than Crichton, a number of comments by him suggest that this was not necessarily the case. In a report to Polanco regarding Mary's proposed marriage to her cousin, Darnley, he expressed the view that: 'At first we shall hear of nothing but disturbance, nor will he [Darnley] be able, as far as human conjectures can go, to pacify the affairs of the kingdom without much blood and slaughter. Then, we hope, a time will follow more adapted to our ministrations'. In May 1566 he advised that Mary required foreign assistance to reduce a few tyrants to order and in the following year he appears to have given his approval to a proposal to execute a number of leading Protestants who were exerting undue influence over her. In light of these comments the allegations made twenty years later that he had hired an assassin to murder the Master of Gray do not appear quite so far fetched.[34]

Hay's abilities were also noted by many outwith the Society. In late 1564 or early 1565 William Chisholm, junior, who had succeeded his uncle as Bishop of Dunblane, had gone to Paris to seek Hay's advice before returning to his new diocese. He had also hoped to obtain permission to take Hay to Scotland with him, but his request to Laínez was never answered due to the general's death. In the summer of 1565 Chisholm was back in Rome seeking financial assistance and papal dispensation for Mary's marriage to Darnley, which fell within the forbidden degrees. In response to Mary's request for 300,000 ducats a Vatican newsletter advised that: 'The pope's ardour is great, but his resources being limited, and having many calls upon him, he will not perhaps be able to grant the queen so much money. It is not doubted, however, that he will never fail to do what he can'.[35] Around this time de Gouda wrote to Polanco on behalf of a number of English Catholic exiles requesting that Hay and Crichton, along with an English Jesuit, Thomas King, be sent to Scotland to advise Mary and Darnley. On his return Chisholm again requested that Hay return to Scotland with him, but Francis Borgia, although under instructions to assist, ducked the issue and referred the matter to Oliver Mannaerts, the French provincial. Hay himself was reluctant to return to Scotland: 'To tell the truth I am perhaps less inclined to my country than may be fitting. I fancy perhaps that this body of mine has a foretaste of the delights that there await'. Despite a temporary improvement in the situation in Scotland in the latter part of the year the Society still refused to release Hay or Crichton until the political situation had been resolved and 'arms have done their work'. However, it was prepared to offer prayers and masses instead.[36]

During the early part of the following year Hay continued to provide Polanco with encouraging reports from Scotland which, coupled with reports from Crichton that there were still widespread celebrations of the Mass, raised the hopes of many observers in Rome. In February 1565–6 the queen's confessor, the Dominican friar, Roche Mamerot, reported that she had appointed Catholic men of learning to preach in public and to teach the Catholic faith, including another Dominican friar, Andrew Abercrombie, the brother of Robert and a kinsman of Bishop Crichton. The appointments appear to have yielded some good results. In May 1566 Hay reported that over 9,000 people had celebrated Easter Mass in Mary's chapel at Holyrood and many more elsewhere in Scotland. This evidence of continuing Catholic worship led Hay to conclude that with a little assistance Mary would be able to return the country to the bosom of the church. Corroboration of sorts is provided by Mamerot who registered 12,606 communicants at Lent. Nevertheless, despite these reports the prospects for the Catholic church were generally gloomy. The Catholic party lacked political support and the likes of Atholl and Lennox, previously Catholic stalwarts, were described as being 'lukewarm in the matter of religion'.[37]

In late March 1566 Chisholm, who had never returned to Scotland due to severe weather conditions and had spent the winter at the Jesuit college in Paris, was instructed to make a further approach to Rome for financial assistance. The newly elected pope, Pius V, decided to comply with Mary's request and news of his decision to grant her a modest subsidy was sent to her via Stephen Wilson. Pius appointed his successor as bishop of Mondovi, Vincenzo Laureo, to disburse the subsidy and gave permission for Chisholm to take two Jesuits with him.[38] Despite confirmation of the appointment from Borgia, Mannaerts was wary of sending a foreign nuncio to advise Mary, especially one from Rome, 'that see which the Scottish hate more than Lucifer', and was concerned about the risk of further unrest directed against her.[39] His preferred choice was Archbishop Beaton, who was in Paris acting as Mary's ambassador to the French court. As a member of the archbishop's household Hay's safety would have been guaranteed. Despite Mannaerts' concerns, Hay and an English father, Thomas Darbyshire from Dillingen, were chosen to accompany Mondovi and Chisholm to Scotland.[40]

Reports of the mission by Mondovi and Hay make no mention of Darbyshire, though he was certainly in Paris in August 1566 with Walter Hay and a Mr James of Valencia. Darbyshire, a former archdeacon of London and a nephew of Bishop Edmund Bonner, the ageing Catholic bishop of London, was a latecomer to the Society, entering on 1 May 1563 at the age of forty five.[41] He was a highly respected teacher and 'a good mixer ready for any talk to the peace or calling for the exercise of kindness and goodwill'. As the two fathers were 'already well tried and known as literary persons and men of great perfection' Mannaerts felt that the Society should consider allowing them to profess their vows. He may also have been worried that on returning home Hay might be tempted to accept one of the offers of a Scottish bishopric which he had previously refused. Despite his concerns Mannaerts' suggestion was not acted on and Hay did not profess his vows until 18 April 1568 and Darbyshire until 1 May 1572.[42]

Mondovi, who aspired to his predecessor's high office, went on to become a cardinal, but lacked the ability to progress further. Although genuinely religious, he was vain and ostentatious, and his lack of diplomacy and tact were painfully exposed during the course of the mission. His shortcomings were no doubt well known to the Society, though the official line was that he was 'an old, true, and devoted friend'.[43] While the principal aim of the mission was the disbursement of the papal subsidy negotiated by William Chisholm, Mondovi's exact instructions are unclear. George Thomson writing in 1594 suggested that the nuncio was also instructed to negotiate with Mary for the restoration of Catholicism in both Scotland and England. Hay was tight lipped about the purpose of the mission and the prospects of success, although he did 'dread lest a certain desperation and imbecility on the part of those, who ought to be foremost in this business should cause this great and opportune subsidy of the Supreme Pontiff to be of little avail for the object intended'. He clearly had no illusions about the Society's true and devoted friend, nor did Polanco, who prior to the party's departure issued Hay with specific instructions about how he should conduct himself. As well as advising tact and secrecy he also reminded him that he should continually be aware of Mary's precarious position: 'you may give him [Mondovi] such counsels as shall seem to you expedient, nevertheless... you must proceed with tact, and as far as possible covertly in matters of this sort which are not proper to our Society, and still more so when you understand from persons at court they may be taken amiss'.[44]

The party arrived in Paris on 10 August and over the next few days Mondovi attempted to compile an assessment of the situation in Scotland. His report to Rome on 21 August advised that Mary had requested him to delay his arrival until after the baptism of her son James, at which stage she would feel more confident about welcoming him. He also referred to Mary's quarrel with Darnley, 'an ambitious, inconsistent youth', and the fact that they had not co-habited since James's birth. He also warned that although Darnley was attending Mass he was on good terms with a number of leading Protestant nobles. As a result Mary, in the absence of any reliable Catholic advisers, was forced to rely on other leading Protestants, including her half-brother Moray, to counter these 'persons of influence... who foster this division and distrust, in order to enfeeble the kingdom and bring it to ruin'. Mondovi also advised that he was being put under pressure to pay over the whole subsidy of 20,000 scudi, even though his instructions were to pay it in five instalments. Although an initial payment of 4,000 scudi was authorised and delivered to Mary further payments were withheld on the instructions of the pope.[45]

In late October orders were received from Rome instructing Mondovi to return to Italy. As much of the groundwork had already been done he decided to ignore these and to proceed with his original instructions. No response to his numerous letters to Mary was received until Stephen Wilson's arrival in Paris *en route* to Rome to thank the pope for the subsidy. His departure from Scotland had been delayed until early November on account of Mary being laid low with illness. He passed through London some time prior to 13 November and arrived in Paris a week later. Having tracked down William Chisholm in Dieppe he departed for Rome on 15 December, where he arrived sometime towards the end of the following month. He was well received by Pius and having conveyed Mary's thanks to him and the College of Cardinals he returned to Paris in late February. Mary meanwhile urged Mondovi to continue with his mission, but distanced herself from some of his more outrageous proposals, which appear to have been endorsed by Chisholm and Hay. Despite her encouragement the nuncio's departure for Scotland was delayed until late November when it was decided that Chisholm and Hay should go on ahead to make the necessary arrangements for his arrival. Their departure from Dieppe on board a ship manned by 'cruel heretics' was further delayed by bad weather and they finally arrived in Edinburgh on 13 December after ten days at sea. Mary was in no rush to grant them an audience, being too preoccupied with the preparations for James's baptism on 17 December. Although he was invited Mondovi remained in Paris waiting to hear from his envoys. When Mary eventually received Chisholm and Hay on 14 January she expressed misgivings about the nuncio's plans, including his suggestion that she execute a number of her leading nobles, 'who go making mischief in the queen's own household'. Mondovi believed that their execution would be seen as a sign of Mary's commitment to Rome.[46] In a subsequent letter to Cardinal Alessandria, he reiterated his belief that Mary's cause would have been furthered by a few summary executions, 'but being too prone to pity and clemency she has exposed herself to the risk of being the slave and prey to those heretics, with danger even to her life'. Despite their differences of opinion Mondovi was later asked by Mary to be cardinal protector of Scottish affairs on the death of Cardinal Sermonetta in 1586. Although Mary had been reluctant to meet them Chisholm was hopeful of Mary's good intentions, though it is interesting that no separate report of the audience was received from Hay, 'perhaps because he sees things in a different light from that in which the bishop describes them'. This would appear to have been the case as his report on the other aspects of the mission, unlike his optimistic reports of the previous year, was more circumspect.[47] Perhaps the most significant feature of Mondovi's mission is the fact that it marked the end of official papal contact with Scotland until 1622 when Scottish affairs were put in the hands of the *Congregatione de Propaganda Fide*.

Hay remained in Scotland for a number of weeks after the audience with Mary and was in hiding in Edinburgh on the night of Darnley's murder at Kirk o'Field in early February. As well as preaching, disputing and making 'many wise [answers] to the calumnies of the wicked' he also converted a number of prominent kinsmen, including

George Hay, 8th Earl of Errol. He left Scotland soon after Darnley's murder in the company of Bertino Solaro Moretta, the Savoyard ambassador, and while passing through London visited Darbyshire's imprisoned uncle, Edmund Bonner. The reports of the mission make no reference to Darbyshire himself which suggests that he must have remained in Paris with Mondovi. On his return to the continent Hay was accompanied by a number of hopeful recruits, though there is no record of their identities. On 15 March he and Moretta were in Paris from where they confirmed the rumours of Darnley's murder, and in the following month Mondovi left to return to his see. In one of his last reports to Cardinal Alessandria he spoke of confusion in the country and of Mary's reliance on James Hepburn, 4th Earl of Bothwell, 'a courageous man, much trusted and confided in by the queen'. Lennox and Atholl were identified as the only remaining Catholic nobles, but even they were criticised for being too preoccupied with safeguarding their own interests. In response to a request from Mary for another nuncio Mondovi suggested that Hay should return to Scotland, but any plans were soon abandoned when news of Mary's marriage to Bothwell on 15 May 1567 reached Paris. A few months later Hay, following his recovery from a bout of illness, gave an account of the marriage and although he was critical of 'that sinner' he was still hopeful that Mary would be able to rally support and regain power.[48] Such hopes were ill-founded and following defeats at Carberry Hill and Langside Mary abdicated the throne in favour of James and fled to England.[49] Her abdication signalled the end of the Society's involvement in Scotland until the early 1580s when the political situation had improved sufficiently for the pope and the Society to consider the establishment of a formal Scottish mission.

Hay continued as rector at Paris until 1571, when he was appointed provincial of France. In 1573 he attended the third General Congregation of the Society and along with Salmerón, Canisius and Nadal sat on a committee to review those sections of the Constitutions which were considered to be inconsistent with the edicts of the Council of Trent. In the following year he was appointed as the first rector of the new Jesuit college at Pont-à-Mousson, where he remained until shortly prior to his return to Scotland in 1582.[50]

While Hay and Crichton made their way to Rome Abercrombie, Gordon, Murdoch, Tyrie and John Hay remained at Louvain. Abercrombie spent less than a year there, before being sent to Rome, along with William Murdoch.[51] He entered the Society on 19 August 1563 and was assigned to the Roman College. In November 1564 he was sent to East Prussia to help establish the Jesuit college at Braunsberg (Braniewo), with his friend, Cardinal Stanislaus Hosius, one of the great figures of the Counter-Reformation.[52] Abercrombie was one of a number of fathers from Rome originally instructed to go to Vienna, via Prague, where they were to join up with other fathers from Cologne, Mainz and Dillingen, including Canisius, Tyrie, Murdoch and an Englishman, John Wick. During 1563 Germany had been ravaged by the plague and travel across the Alps was severely restricted. With great difficulty the party reached the college at Innsbruck, where it was turned away by the over-cautious rector, Johannes Dyrsius. Following a change of instructions Abercrombie was sent back to Prague and then on to Braunsberg. Although still very junior he was soon considered suitable for promotion, his former tutor Laínez describing him as 'an excellent man not wanting in knowledge, even in theology and prudent. In his own country he is of good birth. He might perhaps do useful work with the English and Scots who come to Danzig'.[53] Abercrombie settled in quickly at Braunsberg and although he expressed a desire to learn the local language as quickly as possible he never fully mastered it. He hankered to return home and 'if a door were opened in Scotland, he will not be too preoccupied [to go]'.[54] Unfortunately no opportunities arose and he did not return home for a further sixteen years. He was ordained in 1565 and in 1569 became the first novice-master at Braunsberg where he also taught grammar and rhetoric. He professed his four vows in May 1585 and aside from a spell at Vilnius between 1575 and 1580 and a short trip to Scotland in 1580 remained at Braunsberg until 1586.[55] Despite his keeness to serve in Scotland he was forced to accept that the increasing demands on staff in the Jesuit colleges and the deteriorating situation in Scotland meant that a permanent Scottish mission was not initially feasible. He was perhaps slightly envious when he received news of Edmund Hay's mission, but any hopes he may have harboured of returning home were dashed with the further news that while Scottish affairs were still on the agenda they were no longer a priority for the Society. His main tie with the pre-Reformation church in Scotland was severed in 1573 when he was replaced as treasurer of Dunkeld for his failure to subscribe the Articles of Religion and to take the oath acknowledging the king's authority, and for being 'ane Jesuit beyond the say'. In the following year he and a number of other exiled Catholics, including William Chisholm, were denounced as rebels. Nevertheless, he managed to retain a number of minor benefices for a further fifteen years.[56]

His earlier travelling companion and colleague from Dunkeld, William Murdoch, entered the Society in Rome on 29 August 1563 and then headed north with Abercrombie to help with the establishment of the college at Braunsberg. Sometime before 1565 he returned to Rome and entered the Roman College where he remained until 1568 when he was transferred to Paris. He appears to have been ordained there around 1571 and professed his vows the following year before moving on to Pont-à-Mousson, where he served as assistant to the rector, Edmund Hay. He remained at Pont-à-Mousson until 1588 when he joined the Scottish Mission.[57]

James Tyrie entered the Society on 19 August 1563. He studied at the Roman College where it was reported he was making good progress. Polanco in a letter to Hay in November 1564 advised him that his protégé was 'a very promising subject, and keeps in good heath. This year he is repeating his philosophy, and will attend lectures on [Aristotle's] *De Anima* again or the *Metaphysica* which he has not yet heard. For he is so talented and well informed that with his grounding, after hearing a little theology, he will be able to lecture on both books. It is his own desire that he should spend this year in forming himself in the studies I have mentioned and the other Scots approve'.[58] After a spell teaching at Innsbruck he was sent to Paris in 1567 to study theology. He remained there for the best part of twenty five years as a student and then as a professor of philosophy and as rector. He was ordained in Paris in 1572 and professed his four vows there three years later. During his early years in Paris he entered into correspondence with his brother, David, in the hope of reconverting him and a number of other family members. However, his brother brought their correspondence to the attention of John Knox with whom James entered into a debate over the issue of the visibility of the church. His letter to Knox in 1567 arguing that the Catholic church was the visible church on the grounds that it was universal and enjoyed doctrinal apostolicity provoked an immediate response, which was published shortly before Knox's death in 1572 in a manuscript entitled *An Answer to a Letter of a Jesuit named Tyrie be Iohn Knox*, in which Knox argued that the church was an object of faith not of right. A further response, *The Refutation of Ane Ansuer made be Schir Iohne Knox*, was issued by Tyrie, but despite the General Assembly's proposal that replies be drafted by John Duncanson and later George Hay his response remained unanswered. Two draft replies by Duncanson were presented to the relevant General Assembly committee for scrutiny, but there is no record of its findings, or those of a later committee set up to consider a book by Edmund

Hay. John Hamilton, the Scottish regent of the college at Navarre, was highly critical of the fact that 'nether Knox nor any of his factione sen his dead dorst tak in hand to writ ane answeir to Maister James Tyries beuk concerning the visibilite of the Kirk'.[59] The visibility of the church was a recurring theme in the writings of the period and cropped up again in the dispute between Archibald Hamilton and the former Jesuit, Thomas Smeaton, and in John Hay's *Certaine Demandes concerning the Christian religion and discipline*.[60] In 1574 Tyrie also locked horns with Andrew Melville, the celebrated Scottish Presbyterian, who was persuaded by Lord Ogilvie to take up the challenge while passing through Paris *en route* from Geneva to Scotland.[61]

James Gordon left Louvain some time in 1562 and entered the Society in Cologne on 20 September 1563. After a short spell in Mainz he was transferred to Rome where he served as notary and as a theologian. He was ordained there in 1568 before being sent to Vienna, where he professed his vows and served as professor of theology. His work *De Puro Dei Verbo*, written in Vienna in 1572, remained unanswered until 1588 when Gordon was working in Scotland. Andrew Melville was impressed by Gordon's arguments which he thought demonstrated 'great diligence and sophistrie'. Again there is no record of the publication of the response by Peter Blackburn, one of the ministers of Aberdeen and a future bishop of the diocese. James Gordon of Huntly should not be confused with James Gordon of Lesmoir, who entered the Society on 29 September 1573 and served as rector of Toulouse and then Bordeaux. He was also confessor to Louis XIII of France and died in Paris in 1641 aged eighty eight after sixty eight years in the Society.[62]

Another young Scot who arrived on the continent in the early 1560s was Edmund Hay's brother, Walter. Jesuit sources refer to the two as brothers, though *The Scots Peerage*, which is comprehensive, but not definitive, states that Edmund had four siblings, none of whom was called Walter. He entered the Society on 2 October 1562 at the Jesuit college in Cologne, where he had previously been a student. In April 1564 he arrived in Rome and was placed in the German College, from where it was reported that 'he seems to be a good lad'. In August 1564 Polanco advised Edmund, who was in Innsbruck at the time, that his brother was ill in Rome and was to be sent to Ingolstadt or Dillingen, in Bavaria, to recuperate.[63] A few months later Polanco confirmed that Walter had arrived in Vienna and would be sent on to one of the other colleges. Polanco also sought Edmund's advice about what should be done in the longer term with his brother and together they decided that he should travel to Paris with Crichton so that Edmund could keep an eye on him. Over studying was blamed for his ill health, which prevented him fulfilling any early promise and plagued him until his death in Paris in 1584.[64]

Another Hay who joined the Society in the aftermath of de Gouda's mission was John Hay of the Delgaty branch of the family.[65] Having completed his studies at Louvain in 1565 he travelled to Rome and after a short stay at the German College entered the Society on 24 January 1566. After completing his studies at the Roman College and at Louvain, where he professed his simple vows, he was sent to Poland. He was accompanied part of the way by Thomas Zdelaric, who had been appointed professor of philosophy at the college. They arrived in Vilnius in the summer of 1570 and by the autumn Hay was lecturing in rhetoric and dialectics and running the library. He spent the majority of the next five years in Vilnius, apart from a few months at Braunsberg as a temporary professor assisting Abercrombie. On his return to Vilnius he started lecturing in philosophy and was appointed as adviser to the rector. During his time in Poland Hay acquired a reputation as a skilful teacher, writer and debater and in December 1574 in recognition of his achievements Francisco Sunyer, the vice provincial of Poland, asked Mercurian to grant him the title of doctor. In the following year his colleague, Stanislaus Rozdrazewski, described him as: 'a very educated man, ... his mind is so outstanding that it would be difficult to find another like him, at least in Poland. Philosopher, rhetorician and – what is more important – good theologian, as many sensible people in Vilno will confirm. The heretics call him 'The God of the Jesuits'. He has well-trained pupils among his domestics [the Jesuit seminarists] and his external students. It is particularly noteworthy that here (where the study of philosophy is either despised or neglected) during these three years not only did he not lose any of his pupils but on the contrary he added to their number'.[66] His writings during this period included a collection of philosophical theses written for public debate in Vilnius and a commentary on Book III of Aristotle's treatise on the soul.[67]

In common with many of his colleagues Hay suffered from ill-health which dogged him until his departure in 1575. His well-being was not improved by the squabble with his colleague, Pedro Viana, who taught moral philosophy and polemics, over the respective virtues of Aristotle and Aquinas.[68] In 1574–5 he was responsible for a report on the state of the Scottish college at Ratisbon, in which he was highly critical of the canonical position of the abbot, Thomas Anderson. While the criticism was no doubt founded the report's impartiality is somewhat questionable as the Society was keen to take over the control of the college.[69] In February 1575 he asked to leave Poland and return to Scotland, but before doing so travelled to Strasbourg to recuperate and while there engaged in the celebrated dispute with the Lutheran, Johannes Pappus, on the issue of transubstantiation. Embarrassed by the unwilllingness of the local Catholic community to respond to the challenge thrown down by the Protestants, Hay, pretending to be a layman, took up the mantle. He won the first round convincingly and then the rematch, which was demanded when it was discovered that he was a Jesuit. During the course of the first debate Pappus is alleged to have become somewhat exasperated and to have cried out 'Ou tu es le diable, ou tu es Jesuite'. In 1578 his request to return to Scotland was granted and preparations were put in hand for his mission of the following year, of which more later.[70]

Thomas Smeaton of Gask, near Perth, was another contemporary of John Hay during his novitiate. Smeaton was a cleric of Dunblane and a student of Perth Grammar School and St Salvator's College. He was subsequently a regent of the college and on account of his continuing Catholicism left for France following his graduation. Calderwood relates that 'He went to France about the beginning of reformatioun, at what time he was removed from the Old Colledge of Sanct Andrewes. He was desirous to know the right way to salvatioun and left no meane untried. Understanding that the order of the Jesuits was the most learned and exquisite order in Papistrie, he resolved to enter in their order during the yeeres of probatioun; and at the end thereof if he found all his doubts removed, he would continue a Jesuit; if not he would yeeld to that light which his loving freinds, Mr Thomas Matlane [Maitland], Mr Andrew Melvill, and Mr Gilbert Muncreif showed him when he was in France'.[71] Before entering the Society Smeaton was professor of humanities at Paris, where the university records show that he made a disbursement for souls in purgatory while an official of the German nation.[72] In July 1566 he and two other Scots made their way to Rome, where the general, Francis Borgia, had been advised by Edmund Hay that all three were suitable applicants for entry to the Society. Smeaton entered on 22 September 1566 and in October 1568 returned to Paris. He was posted back to Rome the following summer and remained there for four years. Hay, who later showed great compassion for his friend's dilemma, was presumably unaware that he was already beginning to have doubts about his faith, which were reinforced during a visit to Geneva while *en route* to Rome. After a further year and a half his doubts were still unresolved and in Rome he was suspected of being a Protestant sympathiser. These doubts were further fuelled by visits to the city's prisons. On his return to Paris he rejoined Clermont College as a lecturer in humanities and in October 1571 was recommended by Hay for appointment as rector of Billom. James Melville, the diarist, noted that Hay 'nochtwithstanding that he perceavit his [Smeaton's] mynd turned away from thair ordour and relligion, yit he ceased nocht to counsall him frindlie and fatherlie, and suffered him to want na thing'. Soon after he left for Geneva, where, following discussions with the Protestant authorities, and with his doubts still unresolved, he was persuaded to leave the Catholic church. He may also have been influenced by Protestant friends and family whom he met during the course of a visit to Scotland on personal business. On his return to Paris he travelled in the company of his old friend, Thomas Maitland, the youngest brother of Maitland of Lethington. While there he was lucky to escape death in the St Bartholomew's Massacre and took refuge with the English ambassador, Francis Walsingham, with whose help he secured a passage to England. There he renounced the Catholic faith and settled in Colchester as a school master. He finally returned to Scotland in 1577 to take up office in the Kirk as the minister of Paisley and Girvan and shortly after was appointed moderator of the General Assembly. He was subsequently dean and principal of Glasgow University.[73]

Chapter 4

The Establishment of the Scottish Mission

Following Mary's abdication and flight to England in 1568 the sporadic civil war in Scotland rumbled on until 1573. The country was initially governed by Mary's half-brother James Stewart, Earl of Moray, whose regency was marked by 'indecision and mixed motivation'. The Marians, who resented Moray's supplanting of his sister, looked outwith Scotland, and to Charles IX of France in particular, for assistance against the regent and his English backers. They were encouraged by the rising of the Northern Earls in England in November 1569 led by Thomas Percy, Earl of Northumberland, and Charles Neville, Earl of Westmorland, which they hoped would culminate in the marriage of Mary and Thomas Howard, Duke of Norfolk, and the overthrow of Protestantism throughout the British Isles. Their optimism was shortlived and any hopes of a Marian revival evaporated with the ruthless supression of the northern rising during the following month. Although Moray's assassination on 23 January 1570 by James Hamilton of Bothwellhaugh was celebrated by his opponents there was no long term improvement in their fortunes.[1]

The appointment of a new regent, Matthew Stewart, 4th Earl of Lennox, the young king's paternal grandfather, in July 1570 put an end to the short-lived Marian resurgence. The following year the Marian cause suffered a further set back with the uncovering of the Ridolfi Plot, orchestrated by Roberto Ridolfi, a Florentine banker, who, with the assistance of Bishop Leslie of Ross, devised a further scheme involving a Catholic uprising supported by Spanish troops from the Netherlands, the marriage of Mary and Norfolk and the overthrow of Elizabeth. Doubt has been expressed about the role played by Ridolfi, whom some suspect of having been a government agent. Fortunately for Ridolfi he was abroad when the plot was uncovered, though Norfolk was less fortunate and was executed the following year. Lennox's short lived regency was followed by the equally brief regency of John Erskine, Earl of Mar, who ruled from early September 1572 until his death the following month. He in turn was succeeded by the staunchly pro-English James Douglas, 4th Earl of Morton, who held office almost continually until 1580. At first his appointment was viewed with some optimism by the Catholics, who in the early 1570s, when Morton had initially refused the regency, had looked on him as a potential ally. According to a Jesuit report written over twenty years later: 'He did not persecute the Catholics; and if any of them came into the realm, not only did he permit them to remain there unmolested, but even showed them a certain amount of favour'. Although this proved to be a fleeting friendship, it is clear that Morton had equally little time for the reformed clergy: 'As for the ministers of his own religion, he treated them as men of no character or consideration. He was in the habit of continually repeating that there was no room for comparing the most wealthy of the ministers with the poorest among the priests whom he had ever seen; that in the priests there was more fidelity, more gravity, and more hospitality, than in the whole herd of the others'.[2]

After the fall of Edinburgh Castle and the collapse of the Marian party in 1573 it was reported that large numbers of Catholics, including prominent figures such as John Stewart, Earl of Atholl, had subscribed the Articles of Religion. Morton's goodwill towards the Catholics came to an end in 1573–4 when a number were executed, including Thomas Robeson, a former Paisley schoolmaster, hanged for persistent celebration of the Mass. In the following year a decree was issued outlawing a number of leading Catholics, including William Chisholm, Edmund Hay, Tyrie, Murdoch and Abercrombie, and forbidding their families from supplying them with 'money, fynance, counsall or uther ayid quhatsumevir'.[3] Morton's hard-line approach had the desired effect and the diarist, James Melville, reported that during his regency 'The name of a Papist durst nocht be hard of'. Henry Killigrew, the English ambassador in Edinburgh, attributed this period of relative calm to the reconciliation which had been reached between Morton and the Kirk, while the Jesuit report of 1594 suggests that it may have been due to the fact that the regent did nothing 'to excite a sharper persecution of the Catholics'. Certainly Morton appears not to have been vindictive, though when dealing with opponents he was by nature a pacifier rather than a conciliator.[4] Although his 'was the first stable government decisively committed to Protestantism', the reconciliation with the Kirk was not easily achieved and Morton's concern about various aspects of the Kirk's economic and political policies made conflict inevitable. One of the Kirk's main weaknesses during this period was the lack of manpower, though during the course of the 1570s it did manage to establish an adequate ministry in most parts of the country.[5] Despite the Kirk's internal problems and its conflict with central government the Catholics were unable to capitalise on the situation and by the 1580s, when the political climate appeared to be changing in their favour, the reformers' position was secure.[6]

Although the privy council decree of 1574 named a number of Jesuits it would be wrong to assume that the survival of Catholicism was solely the result of the activities of the Society. Although Jesuit historians have tended to highlight its rôle, the Society did not become involved in Scottish affairs in any meaningful way until the early 1580s. Thomas Innes, a secular priest and the archivist of the Scots College in Paris in the early eighteenth century, who was no friend of the Society, attributed the survival of Catholicism to the activities of the secular clergy, such as Bishop Crichton and the priests who formed his Catholic circle. Innes suggested that during the post-Reformation period 'though not all publicly declared, [the Catholics] were as yet as numerous as the Protestants, and that the Catholics had, for the most part, priests of the ancient clergy in their families'.[7] This was particularly common amongst the leading Catholic families of the north east and the south west where the Gordons and the Maxwells respectively held sway, while in Dunkeld Lady Atholl employed a number of priests in her household and was under constant pressure from the Kirk to replace them with a Protestant minister. Although there was a considerable number of recusant priests they lacked leadership, especially after the early 1570s when a number of Catholic bishops were removed from office and Protestant clergy appointed in their places. At Dunkeld John Winram, the Superintendent of Fife, carried out a systematic reorganisation of the chapter, appointing twelve new Protestant canons alongside the existing three. According to Innes: 'The clergy, thus deprived of a Bishop, their natural head, and so of an immediate centre of union, and of a common superior to give motion to their body and govern them, were left, as it were in their own hands, each man to act as his own zeal prompted him, but without a common concert and unable to take any joint measures'.[8] However, the removal of Catholic clergy did not always make the Kirk's task any easier. Crichton's successor as bishop, James Paton (1571–96), was continually being admonished by the General Assembly for his failure to act against recusants within his diocese, including the formidable Lady Atholl.[9]

Despite the pressing need for spiritual leadership within the Catholic community proposals put forward in 1571 for a Scottish mission to assist the embattled secular clergy were rejected. Likewise, although there was considerable interest in the establishment of an English mission, it was a further five years before any realistic plans were drawn up. The lack of progress is perhaps surprising given that Loyola and another senior father, Pedro de Ribadeneira, had visited England earlier in their careers.[10] For reasons which are unclear the training of English students at the Roman and German Colleges for entry into the Society and the establishment of an English mission was blocked by Cardinal Reginald Pole, who was, nevertheless, an early supporter of the Jesuits. Loyola's successor as general, Diego Laínez, was equally unenthusiastic, as was William Allen, the leader of the English Catholic exiles, who, because of the uncertainty of the situation in England, was wary of the prospects for any mission. He was also concerned that the number of English students at the college at Douai, founded in 1568, was much lower than had been anticipated. As well as the Scots and Irish only 170 young Englishmen had been attracted to the college.[11]

Despite these concerns there was a ground swell of opinion amongst the English exiles in favour of an English mission. Much of the initial planning was done by a young Englishman, Robert Persons, who had been forced to leave Oxford University in 1575, despite having twice taken the Oath of Supremacy. While *en route* to Padua to study medicine Persons stopped off at Louvain where he completed his Spiritual Exercises under an English Jesuit, William Good. After visits to Rome and Padua, where Persons decided against studying medicine, he returned to Rome and on 4 July 1575 entered the Society. During the course of his novitiate Persons began to develop his ideas for an English mission, which received little support from Mercurian.[12]

However, Mercurian was not allowed to procrastinate for long and he soon found himself under considerable pressure from various quarters to give Persons' plans serious consideration. Allen's earlier doubts were resolved by a fellow exile, Doctor Nicholas Sander, who persuaded him that 'The state of Christendome dependethe uppon the stowte assallynge of England'.[13] Allen urged Mercurian to send a number of fathers to England, including Persons, but he remained reluctant to do so in case it was misinterpreted by the English government as having political connotations.[14] Despite a number of other sound reasons for his refusal to authorise an English mission pressure was mounting on Mercurian from senior colleagues within the Society, including Oliver Mannaerts, the assistant for Germany, and Claudio Acquaviva, the Roman provincial.[15] Another interested party was Henry, Duke of Guise, who had succeeded his uncle, Charles Guise, Cardinal of Lorraine, as the leader of the extreme Catholic faction in

France. In April 1578 Henry met with Juan de Vargas Mexia, the Spanish ambassador in France, to discuss amongst other matters, the invasion of England. According to the ambassador's report to Philip, Guise's interest was two-fold; the restoration of Catholicism in England and the release of his cousin, Mary.[16] The duke also offered to found a new college at Eu in Normandy to be funded from his own pocket and the revenues of a nearby priory.[17] The Spanish were more wary about a direct attack on England and were already looking into the possibility of an invasion via Scotland. Bernardino de Mendoza, the recently appointed Spanish ambassador in London, advised caution, pointing out to Philip that any invasion would be looked on unfavourably by Spain's continental rivals. He was also reluctant to subsidise the notoriously unreliable Scottish Catholic nobles until he was sure of their unity and loyalty. Furthermore, any involvement with the Scottish Catholics would inevitably require close co-operation with Archbishop Beaton, Mary's ambassador in Paris, who depended heavily on French support. Mendoza's advice to the royal secretary, Zayas, was to avoid any alliance with the French and to explore other ways of uniting the Scottish and English Catholics without endangering Mary, who was 'so given up to the French connection, that nothing can be done without their hearing of it'.[18]

Despite his initial enthusiasm Guise was persuaded to take a back seat in any negotiations on the grounds that Philip would never commit himself to any enterprise if it involved having to collaborate with the French. Guise had little option but to accept this ultimatum as the financial fortunes of his family were precarious and to take the lead in any invasion would undoubtedly have hastened their decline. As well as the prospect of direct subsidies from Spain he also had his eye on a share of the lucrative trade links with America. With the withdrawal of Guise, Mary was advised to place herself under Philip's protection and in February 1580 Beaton informed de Vargas Mexia of her wish to align herself with Spain.[19] Despite the Spanish offer of assistance and pensions for the ever greedy Scottish nobles Scotland was never the main focus of Philip's plans and these moves were merely part of a broader strategy directed against England and involving the incorporation of the whole of Britain into the Spanish empire. Mendoza's warnings about Spanish involvement in Scottish affairs were confirmed by James's subsequent subscription of the Negative or King's Confession on 28 January 1581 and his submission to the General Assembly. However, despite this 'shameful confession', which Mendoza believed would destroy any prospect of any collaboration with the Scottish Catholics, the relationship between them and Spain grew closer.[20]

Calls for a Scottish mission continued during the 1570s. In anticipation of the go-ahead being given Beaton suggested to Mercurian that Scottish Jesuits should be transferred to France to work with their countrymen in exile there. By the end of the decade the majority of Scottish Jesuits were working in France; however, sending them to Scotland was still a step too far for Mercurian. In 1579 Beaton and a number of Scottish fathers pressed him to reconsider his position, and although a large amount of the correspondence from them to the general has been lost, there are frequent references to their proposals in his responses.[21] Despite the pressure he delayed making any decision, not just because he was personally opposed, but also because he was aware that Gregory XIII and Mary were unenthusiastic.[22] Although he turned down a request from James Fitzgerald Fitzmaurice to send a number of fathers to Scotland to stir up support for his rising in Ireland, Mercurian did allow John Hay and Robert Abercrombie to return to Scotland in 1578–9 and 1580 respectively. Hay's visit would appear to have been for health reasons and permission was only granted reluctantly. He was told that his health was to take priority and that he was not to expose himself to any unnecessary danger. Abercrombie's mission appears to have been a fact-finding trip, though on whose instructions is unclear. Hay's and Abercrombie's reports were forwarded to Mercurian's successor, Acquaviva, and, along with news of the subsequent downfall of Morton, were instrumental in persuading him to give the go-ahead for the establishment of a formal mission. The new general, although he had previously supported calls for an English mission, and had even volunteered to go to England himself, was initially opposed to a Scottish one, but from correspondence around this time it is clear that Persons was influential in resolving his initial scepticism.[23]

John Hay's visit to Scotland was the first Jesuit mission since de Gouda's in 1562.[24] He embarked from Bordeaux on 23 December 1578 and disembarked in Dundee almost a month later after a slow and hazardous crossing. To while away the long hours on board ship he engaged in theological debate with two of the crew, who were apparently closet Catholics. His arrival in Scotland caused great consternation but, according to Hay, he was generally well-received:

> I had scarcely left the city [Dundee] when I encountered a number of persons of rank, and was questioned with much curiosity as to

who I was, and where I came from. I would not reply till I had ascertained that I had got beyond the boundary of the jurisdiction of Dundee; and when they learnt that I was a man of education, that I was withdrawing from the control of the magistrate, and that the latter had threatened to detain me in custody at the suggestion of his minister, one of them asked if I was a Jesuit. When I answered frankly that I was one of those whom they call Jesuits, he told me not to be under any uneasiness, and that the minister had better look out for himself, since my kinsmen lived close by, and would be sure to pay him out very handsomely for any wrong done to me… Most of the sailors who came with me from Bordeaux, took up my defence with warmth when they heard that their minister threatened proceedings against me; and they roundly asserted that the members of our Society were far beyond the ministers in holiness of life, and if the question were to be decided by force of arms, many more would stand up for the Jesuits than for the ministers.

The minister of Dundee began to assail the holiness of our institute with great acrimony in his sermons, the result of which was that the people took to making enquiries for themselves, with respect to our mode of life, manners and discipline, from such persons as had lived in France. Several of them commended our rule, and drew this argument in our favour from the name Jesuit. 'Since they imitate Jesus Christ, those who so cruelly oppose them must be under a great mistake, and in profound ignorance of what the Christian religion is'. The word Jesuit was in everybody's mouth, and nothing else was heard at table, among the higher classes, in taverns, in the market, or in sermons delivered in the church. It was reported all over the kingdom that twelve members of the Society, men of the most eminent piety and learning, had landed at the port of Dundee, and had begun to prove that all the ministers were ignorant deceivers. This rumour caused so much dismay among the ministers that they almost dismayed of maintaining influence in Scotland, and set about exhorting their hearers to constancy and perseverance in the cause, since they could not conceal that their Church was threatened with a grave and pressing peril. The Jesuits (they said) were a new race of persons, far worse that the Papists (as they call the Catholics), and so skilful in the use of the controversial weapons, that wherever they go they easily lead the minds of men astray.

The magistrate in Dundee was unsure how to respond to Hay's arrival, being caught between the calls from the local minister for his arrest and the threat of reprisals from his influential kinsman at nearby Megginch. Hay had intended going to his brother's farm just outside Dundee, but was persuaded to stay at a local inn where he only narrowly avoided capture. After staying three days with his brother he made contact with other family members, including another brother, Edmund Hay, an advocate, who had made his name representing Bothwell at his trial for the murder of Darnley and in his subsequent divorce. He spent a further nine days with his brother during the course of which he met with his powerful Catholic kinsman, George Hay, 8th Earl of Errol, who offered to protect him from the ministers and to arrange safe passage to the king. Further assistance was received from another kinsman, Alexander Hay of Easter Kennet, the clerk register, who was also a kinsman of Robert Abercrombie on his grandmother's side.[25]

In March Hay was summoned to appear before the privy council at Stirling, though an audience was not granted until later in the summer. He advised the council that although he had returned for health reasons he was prepared to dispute with ministers from the Kirk at Glasgow University. The discussions with the council appear to have been relatively amicable; nevertheless, he was ordered to leave Scotland. His brother William put up caution of £1000 guaranteeing that he would do so before 1 October, 'wind and wedder servand', and would do nothing prejudicial to the interests of the Kirk.[26] He was later invited by Lord Adam Gordon of Auchindoun, James Gordon's brother, to spend the winter in Scotland, but was reluctant to jeopardise his brother's caution. He was also keen to ensure that he would be able to return to Scotland at some stage in the future as the privy council's order placed no prohibition on him doing so. He travelled north without being given the opportunity to debate with the ministers and began preparing for his return to France. He was permitted to embark from Dundee, but the captain of the ship was persuaded to berth at Leith, where Hay was well received by many of the locals, including the minister, with whom he engaged in a good-natured dispute. He was unable to meet up with Darnley's cousin, Esmé Stewart, Sieur d'Aubigny, but was optimistic about the influence that he was exerting over James.

On his return to Paris Hay wrote a lengthy report to Mercurian in which he spoke of the unpopularity of the ministers and the undercurrent of support for the Catholic faith. He specifically mentioned a visit to the church of Our Lady of Grace on the banks of the River Spey and the open sale of rosaries at the market in Turriff, close to the Hay seat at Delgaty. He also highlighted the need for more religious books written in Scots and in 1580 he published his *Certaine Demandes concerning the Christian religion and discipline* which took the form of 166 doctrinal points to be answered by the Kirk. The book, which is reminiscent of Winzet's *Buke of Four Scoir thre Questions*, was highly popular and influential and was translated into French and German. It provoked a number of replies, including one from the leading Swiss Protestant, Theodore Beza.[27]

Hay's mission was followed shortly after by that of Abercrombie, who left Vilnius in early April 1580. Again the purpose behind the trip is obscure, though on the basis of the format of his post-mission report it would appear to have been a fact-finding mission to obtain specific information. Abercrombie seems to have stayed mainly in Perthshire making contact with well known local Catholics, including a number of his kinsmen. The mission, unlike many others, does not appear to have come to the attention of the authorities. It also escaped the attention of a number of later historians who have overlooked it in their accounts of the Society. George Oliver and Henry Foley, two eminent Victorian biographers of the Society, both stated that Abercrombie spent 23 years abroad and made no reference to his visit in 1580. The reasons for this omission in their short biographies of Abercrombie are unclear as details of the mission were readily accessible in the Society's archives.[28]

According to his report, compiled on his return to Braunsberg, Abercrombie sailed up the Tay estuary and disembarked close to his grandfather's castle, which was only a mile from his father's house. Although the Tay is now navigable as far upstream as Perth, in former times vessels could only reach the site of the former Roman camp at Carpow, near Abernethy. John Adair's *Chart of the Forth and River of Tay 1703* suggests that Abercrombie could have reached Megginch, but not Murthly. While the identity of the locations referred to in his report are unclear, they do seem to indicate that his grandfather's house was at Megginch, which in turn confirms the suggestion that the Hays of Megginch and the Abercrombies of Murthly were related.

The report dealt at some length with the political and religious situation in Scotland, but it is clear from the contacts Abercrombie made that he ventured little outwith the safety of his family and their kinsmen. In his report he recommended that assistance should be sent to a number of prominent Catholics, in particular his father, Alexander Abercrombie, John Stewart, 5th Earl of Atholl, who had succeeded his father in the previous year, and the earl's mother, Lady Atholl. The earl in fact played no part in the Catholic revival of the 1580s, and unlike his father, who was described as a 'très grand catholique, hardy et vaillant', he was held to be 'a man of little valeur or accompte, in religion suspected'.[29] Lady Atholl urged Abercrombie to stay in Scotland, while her son wrote to his father asking him to persuade his son not to return to the continent. Robert Crichton, under whom Abercrombie had served for a number of years, was also singled out as needing assistance. He described Crichton as:

> of noble rank, of an important family, of spotless life from his youth, as even the heretics admit. He is so firmly attached to the Catholic religion, that, rather than give up the least ceremony, he allowed himself to be deprived of his Bishopric and all his possessions and was even ready to shed his blood. He now lives in Edinburgh in extreme poverty; he has nothing but the alms which good men give him, so scanty that they hardly suffice for himself and a servant. I am certain he would not go anywhere outside Scotland; for he will not even leave the city to go to stay with some noblemen who would like him to be provided for in their houses as long as he lives; nor is he fit to do so, however much he might wish to, for he is an old man and failing in health; he is 80 years old, perhaps a good deal more. In his youth he spent much time in Rome, conducting a law-suit to get possession of his diocese from which he was most unjustly excluded. When he had at length won his case, returned home and was restored to his diocese, he remained in peaceful possession only six or seven years, when he was again deprived of it and robbed of everything by the heretics.

Abercrombie also mentioned two itinerant Franciscan preachers, Fathers Veitch and Leitch, who had been working in Scotland for a number of years. He also reported that there were numerous secular priests still living: 'many of them are now married, and yet are Catholic-minded, though meanwhile they join in with the heretics in everything; they too eagerly look for a change; others again have remained Catholic, have not married and recite the Office. They teach boys to read, to sing and to play musical instruments; some are bold enough to attack the ministers and to dispute with them. I cannot give their names nor their residences; they are all over the Kingdom, and there is no town where there are not still priests, more or fewer according to its size'. As well as more priests to assist those still working in Scotland Abercrombie recommended that the Scottish Catholics be supplied with suitably instructive literature, such as James Tyrie's *The Refutation of Ane Ansuer*, John Hay's, *Certaine Demandes*, and a variety of other vernacular books by leading English Catholics, including Nicholas Sander, William Allen and Thomas Stapleton. He also claimed that the Kirk's failure to respond to Tyrie and Hay and its refusal to dispute with members of the Society had resulted in a certain amount of hostility between it and the nobles.[30]

Abercrombie also provided a short analysis of James, describing him as being secretly in favour of the Catholic cause despite his Calvinist upbringing, of morally good life, sporty, serious in manner, but cheerful and jovial in private. However, like many of his contemporaries, including colleagues within the Society, his judgement of James was flawed: 'I do not regard him as a heretic, and indeed on account of his youth there can be no question of obstinate heresy, and I do not doubt that, if he had a good instructor, he would become in a year an excellent and devout Catholic Prince'. Despite these high hopes Abercrombie conceded that James's conversion was unlikely in the short term, and as an alternative suggested a Catholic marriage as the best means of ensuring favourable treatment for Scottish Catholics. Ironically James's future wife did become a Catholic and Abercrombie's relationship with Queen Anne will be dealt with later.[31]

Abercrombie was generally critical of the nobility, though, like John Hay, he was optimistic about the rise of d'Aubigny, whose secretary Henry Kerr was an acquaintance of Abercrombie and had been James Gordon's tutor at Louvain. Of the officers of state he only mentions his kinsman, Alexander Hay, the clerk register, who, although he was a heretic, had assisted John Hay during his earlier visit to Scotland. Morton, who detested Robert's father, was singled out as the most dangerous of the Protestants: 'The cleverest of all, and the worst of all the entourage of the King is Morton, who usually supplants all others by his cunning; though a heretic he heartily hates the Ministers, but he is so eaten up with greed that he cares nothing about religion so long as he can accumulate money'. Confirming other contemporary reports Abercrombie advised that there was a large number of potential recruits to the Society in Scotland. Many noblemen had indicated to him that they were keen to send their sons to the college at Braunsberg as the Society's reputation was particularly good compared with that of the Kirk, whose ministers were widely disliked for displaying the same traits which had made their Catholic predecessors so unpopular. As well as snapping up the best properties the ministers also married the prettiest daughters of the nobility and burgesses and sometimes even bought them! Naturally everyone had 'a good opinion of the Society, except the Ministers and some men of little account who support them. A sign of this is that though everyone believed me a Jesuit, and knew I was a member of the Society I was never welcomed with such kindness as on this occasion, so much honoured and so well treated, not even when I was a layman and formerly attended Court'.

In concluding Abercrombie surmised that there was still a large number of Catholic nobles and that the Scots were in general 'very well disposed to return to the Church, but the one obstacle is that the chief men of the Kingdom have taken possession of Church lands'. Somewhat naïvely he thought these men could be won over with offices, services and presents, such as 'a book containing pictures of the Roman Caesars or Roman Antiquities; boxes or little chests of steel... fine swords, guns etc., tiny watches for pendants, or for bedrooms, striking or marking the hours, alarm clocks etc., also those brass sun-dials which Father Clavius used to make in the form of a cross'. He also made a number of further general recommendations, including the sending of gifts and alms to rich and poor Catholics and the granting of dispensations for priests working in Scotland, permitting them to celebrate Mass in unconsecrated places, discard their habits and attend Protestant sermons and prayers.

At some stage after completion the report was forwarded to Father William Good in Rome, who made a number of further suggestions for future missions, such as the need for greater secrecy and adequate financial resources. He pointed out that due to inadequate funding John Hay had previously had to rely on help from strangers. He also expressed some concern about the various dispensations suggested by Abercrombie, but agreed that the Franciscans, Veitch and Leitch, should be allowed to discard their habits and preach in unconsecrated places and should be provided with small chests in which to carry their Mass vestments and a portable altar stone.[32] Abercrombie returned to Braunsberg in late August accompanied by two students wishing to enter the college. He resumed his duties as novice-master and after a spell as assistant to the Bishop of Wlocawek professed his vows in May 1585.[33]

Abercrombie's report, despite its somewhat limited scope, was highly influential and was subsequently relied on by Robert Persons, who after fleeing from England in the aftermath of the first English mission began to take a much closer interest in Scottish affairs. There has been some debate about the reasons for Persons' interest in Scotland, but it would appear that he simply viewed the country as a springboard for the invasion of England. Whatever his motives the increased persecution of the Catholic community in England during the course of the 1580s meant that Scotland began to play a more important role in Spanish and Papal foreign policy and in the plans of the English exiles.[34]

Chapter 5

The Sacred Expedition to Scotland

Robert Persons' interest in Scottish affairs was shared by other influential figures within the Society, who persuaded Claudio Acquaviva that a 'sacred expedition' to Scotland was feasible. Although previously sceptical Gregory and Mary had also been won over, the former as the result of an enthusiastic briefing from Crichton, who was in Rome as a delegate at the Third General Congregation of the Society convened to elect the new general. Acquaviva's main concern before sanctioning any mission was to obtain assurances from the Scottish Catholics that any fathers sent to Scotland would receive the necessary protection. With the arrival of further encouraging reports from Persons he was persuaded, despite the absence of such assurances, to give his consent. While the situation in Scotland may not have been as favourable as suggested by Persons or by Hay and Abercrombie in their post-mission reports, there was good reason to believe that it was improving. Dramatic changes were taking place at court where d'Aubigny was starting to exert his influence over the impressionable young king to such an extent that in April 1580 English intelligence warned of the threat posed by this ambitious young nobleman, who 'yf he prosper shalbe an instrument to overthrowe the religion there'. Bishop Leslie of Ross, while lamenting the death of Atholl, that 'illustrious protector of the Catholic party', was optimistic that d'Aubigny would take his place to lead the 'many left who have not bent their knees before Baal'.[1]

English concern increased over the following months, partly fuelled by further reports from Francis Walsingham, the English spy-master, who in May advised that it was common knowledge in Spain that plans were being discussed for the re-establishment of Catholicism in Scotland. He also reported an air of optimism amongst the exiled Scots in the Low Countries and France and advised that his intelligence reports indicated that any Catholic counter-offensive would begin in Scotland:

> This ill disposcion in the common sorte there maketh me more to doubt that there is some great and hidden reason not yet discovered, and to feare that the speches cast abroade in Spaine, whereof late adverstisement hath bene sent hither, are not altogether vaine; which be theis, that alreadye armes are taken in Scotland, and that the masse and Romish religion is set up in that realme. It is further reported also, that such rebelles and fugitives, boeth of that and this realme, as be eyther in the Lowe Countryes or France, are in great hope and expectacion that the matter of religion shall presently and first be pushed at in Scotland, ... And by sondry other advertisements from divers places it is declared that the first attempt to alter religion will begin in Scotland.

The English government was alarmed and confused by reports throughout the summer of 1580 suggesting that d'Aubigny and his servant Henry Kerr, previously 'stiffe Papistes', were beginning to exert some influence over the Protestant ministers in Edinburgh. In a letter to the General Assembly d'Aubigny claimed that God had called him 'by his grace and mercy to the knowledge of [his] salvation'.[2]

Such was the growing confidence of the Catholics in Scotland that in July 1580 Nicol Burne, a former Protestant professor of philosophy at St Andrews, challenged the former Jesuit, Thomas Smeaton, now minister of Paisley, to a public debate. A panel of twelve judges was agreed, but before the parties could meet Smeaton excommunicated Burne and had him imprisoned in the Tolbooth in Edinburgh. Smeaton's attitude towards Burne was in stark contrast to the sympathetic treatment he had been shown by Jesuit colleagues when trying to resolve his own religious doubts. He certainly displayed none of the 'auld Parisiane kyndnes' shown to him by Edmund Hay. After his release from jail Burne made his way to Paris where in 1581 he published his *Disputation concerning the Controversit Headdes of Religion* before joining the Scots College at Pont-à-Mousson. The *Disputation* deals with similar topics to those in John Hay's *Certaine Demandes*, including the nature of the Papacy, the universality of the Catholic church and the validity of the Protestant ministry. Attached to the *Disputation* was a work which has been attributed to Burne, *Ane Admonition to the Unchristian Ministers of the Deformed Kirk of Scotland*, a satirical poem attacking the leading figures in the Kirk, in which the writer, somewhat prematurely suggested that the Protestants should 'to geneve haist with speed'. Amongst those on the receiving end of Burne's caustic wit were his former sparring partner, Smeaton, and

'Wynrame the loun', the superintendent of Fife, who had been criticised by de Gouda in his report in 1562.[3]

The Scottish government's reaction to this Catholic revival was a new act of parliament denouncing papistry and introducing harsher penalties for recusancy and the Negative or King's Confession, drawn up at James's request by his chaplain, John Craig. The confession required signatories to publicly endorse Protestantism, affirm their support for the Confession of Faith and reject 'all contrare religion and doctrine: but chiefly all kynde of papistrie in generall and perticular headis' and the 'fyve bastard sacramentis'. It was signed by James, d'Aubigny and other members of the royal household and was reintroduced during later Catholic scares in 1587–8 and 1595–6.[4]

* * *

Meanwhile in Rome the English mission was finally given the go-ahead, though some, including Mercurian, were sceptical about the prospects of success.[5] Acquaviva was concerned, as his predecessors had been, that the mission would be seen as a political move by the Papacy and that the martyrdom of the Society's fathers, rather than any meaningful missionary work, would be the inevitable outcome of their involvement.[6] Despite his concerns the mission proceeded, and as he had feared the government's reaction was hostile. Persons arrived in England on 16 June disguised as a soldier returning from Flanders and ten days later was joined by Edmund Campion and a lay brother, Ralph Emerson, 'his little man', who was to act as his secretary. Emerson, a native of Durham, entered the Society around 1569 at the age of eighteen and took his vows as a temporal coadjutor in 1579.[7] Campion's disguise as a jewel merchant would appear to have been less than convincing as he had to rely on help from Catholic sympathisers to avoid capture. It is clear that the government was fully aware of the mission as details of it were relayed by its spies in Rome. It was with good reason that Mendoza was continually bemoaning the lack of secrecy shown by the Society and while disguises, aliases and ciphers may have caused some temporary confusion, they were no guarantee of anonymity.[8]

Although the arrival of the Jesuit fathers, followed by a number of secular priests, was hailed as a great success, the mission soon ran into difficulties. Persons and Campion spent a year trying to keep one step ahead of the authorities and after a tour of the provinces Persons returned to London in October 1580, where he was forced to seek assistance from Mendoza. During the course of the winter of 1580–1 the ambassador briefed him on the plans for the invasion of England and from this time on Persons became a keen advocate of Spanish interests. After months of evading the authorities he fled to Sussex and then to Rouen in northern France, where he lived disguised as a merchant under an assumed name and enjoying the protection of Michel de Monsi, Archdeacon of Rouen and vicar general of Archbishop Charles, Cardinal Bourbon. Campion was finally captured in July 1581, tortured and soon after executed at Tyburn along with two secular priests, Alexander Briant and Ralph Sherwin. Campion's famous *Brag and Challenge* failed to convince the English authorities that the aims of the mission were purely spiritual, and while his subsequent martyrdom has been a source of great inspiration to many English Catholics and to future generations of missionaries, it is difficult to disagree with Henry More's assessment of the mission that: 'The two grains planted in the island in 1580 had scarcely produced, in all the 20 years, the 20th Jesuit who could be employed in sustaining Catholicism in so great a country'.[9]

* * *

In light of the harsh treatment meted to Campion and the other English missionaries and the increased persecution of the Catholic community in general the English exiles looked to Scotland where a more liberal regime appeared to offer greater prospects of success. Persons, although not advocating a Scottish mission, recognised the importance of events north of the border and argued that: 'the greatest hope we have lies in Scotland on which country depends the conversion not only of England, but all the lands in the North'.[10] In the autumn of 1580 he instructed William Watts, a secular priest, to find out whether or not Scotland would indeed provide a refuge for English Catholic clergy. Although Watts was described by Mendoza as 'an English clergyman … who was brought up in Scotland', he was in fact Welsh. He was known to have had associations with the borders, though there is no evidence to corroborate either part of Mendoza's statement. He was clearly a resourceful man and was noted for his 'prudence, charity and knowledge'. Physically he was 'short of stature and thick, his beard yellow and thick, his face white, the tip of his nose going downward like unto a hawk's bill'. Originally from St David's Diocese in Wales, Watts studied at the English seminary at Rheims and in August 1578 was sent to England. He was imprisoned for a spell in York Castle, but escaped. It is highly likely that as well as working for Persons, Watts also acted as a messenger for Mendoza and a small faction of English Catholic nobles, who were keen to make contact with their Scottish counterparts. Their plans included an assault on England via Scotland, the conversion of James, the liberation of Mary and the removal of Elizabeth, and without being in a position to give it they were prepared to offer the Scottish nobles an assurance of support from the English Catholic community. There is some confusion as to Watt's exact movements during this period as there are a number of reports compiled around the same time referring to various unnamed priests. However, by a process of deduction it would appear that in the majority of cases it is Watts who is being referred to.[11]

In the summer of 1581 after ten months in the north Watts returned to London to find that a number of the English Catholic nobles had been imprisoned along with Edmund Campion. His favourable reports of conditions in Scotland and the ease of cross-border travel were in stark contrast to the position south of the border and prompted Persons to send Watts back to Edinburgh to offer James the support of both the Scottish and the English Catholics. He was also instructed to emphasise to James that the support of the English Catholics was vital in securing the English throne, and to remind him of his mother's predicament and of his father's murder at the hands of the Protestant nobles who were now vying for his patronage. He also received fresh instructions from Mendoza and the remaining nobles to make contact with their Scottish counterparts.[12]

Watts crossed the border in late August and met with William Kerr of Cessford, the Warden of the Middle Marches, from whom he obtained a grant of safe conduct throughout Scotland. He then travelled on to Edinburgh and from there retired to the safety of Seton House, a few miles outside the city. Within a few weeks Watts sent his first report to Persons, which was to be delivered by Watts' servant along with a separate verbal message. On reaching London the messenger found that Persons had already fled to the continent, and as a result was not prepared to disclose the message to anyone else. The letter, which was sent to Persons in Rouen and then forwarded on to Acquaviva, confirmed that Watts had identified Lennox, Huntly, Eglinton, Caithness, Seton, Home, Ogilvie and Kerr of Ferniehurst as Catholic sympathisers, who had all assured him of their support and had appealed for more priests to be sent north. However, although they were prepared to guarantee the safety of these priests they were reluctant to meet the cost of supporting them once they had arrived.

They were also keen that Persons should go to Scotland, with a number of colleagues, including Jasper Heywood, who were to bring with them two letters from Mary as proof of their identity.[13] Heywood, who had a history of mental and physical instability since the early 1570s, was the nephew of Henry VIII's lord chancellor, Sir Thomas More, and the uncle of John Donne, the poet. He was a former Oxford don who had entered the Society in 1562 and professed his vows at Dillingen in 1570. He was described by a contemporary as 'so grave a man as I ever sett my eyes upon, he wore a coate of black very low and upon the same cloke of black, downe almost to the grounde. He had in his hand a black staff and upon his head a velvet coyfe and there upon a broade seemly black felt'. It is unclear why the Scottish Catholics were quite so keen to become involved with this strange and unpredictable character and one can only assume it was due to the considerable success he had achieved south of the border.[14]

Due to his departure to France Persons did not receive the letter from Watts until 15 September, by which time he was unable to make the meeting scheduled for later that month. On receiving the letter Persons wrote to Seton explaining why he was unable to make the trip. With his reply to Watts he sent further financial assistance and details of the lines of communication between France and Scotland for future correspondence. In the report forwarded to Rome with Watts' letter, Persons explained to Acquaviva that he had left England to confer with William Allen and Archbishop Beaton, to enlist French support and to set up a printing press for the dissemination of Catholic literature. He also requested further assistance from the Society and the pope, including the recruitment of more fathers for a formal Scottish mission.[15]

By 20 October Watts was back in London reporting to Mendoza on the favourable reception he had received in Scotland. He was especially optimistic about the involvement of Seton, who had promised to negotiate with James on his behalf and to update him on his return to Scotland. However, he was not so confident about Lennox or James and was reluctant to compile a full report on the latter until he was certain of his sincerity, which he hoped to be able to confirm before Christmas. However, he did advise that James had confided in him that he favoured a Spanish rather than a French alliance.[16] Both Mendoza and Persons were encouraged by Watts' account of his mission and wrote in similar terms to their respective superiors, though their reports differed in one important respect. According to Persons, Watts had an audience with James, while Mendoza makes no mention of it. In his report to Acquaviva Persons also sought the general's advice about his own involvement with the English mission and the requests for him to go to Scotland. Watts was in no doubt what he thought Persons should do and indicated to Mendoza that he wanted to return north with Persons and Heywood, who in his short time in England, along with William Holt, had achieved notable success. Mendoza was reluctant to send both fathers to Scotland and 'deprive the brain of its principal support', and so it was decided that Persons would continue as the English superior, but on his return from France would remain in England. Meanwhile Heywood would go to Scotland accompanied by two priests.[17] Despite his instructions Persons was reluctant to return home as both he and William Allen had been declared traitors by the English authorities; he therefore decided to remain in Rouen awaiting instructions from Acquaviva. Heywood likewise never set out for Scotland and stayed in England recovering from a bout of sciatica. Following Persons' departure and his subsequent decision not to return to England Heywood became superior of the English mission, but his overly dogmatic approach soon led to his recall to France. He was arrested when his ship was forced to return to port in England, and after a spell in the Tower was banished in January 1585. On account of his ill-health and his chequered past he was considered unsuitable for further service in England and was posted to Italy where he died in 1598.[18]

Heywood's place was taken by William Holt, a Lancastrian and a student of Oxford and Douai, who as a priest had entered the Society in 1578, and following completion of his novitiate was sent to England. In a later account Holt was described as being 'of a somewhat unsociable disposition, he is a man of tried virtue and good intelligence, and... well able to accommodate himself to other people's views'.[19] In late October 1581 he accompanied Watts to Scotland, but fell ill with dysentery *en route* and was laid low for ten weeks. It would appear to have been a recurrence of an illness which had left him unconscious for fifteen days on his journey from Germany to England. Holt remained in the border region recuperating and on his recovery joined his companion in Edinburgh.[20] In November a report was received from Watts requesting more assistance, but Persons was too preoccupied with his writing and was unwilling to act in the absence of instructions from Rome. However, Philip was in favour of sending more priests and sent a draft for 2,000 crowns to cover their expenses. Mendoza, frustrated by the Society's inactivity, and no doubt prompted by Philip, sent messages to Allen and Persons requesting that the latter be sent to Scotland without delay: 'it was no time to be occupied in writing books when it was a question of the salvation of kingdoms'.[21] Allen also wrote to Persons in similar terms, and in fact the Jesuit was on the point of departing when, no doubt much to his relief, he was visited in Rouen by William Crichton, who along with Edmund Hay had been assigned to the Scottish Mission. Meanwhile Holt and Watts and others were 'showing themselves boldly there [Scotland] without fear, far contrary to the late order', and on Christmas Day gave communion to 100 people in Edinburgh as well as saying Mass and preaching daily in Seton's household.[22]

⋆ ⋆ ⋆

In late December Acquaviva relented and authorised the establishment of a Scottish Mission. Jesuit accounts of the mission suggest that the impetus for its foundation came from the Scottish Jesuit fathers. However, according to Thomas Innes 'it was the ancient clergy who, on account of the zeal they observed in the first Scots Jesuits, procured their coming to Scotland, employed all their credit abroad to have them well provided of all necessaries in the country, who conducted them to it, and who were their guides through the country, to introduce them to Catholics, and to provide for their security in these dangerous times; the ancient clergy being well acquainted in the country with those who might be trusted and who not. These first Jesuits, after a long absence from their youth, were, at first entry, generally strangers to the country'. In fact the mission was the result of pressure from various quarters, and once up and running the Society relied heavily on the support of other clergy operating in Scotland.[23] In mid January Crichton and Hay arrived in Paris to consult with Archbishop Beaton and Gian Battista Castelli, the papal nuncio in Paris, about the arrangements for their mission. They then travelled on to Rouen to meet Persons, who despite his reluctance to do so, was still planning to go to Scotland. Not surprisingly he was persuaded to delay his departure until the Scots had reported back to him on the situation there. Following a further conference at Rouen prior to 3 February and a meeting with Guise at Eu it was decided that Crichton should go to Scotland alone to assess the situation. Hay was to follow later, perhaps accompanied by Persons, depending upon Crichton's evaluation of the position.[24]

Although the appointment of the Scottish fathers had been confirmed by the pope and was approved by Mary there was still considerable controversy about who should be sent. Mendoza and many of the Scottish nobles favoured foreign or English priests, such as Robert Bellarmine or Richard Barret, while Persons suggested Pedro Jiménez or Manuel de Vega, the professors of theology at Vienna and Vilnius. A contemporary report on the condition of Scotland recommended that English priests should be sent, and until the mission was established it was decided that an English Jesuit should continue to be responsible for Scottish affairs. A later Jesuit report was critical of the reluctance to send Scottish priests whose number in Paris was considerable: 'they were men of high character and admirable learning; and they would most gladly have undertaken the mission. But the persons, who measured everything by the dictates of human prudence, fearing that the king might possibly incur some danger thereby, decided that the attempt should be postponed until some other opportunity'. Mary's preference for Scots was based on the unpopularity of the English and their problems with the language, and although Beaton was her preferred choice, Crichton was an acceptable compromise.[25]

Prior to their departure the two fathers received letters from Acquaviva wishing them a successful mission and warning them of the dangers facing them.[26] Crichton left for Scotland before the beginning of Lent, sometime in late February or early March, accompanied by Emerson, who was to act as his servant. Emerson, who had been transferred from the English mission, had some experience of Scotland having previously acted as Watts' servant on an earlier visit. A lack of finances would appear to be behind the decision that Hay should remain in France, though there was also a suggestion that he withdrew in protest at the proposed invasion plans.[27] While Crichton and Hay were making arrangements to travel to Scotland Holt returned to London in February 1582 for an update on the situation south of the border and to make contact with the remaining Catholic nobles. On arriving in London, and having made contact with an unidentified priest, he was taken to Mendoza's house where he unexpectedly found himself reporting to the Spanish ambassador in person. He stayed with Mendoza for two days during which time he, like Persons and Watts before him, was well briefed on Spanish affairs.[28] He advised Mendoza of the favourable reception he had received from Lennox, Huntly, Eglinton, Argyll and Caithness and warned him of the dangers posed by the Protestant nobles, and in particular Arran. He also made a number of recommendations regarding James, whose conversion he thought would be best achieved by preaching and disputation rather than by compulsion. In the event of these proving unsuccessful he recommended the use of force and suggested that James should be compelled to convert or, if necessary, forcibly removed from Scotland or deposed in favour of Mary. He advised that the Protestant clergy were the main obstacle to achieving these ends, but was hopeful of success in the rural areas where the influence of the Kirk was weakest.[29] Holt was immediately sent back to Scotland with an assurance of assistance for the Scottish nobles and letters of support from Mary and Philip. In his subsequent report to Philip, Mendoza highlighted the scarcity of priests, pointing out that those who remained were old and poor. The numbers had presumably dwindled since Abercrombie's earlier report, which had suggested that there were priests in every town and in the households of the leading Catholics. Mendoza also wrote to Allen advising him of the position and requesting more priests from France where there were apparently plenty of potential recruits.[30]

Holt, armed with the letter from Mendoza, returned to Edinburgh around the same time as Crichton arrived from the continent. Reports in early March from two English agents, Robert Bowes and William Davidson, confirmed that Holt, using the alias Peter Brewerton, was sheltering with Seton. He and another priest, a Yorkshireman, Roger Allmente, alias Vavasor, who was in fact an English spy, were also regular guests at the French ambassador's house in Edinburgh.[31] Crichton, carrying guarantees of assistance from Spain and Rome, was met by Seton and smuggled into Dalkeith Palace, to the south of Edinburgh, where they met with Lennox, from whom the pope required evidence of his commitment to the enterprise. Lennox, aware that his position in Scotland was becoming less secure, needed Spanish and papal support, and was enthusiastic about Holt and Crichton's offers of assistance, which included 15,000 troops. His position had become so precarious that he was on the verge of returning to France, but he indicated his willingness to remain in Scotland if Philip and the pope could provide the necessary support. Inevitably his involvement had a price and he indicated that he was unwilling to jeopardise his personal position without the appropriate assurances and indemnities. As well as troops and sufficient supplies he also demanded compensation equal to the value of his Scottish estates payable in the event of the invasion failing and his property being confiscated. Crichton considered these demands to be excessive, though Lennox, while insisting that his involvement was conditional on them, accepted that Guise was entitled to modify them if he wished. Lennox's proposals followed a familiar pattern and like earlier schemes involved the release of Mary and the imprisoned Catholic nobles, the conversion of James, the invasion of England and the restoration of Catholicism in England,

Scotland and Ireland. One novel element, a power-sharing arrangement between Mary and James was also proposed, though the terms were never agreed.[32]

Following the audience Lennox wrote to Mary confirming the details of his meeting with Crichton and assuring her that further efforts were being made on behalf of her and the Catholic cause. Crichton and Holt returned to France to deliver Lennox's letter to de Tassis and to pass on other correspondence to the pope, Philip, Guise and Castelli. It was also suggested that Mendoza should go to France to be briefed on Lennox's proposals, but the Spanish ambassador was unwilling to leave London and draw attention to himself. In the event of him being unable or unwilling to travel to France Crichton asked Mendoza to send sufficient funds so that he could travel to Spain to seek Philip's support. Mendoza took a dim view of the fathers' return to France and the proposed jaunt to Spain and instructed them to return to Scotland.[33]

Around the same time Watts, disguised as a dentist, was despatched south to report to Mendoza and to deliver Lennox's letter to Mary. In late April the ambassador sent him back to Scotland with a number of letters concealed in a looking glass. In May Watts, dressed in an old grey cloak, managed to escape from a border patrol acting under the orders of Sir John Forster, the Warden of the Middle Marches, which having arrested him and confiscated his money, breviary, letters, dental instruments and looking glass, returned his money and letters and released him on payment of a suitable gratuity. Subsequent examination of the looking glass revealed a number of further letters which resulted in the immediate imprisonment of the feckless border guards. Forster's report to Walsingham described how 'lookinge more circumspectlye unto the glas, [I] by chaunce dyd espie paper within the said glasse. Whereupon I serched the said glas thorolie and openinge the same, dyd finde certen lettres so well compacted together and enclosed within the said glas, thayt it was verie hard to be espied or fownde owte'. One of the letters, 'beinge writen in figures and ciphers, beinge (as yt is to be supposed) of some greate importaunce', was also sent to Walsingham to be deciphered, and was found to contain references to the invasion plans. Forster also confirmed to Walsingham that a Jesuit priest, calling himself Brewerton or Watts, was part of Seton's household.[34]

Crichton and Holt arrived in France in mid April; Holt claiming that he had had to travel to France as cross border security between Scotland and England had been considerably tightened on account of the increased Catholic activity in the northern counties. They were initially welcomed at St Denis by Beaton and Allen, and having joined up with Persons at Rouen travelled on to Eu for an audience with Guise. The duke was impressed with Lennox's proposals and indicated that he was prepared to make the necessary financial and personal sacrifices to ensure the success of the project. Following agreement between the parties that the time was right for more positive action Guise and Crichton returned to Paris, while Persons was laid low for a few days and remained at Eu until he had recovered.[35]

More meetings were held during the course of April and May involving Castelli, Beaton, de Tassis, Guise, Matthieu and Allen, during which it was decided that further appeals for assistance should be made to Gregory and Philip. By this stage both Philip and Mendoza were becoming somewhat exasperated by the lack of progress of the missions in Britain and decided upon a more cautious approach, advocating that the simplest course of action was the conversion of James. Philip was dubious about the Scottish nobles' plans for their king, but was insistent that his ambassador should continue to employ Jesuit agents to give Spanish political activity an air of religious respectability. Nevertheless, he remained wary of Persons' role, and while impressed by his religious zeal was alarmed at the Jesuit's openness about the invasion plans. Philip insisted that they remain secret, but there was little he could do to ensure that this happened. Mary and Mendoza were also alarmed that the fathers' religious enthusiasm was not matched by their tact and diplomacy and feared that their meddling in political activities might jeopardise the whole enterprise, and more importantly put Mary's life in danger. She was also annoyed that fathers had been sent to the pope and to Philip in her name but without her authority, though she did accept that this had been done in good faith on the basis that the opportunity to invade Britain might never arise again. Philip's response to Lennox's plans was lukewarm, though in order to obtain the support of the Scottish nobles he instructed de Tassis to respond to Lennox 'in such a way that it may not seem… that difficulties are being raised as a pretext to refuse him assistance, but that the affair must be solidly grounded in order the better to ensure its succeeding; for it is a thing which so deeply concerns the service of our Lord and the public good that all are bound to further it'.[36]

In mid May Crichton and Persons briefed de Tassis, but the ambassador, of whom both men were suspicious, was wary of their proposals. Nevertheless, despite the ambassador's reservations, it was decided that Persons and Crichton should be sent to Lisbon and Rome respectively with copies of a memorial apparently prepared by the former outlining the proposals for the restoration of Catholicism in both England and Scotland.[37] While the situation was thought to be favourable in both countries an invasion via Scotland was perceived as offering a number of advantages. There was already a large Marian party, including Lennox, Huntly and Seton, which enjoyed the support of the Catholics in both countries. From a strategic point of view Dumbarton Castle and a number of other safe ports were identified as being suitable for disembarking an invasion force. The memorial also stressed Mary and James's legal right to succeed to the English throne and suggested the creation of a bishopric of Durham as a means of overcoming the 'great points of difference and a natural jealousy between the two nations of Scotland and England' which could form a 'considerable stumbling block'. Time was of the essence in implementing the proposals as security was so lax they could be uncovered at any time. There was also concern that James might be murdered or marry a Protestant. Furthermore, it was imperative to act while Lennox held sway at court and the power of the Hamiltons and Douglases was in temporary decline.[38]

After de Tassis and Castelli had met the two fathers both prepared accounts of Crichton's mission and Lennox's proposals. Castelli, like Crichton, considered Lennox's demands to be excessive and thought that the project would realistically require between 6,000 and 8,000 troops for four to five months as opposed to Lennox's projection of 15,000 troops for sixteen months. Castelli tried to flatter Gregory by likening his involvement to that of his predecessor, Gregory I, who had sent the Benedictines into Anglo-Saxon England. De Tassis advised that Lennox's proposals would require 20,000 Spanish, Italian, German and Swiss troops for eighteen months together with the necessary supplies. He also advised that Lennox required additional supplies for his Scottish troops and 40,000 crowns to fortify a number of existing Scottish strongholds.[39] James Anthony Froude, the notoriously unreliable Victorian historian, was rightly critical of Persons and Crichton for even entertaining such demands: 'The Jesuits, with febrile and feminine impatience believed, like Pompey, that armies would spring out the earth at the stamp of the foot'.[40] Guise, Beaton and Allen also felt that Lennox's demands were unreasonable and that fewer troops would be required.[41]

Crichton and Persons both objected to their proposed missions, but were firmly put in their places by Castelli, who had the backing of both Gregory and Philip.[42] Crichton departed soon after 22 May and arrived in Rome around mid June, while Persons, accompanied by William

Tresham, who had previously been involved with the Scottish Catholic exiles, left on 28 May and reached Lisbon around the same time. Crichton's negotiations in Rome achieved little, and although he received assurances of support from Gregory and Como, the papal secretary, they insisted that Philip should take the leading role. It was also made clear to Crichton that his earlier promises of large numbers of troops were outwith the scope of his authority.[43] In Lisbon Persons also failed to convince his hosts and having failed to obtain an audience with Philip, who was preoccupied with Portuguese affairs and a bout of gout, had to settle for an assurance from the royal secretary, Juan de Idiáquez, that the king was in favour of the enterprise. This inactivity was particularly frustrating for Persons who was convinced that 'nearly the whole of Scotland' was on the side of the Catholics. However, he did manage to obtain a royal grant which was to be paid by de Tassis in Paris and forwarded to James. Details of this grant, which never reached James, were later made public, much to the annoyance of Crichton whose principal concern was that its misappropriation would reflect badly on the Society. After a couple of months word finally arrived in Madrid that the pope was prepared to contribute 50,000 crowns, which Philip judged to be insufficient given that the total cost would be in the region of eight times that amount. Persons assured the Spanish that the pope would offer more when Philip made his own contribution, but any decision was deferred until Gregory's intentions were fully disclosed. As a conciliatry gesture he later offered to pay one quarter of the costs.[44]

After months of stalling the final blow to the invasion plans came with reports from Scotland of James's abduction at Huntingtower, near Perth, during the course of a hunting trip. Elizabeth, alarmed by Lennox's activities, had ordered Walsingham to instruct Bowes to encourage a number of Protestant nobles under William Ruthven, 1st Earl of Gowrie, to abduct James and take control of the government. Lennox was at the time planning a strike against his opponents and at the end of August planned to seize Edinburgh and arrest a number of leading Protestants. However, his plan was pre-empted by Gowrie, who along with Thomas Lyon of Baldukie, the Master of Glamis, Mar, Glencairn, Crawford and a number of supporters seized the king on 22 August in what has become known as 'the Ruthven Raid'. James was clearly shaken by the incident, which led one of his captors, Glamis, to make the much quoted comment: 'Better bairns greet [cry] than bearded men'.[45] Following the raid James was forced to order Lennox to leave Scotland before 20 September, but out of loyalty to James, or perhaps self interest, he ignored the order and sought refuge in Dumbarton Castle from where he planned to rescue the king. However, Lennox dithered and lost his nerve, and on being deserted by his supporters surrendered Dumbarton. In January 1583 he fled to France, with an assurance from James that he would be permitted to return to Scotland to exact his revenge. He travelled via London, where he met with Mendoza. He was also granted audiences with Elizabeth and Walsingham, who 'rattled him up' and left him in no doubt that he would be better off across the channel. His downfall was a considerable blow to the exiles who were receiving little encouragement from the French government. Lennox died on 26 May, supposedly broken by Henri III's refusal to assist him. There was also a rather far fetched and unsubstantiated suggestion that he had been poisoned while in London. Shortly before his death he had refused the last rites and died a Protestant.[46]

Persons and Crichton were understandably alarmed by the implications of Lennox's downfall as his influence over James had been central to their plans for the invasion of England. Philip's attempts to regain control of the situation through de Tassis in Paris and Mendoza in London failed. The former was convinced that James's conversion was improbable and the latter, worn out and in ill health, was under continual surveillance by the English authorities. Despite his poor health Mendoza's request to be relieved of office was turned down by Philip at Mary's request. An offer of support was received from the French, who despatched their ambassador, de la Mothe Fénélon, to Elizabeth to warn her to stop meddling in Scottish affairs. The ambassador also rebuked Gowrie and his accomplices over their treatment of James and threatened French intervention if they did not release him. His appearance caused a certain amount of consternation as it was suspected that the real reason for his visit to Scotland was to suggest a marriage between James and the daughter of Charles of Lorraine.[47]

* * *

In Scotland the activities of the Jesuit mission were brought to a standstill by the arrest of Holt and the seizure of incriminating correspondence. He was apprehended on 1 March 1583 having laboured 'usefully in that vineyard' [Scotland]. His whereabouts were revealed to the authorities by the English spy, Allmente, who for a time had lived in France with the English Catholic exile, Thomas Stapleton, and on returning to England had been arrested at Dover, but released after agreeing to help hunt down Holt. The Jesuit managed to escape to the house of the French ambassador, François de Roncherolles, Sieur de Maineville, where he had previously been a regular guest. De Maineville was an agent of the Guise family and had been sent to Scotland to negotiate with those Scottish Catholic nobles who had indicated their willingness to align themselves with Spain. It is unclear whether the Scottish authorities were aware of Allmente's cover, but if so he was presumably arrested and detained following Holt's escape to conceal his identity. From the ambassador's house Holt and a servant tried to flee to the continent, but were arrested at Leith on the instructions of Bowes.[48] In Holt's possession were a number of incriminating letters, including one from Alexander Seton to his former tutor at the German College in Rome. Seton, who made little effort to disguise his views on the need for foreign aid, managed to avoid arrest, though his opponents were in no doubt where the loyalties of 'this papistical prelate and pensioner of the Pope' lay.[49]

Following Holt's arrest a tug of war developed between Bowes and de Maineville for custody of the prisoner. Before being handed over to either Holt was interrogated by the Scottish authorities; however their initial questioning ascertained little except his identity. Reports varied as to the nature of the interrogation, but it would appear that, despite pressure from Elizabeth torture was not used. James, who remained under arrest until the end of June, also joined the unseemly squabble for control of Holt, but despite the royal request to hand him over it was decided that he should remain in prison. As the initial interrogation revealed little the authorities were reluctant to hand him over in the hope 'by fear of the boots he beginneth to yield'. With the chief prize safely in jail, Holt's servant and Allmente were released, the latter being commended to Walsingham for his good service since being apprehended at Dover. Allmente, aware of the need to preserve his own skin, offered to use his earlier contacts to infiltrate the English Catholic community in France.[50] Bowes meanwhile kept up the pressure on the Scottish authorities to torture Holt and to transfer him to England, while the French ambassador pressed to have him deported to France. Seton also became embroiled in the dispute and sometime prior to 6 April was involved in an attempt to free him by force. Shortly after reports started filtering out that Holt had finally been tortured, and although James had arranged for him to be transferred to Edinburgh Castle and had agreed to the use of torture, there is no evidence of it actually being applied. Persons was certainly of the view that it had only been threatened. During the late spring and early summer French influence seems to have ensured better treatment for Holt. On 27 April James wrote to Henri III confirming an earlier promise to de Maineville that Holt would be freed, which was followed by a request from Henri that Holt be well treated by the authorities. In late July James again granted permission for the use of torture, but at the same time connived in a plan to allow Holt to escape from Edinburgh Castle. Holt was given twenty four hours to decide whether or not to co-operate, but the following day, with the assistance of a servant of one of the captains of the castle, he slipped over the castle wall and made his escape. He embarked from Leith along with Francis Mowbray, the laird of Barnbougle, yet another English double agent, who was eventually executed by James for his duplicity. It is unclear where they fled to, but within a few months Holt was back in Edinburgh enjoying the protection of the king. In response to criticism from Walsingham James pointed out that he would have been happy to hand over Holt if Elizabeth had reciprocated by extraditing Archibald Douglas of Whittinghame, described by a contemporary as 'ane serpaint in ane manis lyknes', who had been involved in the murder of Darnley.[51]

* * *

With the downfall and death of Lennox it became clear to the exiles on the continent that fresh plans were required. Guise, Matthieu and Beaton set about drawing up a new scheme, which was less reliant on events in Scotland. This was discussed at a meeting in June at Castelli's house in Paris and was subsequently communicated to Persons on his return from Spain where he had been delayed following another period of ill health. Persons and Allen now believed that any invasion should avoid Scotland and would need to be executed prior to the onset of winter. At a meeting with de Tassis on 24 June Persons agreed that as soon as the plans were approved preparations would begin to ensure that the English Catholics were ready to welcome the invasion force. David Graham of Fintry, Archbishop Beaton's nephew, was sent to Scotland with sufficient finances to win over new supporters, especially from amongst the ranks of those who were hostile to the pro-English faction at court.[52] Crichton travelled to Rome to canvas support for the new plans, but was sent back to Lyons and told not to meddle in Scottish affairs. With Acquaviva's consent Persons left Paris shortly after 22 August and travelled incognito to Rome using the alias Richard Melino. As well as briefing his superiors on the invasion plans

Persons also requested the appointment of William Allen to the bishopric of Durham and the issuing of a papal bull demonstrating Gregory's commitment to the invasion, the management of which was to be left to Philip and Guise. The pope's reaction was favourable and on 24 September he issued briefs in which the majority of Persons' requests were granted. Not surprisingly he returned to Paris in a buoyant mood and set about concluding the negotiations with Spain.[53]

Despite Spanish and Papal assurances of support nothing further was done during the winter of 1583–4. The new invasion plans received a set back with the arrest of Francis Throckmorton, an intermediary between Mary and Thomas Morgan, who under torture revealed details of the project. He was executed in July 1584 about the same time as Mendoza was expelled from London. Meanwhile Philip had instructed his ambassador in Paris to continue stalling Persons, which he succeeded in doing for a number of months. Crichton was appointed rector of Chambéry, no doubt in the hope that the appointment would keep his mind off Scotland. However, his influential friends, including Beaton, protested to the general that his talents were wasted there and called for him to be sent to Scotland. Although Acquaviva advised Edmund Hay that he felt a Jesuit presence would be of little benefit in Scotland and that he was considering disbanding the English mission he did allow Crichton to absent himself from Chambéry to work on the Scottish Mission, but on the strict proviso that he did not leave France. The general was especially worried about the reaction from Henri, who wanted Crichton banned from Paris. Crichton rashly decided to visit Beaton in Paris and as a result incurred the wrath of his superiors. When asked to explain his actions he claimed to have spoken to no one except Beaton, an explanation which appears to have been initially accepted by them. In the summer of 1584 he received a stronger rebuke from Acquaviva in which the general passed on the pope's disapproval of the Society's involvement in political matters.[54]

While Crichton was trying to extricate himself from Chambéry, Persons and Allen sent a memorandum to the pope to try and get the invasion plans back on track. Despite James's leniency towards his Catholic subjects and his connivance in Holt's 'escape' the situation in Scotland was critical and prompt action was required if it was not to deteriorate further. They continued to assure Philip that the English Catholics were in favour of a foreign invasion, but that domestic politics prevented Guise leaving France to lead it. In Scotland James indicated that he was reluctant to allow foreign troops to participate in any invasion or to be party to any scheme involving the Papacy. In fact he claimed to be sorry he had ever become involved with the Jesuits; this change of heart having apparently been brought about by the influence of the Master of Gray, who had persuaded him to allow Holt to remain in Scotland and had then fallen out with him after Holt denied Gray absolution because he refused to divulge everything he knew about Mary's activities. Thereafter James resolved to have nothing to do with the Society, at least temporarily until it suited him otherwise.[55]

⋆ ⋆ ⋆

As 1584 progressed events took another turn and the plight of the Catholics, despite James's change of heart, appeared to be improving. In April 1584 there was a second attempt to kidnap James by the pro-English party, led by Gowrie, Angus, Mar and Rothes. The attempt was foiled by Regent Arran and in the aftermath Gowrie was executed and the other nobles exiled to England. They were only allowed to return with assurances from Elizabeth of English aid. The attempted coup was followed by a series of statutes known as 'The Black Acts' which asserted royal control over the Kirk, in the form of royally appointed bishops under the control of Patrick Adamson, Archbishop of St Andrews. As well as the restoration of a number of former bishops, including 'Dunkelden, an old dotted Papist', the system of presbyteries was abolished and the ministers forced to subscribe to the Acts. James also let it be known that English Catholics would be allowed to take refuge in Scotland.[56]

To take advantage of the more relaxed regime two ships were berthed at Dieppe waiting to carry a number of Catholic sympathisers to Scotland. Persons, who had returned to Paris from the Low Countries, where he had been advising Parma on English affairs, was pressed by Matthieu and Crichton to travel to Scotland, where the Scottish Catholic nobles still felt that he could persuade James to support their cause. The party, minus Persons, which reached Scotland in early June, included two young priests from the new Scots College at Pont-à-Mousson and James Cheyne, the head of the college and a canon of St Quentin. Cheyne was reported to be a Jesuit seeking leave from the authorities for the return of a number of his colleagues; this incorrect assumption being based on the misconception that as head of the college Cheyne had to be a Jesuit.

Holt also returned to Edinburgh and again took up residence in Seton's household. Persons reported that 'Father Holt is very well in Scotland secured against the ministers by the public protection of the

King', though this rather contradicts other reports of James's antagonism towards the Society. Holt misinterpreted this benevolence as an indication of James's willingness to convert, and, having convinced himself of James's sincerity, felt that freedom of worship was only a matter of time: 'He shows me greater marks of favour every day, and has not only permitted, but even approved of my remaining in the kingdom... He has evidently made up his mind to grant full liberty of worship to all the inhabitants of the kingdom, provided he can do so consistently with his own personal safety, and the peace of the country'. For the moment James was apparently keeping his change of heart to himself to prevent a public outcry. However, Holt was more astute in his judgement of the leading nobles, such as Argyll, Glencairn, Arran and Marischal, who although they appeared to be moderates, were not to be trusted.[57] For reasons which are not altogether clear Holt fell out with his host, Seton, whose son Alexander requested that the Jesuit be recalled to Rome, though he grudgingly admitted that Holt's presence was preferable to having no one at all. His request was denied as no replacement was available. Persons, who had no intention of travelling to Scotland as had been requested by the Scottish nobles, suspected that Holt and Seton must have fallen out over some private matter as the Jesuit's safety was not an issue. Further investigation by Persons, in consultation with Matthieu and Crichton, suggested that Alexander Seton was unhappy with Holt's departure from the Seton household to be nearer court and his growing links with Gray and Graham of Fintry. In view of Holt's problems and his over involvement in political affairs it was decided that the mission required some new faces – fathers who had not become embroiled in the manoeuvrings of James and his nobles.[58]

* * *

Despite the uncertainty regarding the position in Scotland the decision was taken to press on with the preparations for an invasion. Acquaviva informed Matthieu that Persons was to take charge of both the English and the Scottish missions, though Persons and Odo Pigenat, Matthieu's successor as French provincial, pointed out various reasons why this was a bad idea. As well as the traditional hostility between the two nations there were also a number of more senior Scottish fathers, who would be offended by Persons' appointment. Pigenat, who was the eventual choice, was also unhappy with the fact that Persons, who was from outwith the French province, would have jurisdiction over those within it. Nevertheless Acquaviva refused to back down pointing to the fact that the futures of the two nations were inextricably bound together and that Persons had been the preferred choice of the Scottish nobles. There is little evidence to suggest that the Scots had any particular preference for Scottish priests; they had been more than happy with the services of Holt and Watts, neither of whom were Scots. Although he was persuaded to authorise the dispatch of more fathers the general was wary of antagonising the Kirk and prejudicing any rapprochement with James. Gregory was of the same view and to avoid any criticism it was left to those in Paris to make the important decisions. The pope's only provisos were that Allen's opinion was to carry the most weight and that Persons was not to travel to Scotland for fear of inflaming the situation. This further confirmed Persons' belief that Matthieu or a Scotsman should be appointed as superior of the mission and that his own appointment 'would be an enormous pain and distraction'. He did not suggest Crichton as an alternative candidate perhaps on account of the Scotsman's strained relations with Seton. In fear of his life Persons left Paris for Rouen, and in response to alleged plots to assassinate him, Edmund Hay suggested that he should take refuge in Flanders and leave the Scottish Mission in his hands. Persons himself felt that Rome was the safest place, but despite his fears for his safety he felt compelled to visit Paris to discuss the financial difficulties of the English college at Rheims and the preparations for the mission. Following these discussions he returned to Rouen and after spending the summer at St Omer left for Rome to undertake his tertianship.[59] With Persons' departure Pigenat took up his appointment as superior of the British missions, despite his warning to Acquaviva that foreign superiors were not popular with the Catholics in Britain. Tyrie was appointed as his assistant and was to be used by Pigenat as a shield to deflect any criticism. Persons, although he was happy to turn down the appointment, was quick to criticise the appointment of Pigenat and Tyrie. He felt Pigenat was too busy to devote sufficient time to the post and lacked the hard edge required for such a rôle, while Tyrie possessed many fine qualities, but was politically naïve.[60]

* * *

During the late summer of 1584 reports of Holt's activities dried up. In October Persons reported to Acquaviva that there had been no news from him for three months, though it was thought he was in the north of Scotland. In November Persons still had little information, but as far as he was aware Holt was in good health, though less optimistic about the situation in Scotland.[61] Holt also spent some time in the south west of Scotland with John, 8th Lord Maxwell, who had been a Catholic since the early 1580s. As well as having Mass said daily in his house Maxwell allegedly paid his retainers in French crowns, delivered to him by an unidentified English Jesuit aspirant. This allegation and the suggestion that Holt had been in France arranging financial assistance for Maxwell, which was subsequently delivered in September 1586, should be treated with some caution, though it is known that Holt left Scotland in the spring of 1586 heading for Paris.[62] Tyrie informed the general that James Gordon had advised him of Holt's departure, although he had not arrived in Paris by the date of Tyrie's letter in early May. In late June Castelli reported that Holt had arrived a few days earlier. He was subsequently appointed rector of the English College in Rome, a post which it became clear did not suit him. Despite his fall out with Seton there were still calls for him to return to Scotland, where his encouragement of closer links with Spain had been popular with the Catholic nobles, who were becoming increasingly impatient with their traditional dependence on France. Despite these requests and his restlessness Holt remained at the English College for six years and never returned to Scotland.[63]

Chapter 6

Shaking off the Yoke of the Heretics

Despite the problems encountered by Holt Archbishop Beaton continued to press Acquaviva to send more fathers to Scotland, though it remained the general's view, and also Gregory's, that a Jesuit presence there would do little to improve the plight of the Scottish Catholics. Nevertheless, Beaton persisted and in June 1584 he wrote to the pope requesting that Edmund Hay, Tyrie, Gordon and Crichton be sent to Scotland.[1] Crichton, despite the attempts to silence him, also pressed the general for a decision. Their persistence eventually paid off and Acquaviva granted permission for preparations to begin. An indication of the Society's reluctance to be involved was the devolution of responsibility to William Allen and fellow exiles in Paris, who decided that Crichton and Gordon should be sent to Scotland. In view of Persons' unwillingness to head the Scottish mission Crichton as the senior Scottish Jesuit was the obvious choice, though concern was expressed about his poor relationship with Seton. Crichton later confessed to the English authorities that in his opinion Seton had 'neither capacity, secrecy or any other good government'. In his memoir of the Scottish mission Crichton was slightly more diplomatic and described Seton as the only noble 'steadfast in the Catholic faith'. He also mentioned the hospitality shown to him by Seton following his arrival in Scotland. These comments were made many years after the event, but at the time the strained relations between the two posed a serious threat to the success of the mission.[2] Persons, on being presented with a further opportunity to avoid an arduous journey to Scotland, approved the appointment of Crichton and Gordon, describing his colleagues as: 'men of importance, and besides being very virtuous and prudent, they were held in great estimation, belonging as they did to the first families of Scotland'.[3]

In early August the preparations were completed and the two fathers, along with a secular priest, Patrick Addy, embarked from Dieppe. The exiles in Paris were optimistic about the prospects of success, but, as was often the case, the English authorities were one step ahead of them. Sir Edward Stafford, the English ambassador in France, forewarned Walsingham of Crichton and Gordon's mission, and soon after embarking the party was arrested by the merchant who had chartered the ship on their behalf.[4] In fear of retribution from Gordon's nephew, the earl of Huntly, or perhaps recognising a good deal, the merchant released him in exchange for 100 crowns. Crichton and Addy were taken to Ostend and handed over to the Dutch authorities, who accused Crichton of having participated in the assassination of William the Silent, Prince of Orange, in July of the previous year. He was sentenced to be hanged, but was saved from the gallows by the intervention of Elizabeth, who demanded that Crichton be handed over to her, as part of the terms of a treaty being negotiated with the Dutch.[5]

The account of the fathers' capture at sea has generated some controversy. It would appear that immediately prior to his capture Crichton attempted to destroy a letter containing proposals for the invasion of England. The various accounts of this episode are based on a letter by Walsingham to Sir Ralph Sadler, in which he reported that 'Of late one Creighton, a Scottish Jesuite, was taken by a shippe sett forth by the admiral of Zeland, and sent hither by him unto her majestie, about whom was found a very daungerous plott set down abowt two yeares past in the Italian tongue for the invading of this realm. And although it was torne in pieces and divers parts thereof lost, yet we have gathered the sense thereof, which I send you herewith'.[6] The events were also depicted in a montage of 'Popish Plots and Treasons, From the Beginning of the Reign of Queen Elizabeth' by the Dutch engraver, Cornelius Danckerts, and described in an accompanying verse:

> View here a Miracle – A Priest Conveys,
> In Spanish Bottom o're the path less Seas,
> Close treacherous Notes, whilst a Dutch Ship comes by
> And streight Engag'd her well-known Enemy:
> The Conscious Priest his Guilty Papers tears,
> And over board the scatter'd fragments bears:
> But the just winds do force them back o'th' Decks,
> And peice meal all the lurking plot detects.[7]

The story has been dismissed by many historians, including Father John Morris, SJ, who described it as 'a ridiculous story… put in circulation that a letter, torn up by him and thrown away, had been blown on board ship again and pieced and read'.[8] Bellesheim was equally sceptical, while Thomas Graves Law expressed doubt about Froude's version of events in his voluminous history of England.[9] Sir William Waad, Walsingham's secretary and the clerk to the English privy council, was apparently responsible for piecing together the parts of the letter which were retrieved, and upon which Crichton's subsequent prosecution was based.[10] Although it has been challenged there is evidence to suggest that there was some basis to the story as the torn letter, which is printed in Knox's *Letters and Memorials of Cardinal Allen,* is corroborated by a confession extracted from Crichton in which he admitted that the letter had been delivered to him by Claude Matthieu, the French provincial. It is unclear whether Crichton was tortured to obtain this confession, though the unreliable Froude states that he was examined on the rack. It is strange that Crichton was still carrying details of the proposed invasion two years after its conception, though these were presumably still relevant to the exiles' current plans despite the changes necessitated by Lennox's death. The letter was not only used against Crichton, but was also produced as evidence in the legal proceedings against the earls of Northumberland and Arundel in the following year. Clause 13 of a brief prepared by Sir John Popham, the attorney general, who was present at both trials, referred specifically to Crichton: 'It appearethe by papers found about him, uppon that he was apprehended on the seas to pass into Scotland, that an enterprise was intended against England by the waie of Scotland bothe by forreins to have ben landed there and by the Scotts to have ioyned with them, and shold have been executed by the late Duke of Leneux, but prevented by his deathe, and was thereby to have overthrowen, bothe the gouvernement in England and the Religion'. Although the brief was produced at the earls' trials there was no evidence of any link between them and Crichton, and its production was a further example of the Crown's ploy of citing irrelevant Catholic plots as part of any charge. Popham, who was especially noted for his harsh treatment of Catholics, was also involved in the trials of Throckmorton, Parry and Babington, of which more later.[11]

After being handed over to the English authorities Crichton was questioned by members of the privy council at Walsingham's house in Surrey, where he attempted to negotiate his release through Nicholas Faunt, an under secretary. Faunt, whose uncle Lawrence Faunt was a Jesuit rector in Poland, had spent a number of years in France and Italy in the early 1580s and was fully conversant with the activities of the exiles. In an attempt to ensnare him Crichton was required to answer a written questionnaire, which Nicholas Faunt agreed to help him complete in return for a recommendation to his uncle: 'Hardly quoth he, will you be able to avoid trouble in your replies; but do you befriend me with my uncle the Jesuit, so that he bequeath his possessions to me, and I will help you to answer all these articles without any hurt to yourself'.[12] Somewhat naïvely Crichton demanded to be tried in Scotland, arguing that the English courts had no authority to detain him. In response the privy council claimed jurisdiction on the basis of a letter, which indicated that while at Lyons Crichton had heard the confessions of a number of English exiles, including Thomas Arundell, a kinsman of the queen. When confronted with the letter Crichton refused to identify the writing as his and claimed that the letter, like the invasion proposals which he had attempted to destroy, was past history and failed to implicate him. Not surprisingly the authorities differed to agree and felt he had more to tell them. In a letter written in October 1584 Stafford pointed out to Walsingham the importance of Crichton's capture as he was privy to dealings at the highest level between the pope and Guise. Although he was well aware that 'if well wrung no man can tell us more' he was not confident of getting much out of Crichton and Addy 'so secret be they in their naughty enterprises'.[13]

Despite Faunt's assurances and Crichton's protestations the privy council had no intention of releasing such an important prisoner and in mid September 1585 both Crichton and Addy were sent to the Tower, where they remained until their release in May 1587. Crichton was initially imprisoned in the Martin Tower and subsequently transferred to Coldharbour. In the Tower Bills there is an account detailing expenditure on various prisoners from September 1584 to Michelmas 1586, which includes reference to the two Scots. In an official list of prisoners compiled in 1585 there is the following entry: 'Patrick Adye, taken in Craightons companie, a scott and a priest and Chaplaine to ye Bushop of Rosse: fit to be banished. William Craighton, to be continued for a season in the Tower'. Despite the recommendation regarding Addy's release both men still appear in prison records in November 1586 and were not released until six months later.[14]

During the course of their imprisonment Crichton and Addy were regularly interrogated and there were reports that they had been tortured on a number of occasions.[15] Acquaviva in a letter to the English Jesuit, Robert Southwell, expressed concern for the plight of a number of fathers, but was less concerned about Crichton as 'his heart is prepared to endure every extremity'.[16] Edmund Hay reported to Acquaviva that provision had been made to look after Crichton while in prison through Archbishop Beaton, who had written to Michel de Castelnau, Seigneur de Mauvissière, the French ambassador in London, requesting assistance. If Castelnau was unable to meet Crichton he was asked to see what could be done to provide for his needs and secure his release. Hay also instructed Matthew Zampini to look after Crichton's interests through an Italian friend in London, who for a number of years had been helping imprisoned Catholics.[17]

Despite close supervision Crichton managed to communicate with his fellow prisoners and the outside world, and early in his imprisonment was interrogated about the system for smuggling letters within the Tower. Following the interception of Crichton's account of the initial interrogation by Walsingham an informant, Nicholas Berden, alias Thomas Rogers, one of Walsingham's most able spies and a former servant of the prominent Catholic layman, George Gilbert, was ordered to keep watch on him. With the unwitting assistance of Gervaise Pierrepoint, a former prisoner in the Tower, Berden was able to establish that with the assistance of some of his jailers, including Fish, the Tower butler, Crichton could correspond with the outside world and could communicate with a number of his fellow prisoners. By opening locked doors and lifting paving stones Crichton was able to meet under cover of darkness with fellow prisoners in the Martin Tower, including Nicholas Roscarock, a Cornishman, who for a time occupied the cell below, and Henry Orton, who had been the first of Edmund Campion's entourage to be arrested in July 1580 while *en route* to the Southwark Conference, convened by Persons and Campion to discuss the many problems facing the English mission. Crichton also acted as an intermediary for a French emissary, Monsieur des Trappes, who was captured *en route* to France carrying letters from Castelnau to Henri III. Des Trappes was imprisoned in a cell near Crichton, who, with assistance from a servant of the lieutenant of the Tower, was able to pass messages to him. Information passed to Castelnau by Crichton helped secure the emissary's release, for which Crichton, despite Henri's earlier mistrust of him, was well rewarded.[18]

Another of Crichton's fellow prisoners was the charismatic archbishop of Armagh, Richard Creagh, with whom he had travelled to Rome in 1562. Creagh was responsible for the development of a flourishing recusant community within the Tower, which met on a regular basis to discuss religious issues and to say Mass. On Sundays Crichton heard confessions and celebrated communion. During his time in the Tower Creagh had become something of a figurehead for Irish and Scottish dissidents and in late 1586 the authorities decided to assassinate him. He was apparently murdered with a piece of poisoned cheese given to him by a notorious undercover agent, Robert Poley, of whom more later. After eating the cheese Creagh became violently ill and a urine sample was smuggled out of the Tower to a doctor who diagnosed poison. Creagh died soon after with the last rites being administered by Crichton.[19]

During his imprisonment Crichton was also interrogated about a number of plots against Elizabeth. One involved a papal subsidy allegedly paid over to Matthieu to finance the queen's assassination; however, there is no evidence of any such subsidy having ever been paid and the allegation may simply have been a ploy to induce Crichton to incriminate himself and fellow prisoners. In his memoir Crichton referred to a further plot by Charles Paget, one of Mary's servants, which had been hatched in Paris, while Crichton was rector at Lyons. It would appear that Crichton was confusing Paget's plot with that of Francis Throckmorton, a personable and wealthy young Catholic gentleman, who had been involved with the Catholic party since Campion's mission in 1580. He was arrested in November 1583 and was finally executed on 10 July 1584 following a particularly arduous imprisoment.

While it is debatable whether Crichton was aware of Throckmorton's plot he was certainly privy to William Parry's plans and was fortunate to survive the episode unscathed.[20] Parry, a Welsh Catholic gentleman and a doctor of law, was heavily in debt and agreed to spy for the English to avoid imprisonment. While in Venice gathering intelligence for the English authorities he was persuaded to accept a further bribe to murder Elizabeth. From Venice he travelled to Lyons where he sought out Crichton to ask his advice on whether or not he could murder the queen with a clear conscience. He was advised that his proposals were unlawful: 'Because, that one may be put to death, two things must concur, a [good] cause and [legitimate] power; that perhaps Parry had a [good] cause, but that he had not [legitimate] power, as he was only a private individual'. Crichton also advised Parry that papal approval would not be granted, and in response to Parry's argument that immense good would result from the queen's assassination quoted St Paul's view that '*Evil is not to be done that good may ensue*'.[21] Despite Crichton's advice Parry travelled on to Paris where he made contact with another of Mary's servants, Thomas Morgan, and with Cardinal Como, who was more enthusiastic about his proposal and from whom he obtained a licence to travel to England.[22] On his return home Parry acquired a seat in the House of Commons, but his outspoken opposition to anti-Catholic legislation made the government suspicious of him. Nevertheless, he succeeded in obtaining a private audience with Elizabeth, but bungled his attempt to assassinate her, having apparently forgotten to take his dagger with him. A further opportunity never arose and Parry, unable to keep his secret to himself, confided in a relative, Sir Edward Neville, who in turn advised Elizabeth. While his subsequent testimony cleared Crichton of any involvement, it was not enough to save the hapless assassin from the gallows. John Bossy has expressed doubt about the circumstances surrounding Parry's plot and suggests that relations between him and Elizabeth were quite cordial and she had in fact defended him following his criticism of the government. It would appear that Elizabeth sacrificed Parry to ease the strained relations between her and her councillors over the issue of her personal security.[23]

Crichton was also suspected of being in direct contact with Mary, who through the Master of Gray, had requested Crichton's release. Crichton had also been in correspondence with Gray, 'whom he deemed a very trusty friend', though their confidence in him was misplaced and both were betrayed by him when he disclosed details of their dealings to Elizabeth, including a letter from Crichton to Mary, which, although uncontroversial, contravened prison rules on contact with outside parties. The letter was subsequently used by the authorities as evidence of a further conspiracy against Elizabeth.[24]

In his memoir Crichton also gave an account of his dealings with John Ballard, a secular priest and one of the leading conspirators in the Babington Plot. The origins of the plot are obscure, but it appears to have been concocted by Ballard with the backing of Mendoza. It was subsequently hijacked and orchestrated by Walsingham and his intelligencers, including Robert Poley, one of his most effective agents, who, like Ballard, was a Cambridge graduate. Poley appears to have been an unsavoury character in whose presence the English Jesuit, William Weston, detected 'an unpleasant smell'. Ballard was an acquaintance of Anthony Babington, a young Catholic gentleman with contacts at court, who had first met Mary when he had been a page to one of her jailers, the earl of Shrewsbury. Babington, who was part of the same network of Catholic gentlemen as Throckmorton which had been active since the beginning of the 1580s, agreed to lead the plot and entered into correspondence with Mary. Meanwhile, Poley persuaded Ballard and a number of his co-conspirators, including another secular priest, Anthony Tyrell, to act as messengers to spread word of a rising which would be joined by a number of leading

Catholics. The messengers were invited to dinner by Poley to discuss the arrangements and arrested. Ballard was offered his life in return for testifying against his accomplices, who unknown to him had already done the same. Tyrell confessed that he and Ballard had been in Rome to obtain the pope's permission to assassinate Elizabeth. Their arrest caused great consternation and many of those whom Ballard had spoken to in the confessional before he was arrested wrote to Crichton to find out if they had been betrayed. Crichton, who occupied the cell above Ballard, managed to communicate with him by pushing a thin sheet of paper through the floor of his cell into the closet below. Ballard returned the sheet of paper with a message admitting that he had betrayed some of his accomplices and as a result was worthy of death. Despite being tortured he remained true to his promise to betray no-one else and along with fourteen others was executed in September 1586.[25]

Various efforts were made to secure Crichton's release, though these merely served to prolong his imprisonment. Amongst those pressing for his release was an unidentified Scottish nobleman, who appeared in London in person to appeal on his behalf, the archbishop of Lyons, the president of the French royal council, who despatched a number of letters to Elizabeth, and Monsieur de Cueilly, the curé of St Germain and a doctor of the Sorbonne. In June 1586 the French Jesuit, Alexandre Georges, wrote to Acquaviva advising that de Cueilly had taken a letter from Henri to his ambassador in London, who was assured by Elizabeth that Crichton would be released. Georges was rightly sceptical, though not of the queen but of her advisers: 'I pray God this may not be hindered by her dishonest ministers'. These representations on his behalf had the opposite effect from that intended and convinced the English authorities that Crichton was more important than he actually was. In a further attempt to have him incriminate himself they pretended that Elizabeth herself had ordered his release. However, Crichton was aware of the rumours surrounding his release and his letter to the queen was carefully worded to avoid any misinterpretation. Although not to the authorities' liking the letter seems to have had some effect on Elizabeth and with the assistance of Sir Christopher Hatton, a one-time favourite of the queen, whom Crichton and many others suspected of being a covert Catholic, he managed to secure his release. Crichton and Hatton appear to have struck up something of a friendship and in response to a query from Hatton about how he was perceived by the Catholic community in England Crichton advised him that 'they felt about him, what mathematicians think about the motion of heavenly bodies. They have a natural motion from west to east, but still they are drawn by the primum mobile, and carried by motion to the west. Being a learned man, he at once understood that Crichton would have liked to say, that he had embraced heresy to please the Queen'. On his release in May 1587 Hatton ensured that Crichton was 'most familyarle and friendlye intreated and dismissed withe 100 li *Viaticum*, and a moste lardge and friendly pasport' to cover his passage home. He departed promising to do nothing to bring about his return to Scotland.[26]

* * *

When James Gordon of Huntly arrived in Scotland in the summer of 1584 prospects for the Catholic cause looked more promising than they had for some time, to the extent that there was great expectation in England of a Jesuit success north of the border.[27] An account of the mission reported that: 'Its success was very remarkable, although it had not the approval either of the Queen of Scotland nor of the more prudent ones. From that time the face of the country was entirely changed, and so great was the visible increase among the Catholics that they could easily have shaken off the yoke of the heretics, and their English brethren might have neutralised the power of their enemies in that realm'.[28] In September 1585 James Tyrie was visited in Paris by an Irish bishop, Edmund MacGauran of Ardagh, who had been in Scotland with Gordon and Hay. He advised Tyrie that during his short stay there he had administered the sacrament of confirmation to at least 10,000 people. Corroboration is provided by a later report in the same year which suggested that the same number of souls had been reconciled to Catholicism in the previous six months. An English report written around the same time advised that the number of converts was increasing daily and that the Jesuits, who proceed 'according to their wishes', were hopeful of converting the king. Their optimism was unfounded as Gordon was to discover following two frustrating months in Edinburgh lobbying James. Crichton in his account of events described how Gordon, a kinsman of the king, who was introduced to him by his nephew Huntly, 'not only touched the hearts of many persons by his holiness of life, but, further, being a man of great learning, he openly defeated the ministers of the heretics in the public discussions which were held'. These discussions involved a disputation before James against eight ministers of the Kirk on a variety of topics and a further disputation against George Hay, minister of

Rathven, on the writings of the ancient doctors. James may have been impressed, but he was not won over.[29]

Following MacGauran's visit Tyrie reported to Acquaviva that a small number of priests had achieved reasonable success, which coupled with the change in the political situation could have brought about the overthrow of the Kirk. However, there was great concern amongst the exiles in France about the overthrow of the regent, Arran, and the return of the Protestant nobles who had been banished by James in the aftermath of the Ruthven Raid. The exiles' earlier optimism was soon dampened by this 'fresh outbreak of the tempest'.[30] Their fears were heightened by the lack of communication from the fathers in Scotland. According to Berden, the English spy: 'The change in Scotland hathe made manye here verry melancholy, & hethereto they have no newes butt by generall Reporte from England, that the lords which weare Banyshed have the kynge in there coustodye... There is great expectation of letters from the Jesuyts in Scotland, & they yeeld not good Reason of their doings they will lose there credytt with all our Papists here, for they upon the Jesuyts promyse in there laste letters of the 28 of November, did expect that ther kynge shoulde have bynne in there Saffe custodie with Huntley and Maxfelde. Yet they here are nott altogther in despayer, because they hope lord hambleton will prove for there partie'. Reports from other sources suggested that, despite the changing political situation, the Jesuits continued to enjoy considerable success and in late 1586 Mendoza advised Philip that the Society had converted over 20,000 souls, including three noblemen and other gentlemen of note. It was, in fact, 'raising such a harvest by God's help that more priests were required to garner it'.[31]

In response to these positive reports from Scotland Acquaviva directed Pigenat, the French provincial and superior of the British missions, to send Edmund Hay and Tyrie to Scotland. As it transpired Tyrie was too preoccupied as Pigenat's assistant on British affairs to be spared and remained in France. John Hay was suggested as an alternative, but could not be released by his college at Tournan. Edmund Hay and John Durie were eventually appointed and arrived in Scotland in July 1585. Durie was the son of George Durie, Abbot of Dunfermline and Archdeacon of St Andrews, the nephew of Andrew Durie, the Protestant Bishop of Galloway and the great nephew of Archbishop Beaton. He was probably born in Dunfermline and was one of four brothers, of whom the two eldest, Peter and Henry, acted as guardians to their younger brothers, John and George, both of whom entered the Society. Their cousin John, another former monk of Dunfermline, was the Protestant minister of Leith and St Giles.[32] John, the Jesuit, was educated at Paris and Louvain and entered the Society in 1576. Although he was described as 'vir simplex et humilis' he was in fact a noted classicist, philosopher and theologian and was well known amongst his contemporaries for his famous defence of Edmund Campion in response to the attack by William Whittaker, the Dean of Durham, the *Confutatio Responsionis Gulielmi Whitakeri... ad Decem Rationes P Campiani*, written while Durie was studying at Eu.[33] Berden reported that 'Dureus the ffryr of Eawe hathe allso wrytten a booke declaringe that Papists (Catholeques as he termeth them) cannot dwell in England withoute perill of there lives, and withoute the offence there Conscience, (as the ffrenche men do dayle obiect agaynste the Papists which live abroade)'. After teaching rhetoric at Clermont Durie was transferred to Angers, from where he was summoned to join Edmund Hay.[34]

Hay and Durie were escorted to Scotland by Robert Bruce and travelled disguised as his servants, though they were described by Berden as being 'apparelled in purple like mariners'.[35] They embarked from Le Treport near Eu in Normandy on a ship bound for Newcastle for coal and slipped into Scotland with little fuss. Throughout August there seems to have been some doubt as to whether or not the party had actually arrived, although the English authorities suspected that it had. Further reports from Berden confirmed that the party had left for Scotland in mid July with instructions from Guise to deliver a message to Huntly, which had been approved by the French king. Guise, like many of his compatriots, was still labouring under the misapprehension that James was secretly a Catholic.[36] In mid August Robert Dudley, Earl of Leicester, wrote to James warning him of the fathers' arrival and imploring: 'For the love of God not only beware of them but lett the world know you detest them. I fear your Majestie shall find matter of their coming'.[37] Under pressure from the English government and the Kirk James made the appropriate noises about the need to apprehend Hay and Durie, though the Master of Gray, who was appointed to arrest them, was himself a suspected Catholic, albeit a thoroughly unreliable one.[38] Despite the information received from Berden and Leicester the doubts about the party's whereabouts persisted, though by the end of August it was clear that it had arrived and that James had met Bruce at Falkland and taken delivery of the letter from Guise.[39]

Following Bruce's meeting with James, Hay spent some time at Megginch with his brother, Peter, who was under pressure from the Master of Gray and members of his own family to convert. As a precaution Edmund persuaded his brother to retire temporarily to France until conditions improved. During the course of the mission Archibald Douglas of Whittinghame, a thoroughly disreputable Scottish agent who had been involved in Darnley's murder, alleged that Edmund had hired an assassin to kill Gray: 'The Jesuitis that are in Scotland, specially Father Hay is becummit now colerik and blode tharsty he conducit ane man to shoote the Master of Gray going to his lodgeing at Styrelin'. Although Hay has always been thought of as one of the more moderate members of the Society he appears not to have been averse to the use of force and it is not inconceivable that Gray's animosity towards his brother might lead him to consider such sanguine measures. Edmund further antagonised his Protestant relations by reconciling the wife of one of his nephews to the Catholic church shortly before she died. Having taken care of his family affairs Hay teamed up with Gordon and headed to the north east where he achieved a further minor success reconciling David Graham of Fintry, senior, a few months before his death.[40]

While Hay and Gordon headed north, Bruce and Durie travelled to the south west of Scotland where they may have met with Maxwell, who had been persuaded to join the Protestants in return for an indemnity for his past misdemeanours. Durie worked alongside Holt at New Abbey on the banks of the River Nith where they achieved considerable success in an area which was already noted for being staunchly Catholic. Durie 'by his learning, his indefatigable labours, and the sermons whereby he seemed able to turn the minds of men in any direction he wished, converted to the Catholic faith almost all the inhabitants of Dumfries, together with Lord Maxwell, the governor of the town and district'. At Christmas 1585 Maxwell, now back in the Catholic fold, marched in procession from Dumfries to Lincluden where Durie said Mass. Despite attempts to exclude them the service was gatecrashed by a large number of local Catholics who waded the River Nith to avoid Maxwell's guards. Life in the relatively cosy surroundings of New Abbey may have rather distorted Durie's view of the political situation in Scotland, and while he was correct in reporting that James's position was more secure than it had been for some time, he was perhaps being over-optimistic in predicting that Angus and his pro-English faction would soon be forced to leave Scotland as a result of the efforts of Huntly, Hamilton, Lennox and the other Catholic nobles.[41]

At New Abbey Durie and Holt continued the work of the former abbot, Gilbert Brown, who had been active in the area since the late

1570s. In September 1585 Brown failed to appear before the privy council, presumably to answer charges relating to his recusant activities, and fled to Pont-à-Mousson and then on to Douai. In 1587 he was ordained as a priest in Paris, before being transferred to Rome in May of that year. By the end of the year he was back in Scotland and for the next twenty years continued where he had left off, 'corrupting' the south west. Apart from a few visits to France during periods of heightened tension Brown remained in Scotland until 1608 working in tandem with the Jesuits until old age and ill health forced him to retire to Paris, where he died in poverty in May 1612.[42]

Alexander McQuhirrie, who also worked in the south west disembarked at Leith in mid-January 1586 along with the French ambassador, D'Anville, and a number of 'preistis, clad in blacke, well stored of money'.[43] William Murdoch may have been one of these priests as he was known to be working in Scotland in September of that year. This would appear to be confirmed by James's testimony to the privy council in 1607 that Murdoch had been in the country for about twenty years. McQuhirrie, who may originally have come from Edinburgh, was a former student of St Salvator's, where he had been a contemporary of two well known Catholics, Mark Kerr and Alexander Meldrum, and perhaps George Kerr, of whom more later.[44] In 1582 McQuhirrie was reunited with Mark Kerr and Meldrum at Pont-à-Mousson, where he trained for the priesthood.[45] Intelligence reports provided by Henry Scrope, Warden of the West March, confirmed that McQuhirrie, Holt, Durie and a French priest were all operating in the south west in early 1586, though there has been some confusion as to McQuhirrie's exact whereabouts and his position. Abercrombie's correspondence in the late 1580s and two further letters of 1596 and 1598 to Tyrie and Acquaviva, which refer back to earlier events, make no mention of McQuhirrie, while Crichton's memoir, compiled in 1611, suggests that the young man was not sent to Scotland until 1587. Abercrombie's letter of 1596 states that he had arrived nine years earlier from Braunsberg with William Ogilvie to join fellow Jesuits, Edmund Hay, Gordon, Crichton and the two Duries and makes no mention of McQuhirrie. Although the earlier English report mentioning McQuhirrie's arrival in 1586 described him as one of a group of priests it does not distinguish between Jesuits and seculars. The Scots College records indicate that he did not enter the Society until 1588, hence the reason for his omission from Abercrombie's letters. At some stage, though exactly when is unclear, McQuhirrie appears to have spent some time in prison before his release was secured by the Master of Gray.[46]

While the activities of the Jesuit fathers were shrouded in a certain amount of secrecy the rôle of some of their lay agents, such as Robert Bruce, was even more complex and confusing. Bruce, the son of Ninian Bruce and a nephew of the laird of Binnie, first came to prominence in the late 1570s when he was Archbishop Beaton's secretary in Paris. In January 1585, following a fall out with Beaton over money, he approached Stafford, the English ambassador in Paris, offering to sell his services there and in Scotland. Stafford thought him to be a 'proper wise fellow and well spoken and learned', having studied under the Jesuits at Pont-à-Mousson. The college records include reference to a student of that name, although the identification is by no means certain.[47] Although Bruce may have been a priest, Edmund Hay in his memoir of the period simply refers to him as a nobleman.[48] Around the same time Bruce was also hawking his services to Mary, though it would appear that neither offer was accepted, and six months later he was accompanying Hay and Durie to Scotland.[49] He remained in Scotland for a year before returning to France with the Scottish authorities in hot pursuit.[50] Of particular interest to them were the latest plans for the invasion of Scotland, drawn up by the Scottish Catholic nobles, including Huntly, Maxwell and Hamilton, and the purpose of a number of blank letters, similar to those which were to cause such a furore in 1592–3, bearing the noblemen's signatures, which were to be delivered to Guise to be filled in and forwarded to Philip. The Scottish proposal, which Guise readily endorsed, involved the deployment of 6,000 Spanish troops to protect the Scottish border and the levying of a Scottish army to overthrow the pro-English faction at court, liberate Mary and restore Catholicism. The proposal, having been approved by Mendoza, was delivered to Philip by Bruce, though by November he was back in Paris having failed to persuade the king, who had already decided on an armada against England. As consolation Philip proposed a small expedition to Scotland and consulted Alessandro Farnese, Duke of Parma, who was initially unenthusiastic. Although Bruce eventually persuaded the duke to back the scheme it never got past the planning stage and Bruce, who was to charter the necessary ships, sensing the lack of interest, went into hiding in Brittany.[51]

After a temporary lull in Jesuit activity in Scotland the English authorities detected an upsurge in activity, which was confirmed by Christopher Buxton, an English seminary priest, who reported that 'Everye man thinketh to go in by Scotland is the best, because of great lybertye which is [given unt]o the Catholickes there of late tyme'.[52] In May 1587 Sir Cuthbert Collingwood, an English border official, reported that a number of Jesuits and seminary priests had entered Scotland by Northumberland, including John Boste, another seminary priest, who later appeared in Edinburgh and also attended a meeting of Jesuit fathers, including Gordon, Edmund Hay, John Durie and two other unnamed fathers, convened at Fintry's house in Aberdeen. It is unclear whether Murdoch was one of the unnamed fathers as it is possible that he was in London at the time awaiting Crichton's release from the Tower. Bruce returned to Scotland in late August or early September 1587 and disembarked at Loch Ryan in Wigtownshire with letters from Parma for Huntly and Hamilton. The Catholic nobles decided that it was too late in the year to hire the ships necessary to carry out Bruce's invasion plans; nevertheless he pressed on and obtained a number of audiences with James at Hamilton, Blantyre and Falkland. Within a few months it was clear that his mission was a failure and that James was not prepared to accept any offers of Spanish support which involved the use of military force.[53]

* * *

Meanwhile in England Mary was paying the price for her involvement with Babington. In October 1586 she was tried at Fotheringay before a panel of thirty six commissioners, and although she denied any knowledge of Babington's plot incriminating correspondence and the testimony of Babington himself and her secretaries, Claude Nau de Mauvissière and Gilbert Curle, sealed her fate. After swithering over signing her cousin's death warrant Elizabeth eventually agreed to her execution. The events of 8 February 1587 are well-documented as are the effects of her subsequent martyrdom.[54] However, her death appears to have had little effect on the activities of the Scottish Jesuits, whose contact with her had tailed off during the last few years of her life. Although Crichton had continued to correspond with her, she had fallen more and more under the influence of Nau and Curle and two other servants, Charles Paget and Thomas Morgan, who as a result of being excluded from the exiles' activities during the early 1580s had turned Mary against the Society. Some doubt has been expressed about the rôle of Paget and Morgan and there is a suggestion that they were actually English agents infiltrated into the exiles' organisation to undermine it.[55]

Mary's execution provoked a hostile reaction in Scotland, where rumours of war began to circulate. Any thoughts of a Scottish army storming over the border were quickly quashed by Walsingham who pointed out to James the adverse effect this would have on his claim to the English throne and the continued payment of the subsidies he was receiving from Elizabeth. James, who had always been aware of the implications of Mary's martyrdom and the threat she would still pose after her death, described her as 'a new head, more formidable than a sickly woman'.[56] Similarly, the English Jesuit, Robert Southwell, was aware of her value as a Catholic martyr, and in his poem *Decease Release* wrote:

> Alive a Queene, now dead I am a Sainte
> Once Mary calld, my name nowe Martyr is,
> From earthly raigne debarred by restraint
> In view whereof I raigne in heavenly blisse[57]

Mary's execution rather than solving Elizabeth's problems brought the succession question to the fore. Allen and Persons pressed Philip's claim as a descendant of the house of Lancaster and as Mary's nominee. Others supported James's claim despite the fact that he was a Protestant. In Crichton's opinion James, despite his vacillations, could be cultivated, and ignoring his claim would simply play into the hands of the Protestants.

* * *

Bruce's mission was followed by the visit of William Chisholm, Bishop of Dunblane and administrator of the see of Vaison near Avignon, who was sent to Scotland by Pope Sixtus V (1585–90) along with Crichton and, possibly, McQuhirrie to persude James to support the Armada.[58] Chisholm had been deprived of his bishopric in 1569, but his reappointment at the instigation of James was approved by parliament sometime between March and July 1587.[59] Following his release from the Tower Crichton had travelled to Paris and then on to Rome, where, following a meeting with Persons, he received instructions to return to Scotland. The letters patent issued by Acquaviva instructing his return stressed that he was doing so under orders and that he had done nothing to go back on his earlier promise to the English privy council.[60] The mission was arranged at the instigation of the pope and a likeminded faction in Rome, including Dr Owen Lewis, the Welsh bishop of Cassano, who were becoming suspicious of Spanish policy in Scotland. Enriqué de Guzman, Count of Olivares, the Spanish ambassador in Rome, made every effort to undermine the mission claiming that James was clearly a heretic and that the pope should be promoting Philip's claim to the English throne. Despite the Papacy's efforts to redress the balance Mendoza managed to intercept Chisholm in Paris to ensure that he was made aware of the Spanish perspective: 'I have conveyed to the friar what I have considered it would be most conducive to the interests of the Catholic religion and your Majesty's service to lay before the King. He is thoroughly imbued with this, and is convinced that, if the Catholics do not kill those belonging to the English faction and liberate the King, nothing good will be effected'.[61]

Chisholm and his party landed at Leith in September or October 1587 and in a letter written a couple of years later Crichton reported that he personally took the helm of the French ship as it entered port. There were five passengers on board and the rumour quickly spread that all were Jesuits. To avoid any unwelcome publicity the party immediately travelled north to visit Huntly and *en route* lodged with an unnamed Presbyterian noble, possibly the envoy's brother, Chisholm of Dundern.[62] William Chisholm's requests for an audience with James were refused and his visit restricted to twenty days. With the help of Francis Stewart, 5th Earl of Bothwell, Lord High Admiral of Scotland, his permit was extended and he eventually gained an audience with the king on 11 March 1588, following a preliminary audience with the chancellor, John Maitland of Thirlestane. No account of either audience survives, except for a unreliable report of the audience with James by John Arnold, the prior of the English Carthusians, prepared for Philip some time in or around 1589. It would appear that at the preliminary audience Chisholm offered James the chance of revenge for himself and his mother and advised Maitland that papal support would be forthcoming for James's claim to the English throne. Maitland, not surprisingly, avoided committing himself or James, and instead sought two assurances from Chisholm, firstly, that James would succeed to the English throne if Spanish power prevailed and secondly that James would not be expected to convert to Catholicism. It is unclear whether Chisholm was authorised to give these assurances, but it would appear that both Maitland and James made it clear that they were not interested in his proposals.[63] The failure of the mission came as little surprise to either the pro- or the anti-Spanish lobbies in Rome, and Olivares, Allen and Persons all felt that there was little point in continuing to pander to James, a view which the Papacy was also beginning to share.[64] To many the mission merely confirmed the widely held view that James could not be trusted. Nevertheless, the Society had no plans to withdraw from Scotland, and Chisholm's mission was followed soon after by the reappearance of Abercrombie who had spent the years since his last mission in 1580 serving as the novice-master at Braunsberg and Cracow. He was arrested by Bothwell soon after arriving in Scotland, but was released at the request of Crichton and sent to the relative safety of the south west.[65]

In February 1588 an extraordinary General Assembly of the Kirk was called in response to the increased level of Catholic activity. Andrew Melville in his opening address to the Assembly warned of the threat posed by Philip and the Jesuits. A memorial to James was drafted listing the Catholic agents operating in Scotland and those nobles and lairds assisting them. In the south John Durie was 'seduceing and practiseing [to and fro] under the name of William Leing', while in the north Gordon, Hay, McQuhirrie (still not a Jesuit), John Scot, Alexander Meldrum and Arthur Panton were described as 'Jesuites [incessantly corrupting] mak[ing] residence cheiflie in Murray [Elly, Boyne] and Strathbogie, but seduc[ing] everywhere in Buchan, Garioch, Mar, Aberdein… And to the recepters they are so many that few or no honest men are in the whole countrey, that aither for fear or favour have not recept the Jesuits'. Scot, Meldrum and Panton were either Jesuits using assumed names, or, as is more likely, secular priests. The Presbytery of Edinburgh also complained about the number of priests at large, and was particularly irate that the city magistrates had previously arrested McQuhirrie, James Seton and John Scot (presumably the same priest operating in the north), and subsequently released them.[66] Gordon and Crichton were also in Edinburgh for spells, while John Durie remained in the south west under the protection of Maxwell, who was accused of assisting the Jesuits in organising celebrations of the Mass in Dumfries and ejecting the Protestant minister. Durie was by this stage terminally ill with consumption and died shortly after with Abercrombie in attendance.[67] Others singled out by the General Assembly included Huntly, Sutherland, Graham of Fintry and a number of noble ladies.

Surprisingly James Gordon was not specifically named in the memorial to James despite the fact that in early February he had been involved in a disputation at Holyrood with a number of Protestant ministers in the presence of the king. Gordon had been impressed by the king's eloquence and his understanding of the theories of justification and predestination and other complicated theological issues, and had been pleasantly surprised at the level of agreement between them. Gordon might not have been quite so full of the king's praises if he had been aware of what was said behind his back by James and his courtiers, one of whom boasted that the most learned papist in Europe could not trip the King of Scots. It also came to Mendoza's attention that 'after the disputation the King said in his chamber that Gordon did not understand the Scripture, which is a fairly bold thing to say, only that the King has the assurance to translate Revelation and to write upon the subject as if he were Amadis de Gaul himself'.[68]

McQuhirrie, who was perhaps accompanied by Scot, left Scotland at some stage during the spring of 1588 to enter the Jesuit novitiate, and was replaced by Murdoch and George Durie. By this time there may have been as many as eight Jesuits working in Scotland, of whom the most influential, in the opinion of the authorities, were Hay and Crichton. Spottiswoode in comparing Hay and Gordon dismissed the latter, who despite the disputation at Holyrood and his reputation as the most learned papist in Europe was not much 'feared as being a simple man, and not deeply learned'. Hay was considered to be 'of greater account and more politic and wise'.[69]

The increased Jesuit activity during this period coincided with the formation of a new league of Catholic and anti-English nobles, including Huntly, Errol, Crawford, Bothwell and Hamilton. The origins of this league are to be found in a dispute between James and Huntly, when the latter refused to hand over a kinsman, Gordon of Gight, accused of murdering the Earl Marischal's brother.[70] Links between the Society and the Hamiltons had existed for some time and Lord Hamilton's brother, Claud, may have been the son of the Duke of Châtelherault, who while studying in Rome, was converted to Catholicism by Crichton.[71] Encouraged by the more volatile members of the mission, such as Crichton, the Catholic nobles gathered their supporters at Dunfermline and Linlithgow. In response to a request from the English faction at court Henry Carey, Lord Hunsdon, the governor of Berwick, sent financial assistance with which to raise the necessary troops to quell the rising.[72] It was followed by another abortive uprising in the south west during the late spring under the leadership of Maxwell and Colonel William Sempill, a Scottish mercenary and former veteran of the war in Flanders, who had landed at Kirkcudbright to raise an army in support of the Catholic party. Acting on the instructions of Parma, Maxwell and Sempill succeeded in raising the south west, but by June the rebellion had been quelled and the leading rebels executed or imprisoned. After a few months in Edinburgh Castle Sempill escaped, apparently by shinning down a silk cord smuggled to him in a pie, and with financial assistance from Bruce fled to the continent.[73] As an expression of her gratitude for his decisive response Elizabeth granted James an annual pension from the earldom of Huntingdon, which was soon withdrawn when the threat of the Spanish Armada had passed.

The events surrounding the Armada are well documented and need not be repeated here. Suffice to say that its failure was a great disappointment to the Scottish Catholics, who had seen the overthrow of Elizabeth as a precursor to the collapse of the Kirk. Aside from the failure of the main objective of the Armada they were disappointed that as it fled north round Scotland no further attempt was made to land.[74] In a letter to Acquaviva Crichton complained that 'for many a day did we wait the fleet of the Catholic King, with a longing, a loyalty not less than that which Christ's coming was looked for by those who cried: O but thou wouldst rend the heavens and wouldst come down... the mountains would melt away at thy presence... But here there was melting away of our mountains, they never even touched our shores but fled although none pursued'.[75] Around 1,000 Spaniards were shipwrecked off the coast of Scotland, and with James's consent were cared for by Scottish Catholics, and no doubt many Protestants.[76] Amongst them were a number of Spanish officers who arrived at the lodging of the young earl of Angus in the New Street in the Canongate in Edinburgh, to pay their respects to Crichton. Although Crichton had been amongst those calling for the Spanish to land in Scotland he had envisaged them coming ashore in slightly different circumstances and to avoid unwelcome attention and possible arrest he moved out of his lodgings to a safer refuge. In his letter Crichton also told the story of a Spanish youth who was spat on in the street in Edinburgh by one of the English ambassador's staff and took exception to the fact that the insult had come from an Englishman rather than a Scotsman. Subsequent letters from Crichton and others to the Spanish fleet sheltering in the Western Isles failed to reach their destination as the remnants of the fleet had already departed for Spain.[77]

Plate I
A Bellarmine Jug made in Germany in the late sixteenth century and named after Robert Bellarmine, SJ, found in Berwickshire

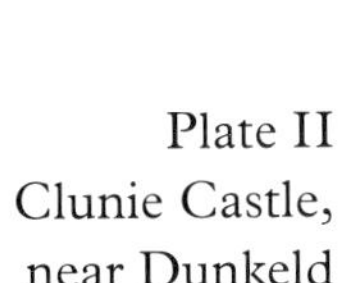

Plate II
Clunie Castle, near Dunkeld

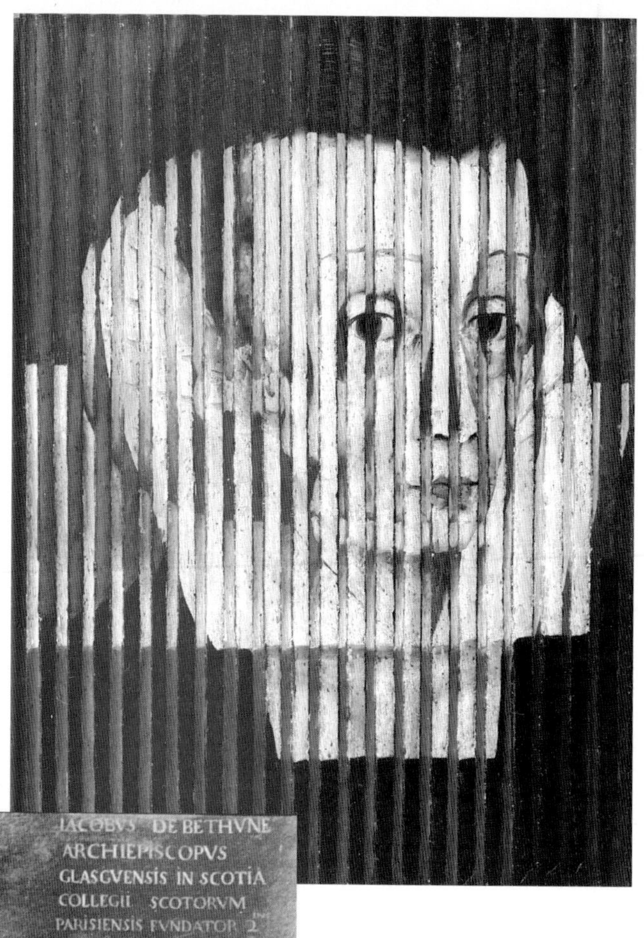

Plate III
Mary, Queen of
Scots, Anamorphosis

Plate IV
James Beaton,
Archbishop of
Glasgow

Plate VIII
Detail from 'Popish Plots and Treasons'

Plate IX
George Gordon, 6th Earl of Huntly, and his wife Henrietta Stewart

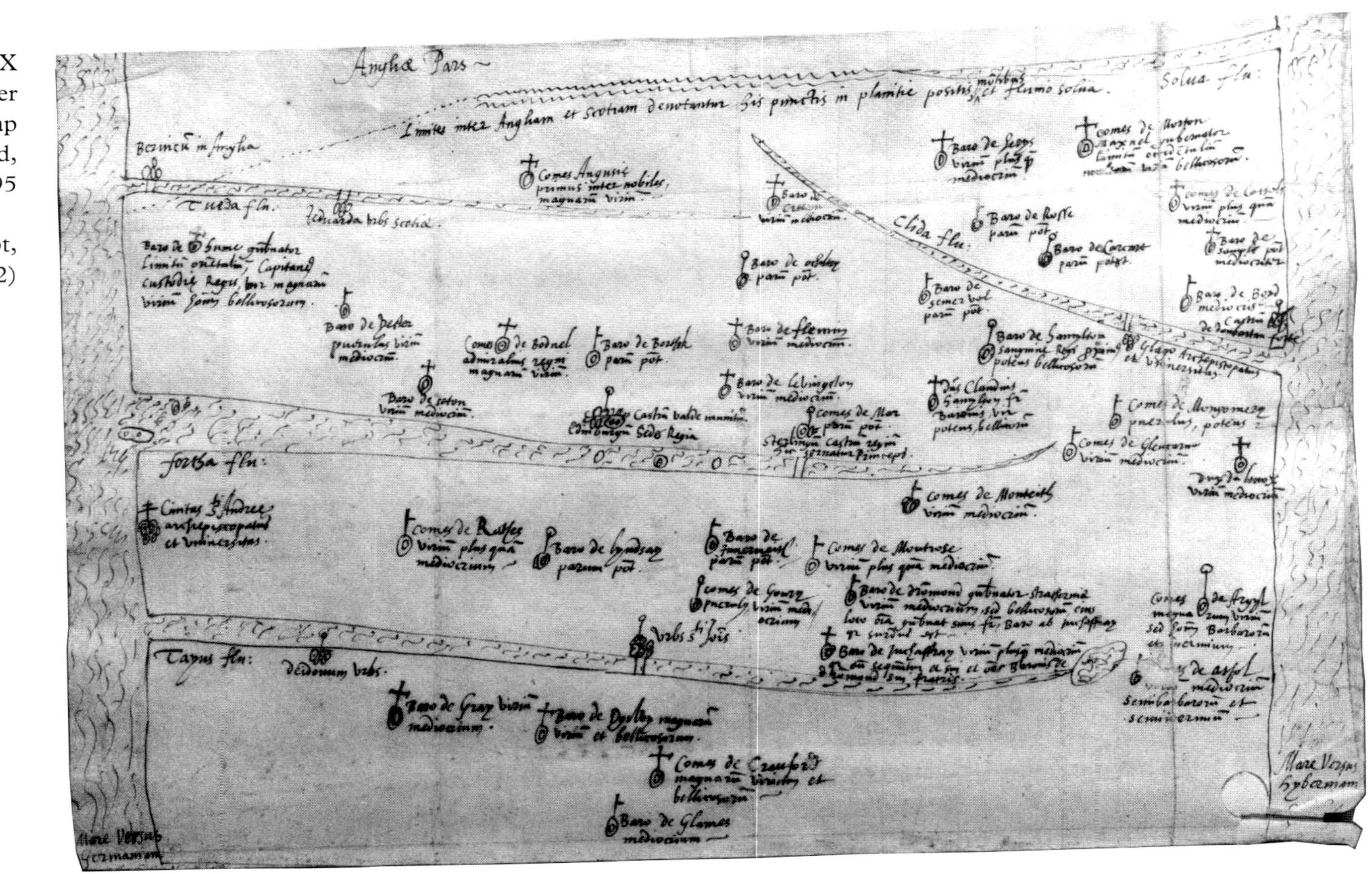

Plate X
Father
Crichton's Map
of Scotland,
1595

(For transcript,
see page 182)

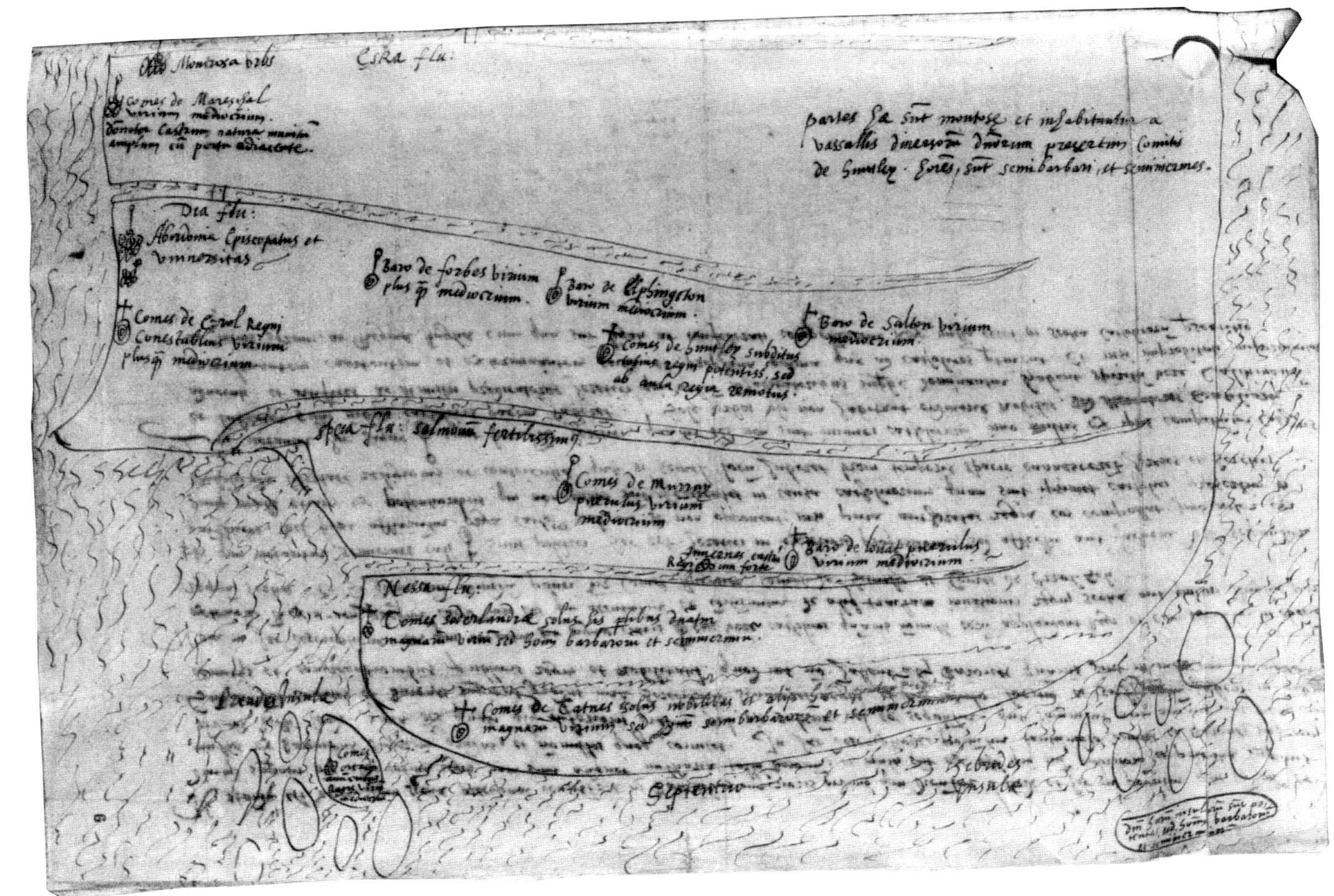

Plate XI
Father
Crichton's Map
of Scotland,
1595

(For transcript, see page 182)

Plate XII
James VI in 1595

Plate XIII
Queen Anne in 1595

Chapter 7

Brig o'Dee and the Affair of the Spanish Blanks

As the Armada fled for home the Catholic party in Scotland turned on the English Catholics for their failure to support the Spanish. It was claimed that two thirds of Scotland would have welcomed the Armada had it attempted to land there. Despite their disappointment Huntly, Errol, Crawford and Graham of Fintry remained active in support of the Catholic cause. Maxwell and Colonel Sempill were still in jail, but Bruce remained at large and in October 1588 received a subsidy of 10,000 crowns from the Duke of Parma, which he and Crichton were to distribute amongst the leading Catholics, including Huntly, who indicated that he was still prepared to lead any rebellion as long as there was sufficient support. However, until he was satisfied that this was the case he decided to concentrate on removing Maitland and Glamis and James's other pro-English councillors and making his peace with the Kirk.[1]

During the winter of 1588–9 Calderwood reported that Jesuits, seminary priests and 'other emissareis of Antichrist' were 'creeping in the countrie [and] ceassed not to pervert and subvert in diverse places'. Specific reference was made to Edmund Hay and William Crichton and the 'rest of that sect there, [who] doe daylie draw men to Poperie, and so to the King of Spain's service in this yland'.[2] James was urged by the General Assembly to act more vigorously to curb this upturn in recusant activity and as a mark of his commitment was called on to remove all Catholics from his own houschold.[3] In February 1589 the privy council passed further legislation against secular priests, Jesuits and 'other excommunicated persons still lingering in the realm', including Hay, Crichton, Bruce and Graham of Fintry. The legislation distinguished between 'twa sortis – the ane alluraris and persuadirs, be dispersing of buikis and prevey ressoning amangis the simple and ignorant people, to declyne frome the treuth and to imbrace superstitioun and idolatrie, and the uthir crafty and politique heidis, trafficquaris in materis of the Estate, surmysaris and forgearis of leying amangis sum of the nobilitie, dispersaris of brutis and rumouris of foreygne preparationis'.[4]

Colonel William Sempill was amongst those in the King of Spain's service, whose servant, Thomas Pringle, was captured by the English in February 1589. In his possession they found letters from Huntly, Errol, Crawford, Maxwell and Lord Claud Hamilton to Philip purporting to be in the name of the Scottish Catholics and requesting military intervention by Spain. James was in a meeting with his councillors, including Huntly and Errol, when the letters were delivered to him by the English ambassador, William Ashby, along with a sharp rebuke from Elizabeth, who was clearly exasperated by his failure to control his Catholic nobles. Pringle was also carrying a letter from Robert Bruce to Parma in which he expressed his disappointment over the failure of the Armada, but celebrated the good news of Angus's death and Errol and Crawford's conversion by Hay and Crichton. Bruce claimed that the Jesuits 'reap much fruit in Scotland, and as soon as a lord or some other person of importance is converted by them they at the same time dispose and incline his affection to the service of the King of Spain and that of your highness, as to a thing inseparably united with the advancement of the true religion in this country'.[5]

Huntly's attempts to maintain his political position by making his peace with the Kirk and outwardly conforming to Protestantism were soon undermined by the arrest of Pringle and the disclosure of the incriminating letters, which provided clear evidence of the continuing negotiations with Spain.[6] Nevertheless, he remained confident in his close relationship with James and offered to stand trial, whereupon he was promptly locked up in Edinburgh Castle and deprived of his recent appointment as captain of the guard.[7] While in prison he was allowed to communicate with Montrose, Errol and Bothwell, and even dined with James, who 'kissed him often, and protested he knew he was innocent'. James was always ready to excuse Huntly, whom he believed to be 'young, merry, disinterested in matters of state'. He was also reluctant to remove him from the political scene as this would create a vacuum in the north of Scotland and an imbalance at the heart of government.[8] It suited James to have a series of checks and balances in place to prevent any single faction dominating Scottish politics. As relations between the two remained close it was no surprise to anyone that Huntly was soon released and restored to favour. Errol, Peter Hay of Megginch and a number of the other conspirators were less willing to take a chance with James and fled from Edinburgh to the safety of their country estates.[9]

Within a few months of his release from prison Huntly was in open rebellion along with Errol, Crawford, Bothwell and Montrose. Their motives are unclear, though religion was apparently not the main issue. More important was the threat posed by Maitland of Lethington, especially to Huntly's political aspirations. In response to the rebels' occupation of Perth and Aberdeen James mustered a small royal army of less than 2,000 men and marched north via Perth and Dundee. Huntly and Errol were outwardly defiant, but when confronted by the royal army at Brig o'Dee, near Aberdeen, the rebel army and its leaders quickly dispersed. The Gordon lands were soon subdued, Errol's stronghold at Slains Castle, near Peterhead, captured and financial securities exacted from the leading rebels. Huntly, Crawford and Bothwell were imprisoned in Borthwick, St Andrews and Tantallon Castles respectively, while the other leading conspirators, who were not captured, such as Graham of Fintry, were denounced as rebels. Fintry was to get short shrift when his subsequent involvement in the Affair of the Spanish Blanks was exposed, of which more later.[10]

The rebellion was followed by a period of relative domestic calm during which James took the opportunity to patch up relations with Elizabeth and the Kirk and to travel to Scandinavia in search of a bride. At home the Catholic party found a new champion in the young earl of Angus, who had succeeded his Protestant father.[11] The Jesuits continued to enjoy royal support, and the freedom they were permitted aroused considerable public resentment. Sir Robert Melville and the magistrates of Burntisland refused to arrest James Gordon as he claimed to have a royal warrant permitting him to remain in Scotland.[12] Nevertheless, Gordon, Hay and Crichton, wary of the ascendancy of the pro-English faction, decided not to rely on James's continued favour and left Scotland in the autumn of 1589. Their position had become very awkward following their implication in the plot revealed in the letters to Philip and Parma, though it was as much out of concern for those sheltering them as for their own safety that they decided to return to the continent. Furthermore, Crichton had almost been arrested in Edinburgh a few months earlier and in the wake of further anti-Catholic legislation and increased efforts by the authorities it would have been merely a question of time before he was finally apprehended. They left Scotland at around the same time as Huntly, and shortly after arriving on the continent met with Parma before departing for Spain.[13]

Crichton made his way to Spain via Genoa, where, in August 1590, he suffered a bout of tertian fever and was bed-ridden for long periods.

He eventually arrived in Madrid in late autumn of that year and remained there until 1592 conducting negotiations at the Spanish court. He was well received, as were the offers of support from the Scottish nobles for the proposed invasion. Crichton argued that Philip provided the best option 'to maintain faith and justice and defend the inhabitants against enemies', unite Scotland and England and 'enable our countrymen to share in his great honours, wide spread Empire and wealth'.[14] He also believed that England was the source of most of Spain's problems and stressed to Philip the financial implications of a successful invasion, including an estimated saving to the Spanish treasury of five to six million ducats: sweep away the spider, he argued, and her web would collapse thereby removing the English threat in France, Flanders and the New World. Although he suggested Scotland as the disembarkation point for any invasion he was not averse to the use of a suitable English port as this would spare Scotland the excesses of an invading army. To move matters forward the Spanish suggested that Crichton or another father should be sent to Scotland to begin preparations, a proposal which was opposed by the general, who was fully aware that the English authorities would quickly learn of the visit. Acquaviva advised Crichton that if Philip insisted on proceeding with the proposal he was to make his opposition known. Instead Robert Bruce's name was suggested, being a man of 'rare parts', who was well known to the Spanish. Bruce was in Flanders at the time, but could be summoned to Spain or sent instructions. Crichton was keen to go to Flanders to make contact with Bruce, but again the proposal was blocked by Acquaviva who felt it would only arouse the suspicions of the English authorities. Despite the general's misgivings Crichton was given authority to reside in Lower Germany, ostensibly to assist with the running of the Jesuit colleges in Belgium and the relocation of the Scots College to Douai.[15] In June 1591 he was instructed to go Rome to meet Edmund Hay, the recently appointed assistant for Germany, whose remit included the three British missions, but before arrangements could be finalised Hay died on 4 November following a long bout of dysentery and colic.[16]

In the autumn of 1591 Philip decided to invite David Graham of Fintry to Spain as the representative of the Scottish Catholic nobles. Crichton spoke highly of Fintry and had specifically mentioned him to Philip in a report on the Scottish nobility. As no response had been received from Fintry by March of the following year Crichton sent William Gordon, the son of the Laird of Abergeldie, to his kinsman, James Gordon, with letters to the Scottish Catholics containing details of his negotiations with Philip. He claimed in the correspondence that Philip was being deceived by his English advisers and that he was relying on Crichton for advice regarding the invasion and the subsequent reconversion of Scotland. He was particularly critical of Robert Persons for his lack of assistance while in Spain, though the Englishman does not seem to have been offended by the criticism and in subsequent exchanges between the two they continued to express the highest regard for each other. In response Persons suggested that Crichton's schemes 'for curing the ills of Scotland.... were not well founded and, indeed, impracticable'.[17]

Crichton, who had delayed his return to Rome in anticipation of Fintry's arrival, wrote to Acquaviva in March 1592 expressing his concern at the lack of progress. His hosts, aware of his frustration, appear to have strung him along with assurances of their goodwill and a small subsidy. In May he sent a further letter to Acquaviva confirming his decision to leave for Rome. In this letter he likened his futile mission to the myth of the Egyptian elephants, which after long labours had given birth to abortions. He had hoped to have something to show for his own labours.[18] His departure was further delayed until August and it was November before he arrived in Rome, armed with a letter of presentation to the new pope, Clement VIII, from Pietro Millino, the papal nuncio in Madrid.[19] With the benefit of hindsight it is clear that Crichton's lack of success was inevitable as Philip, although keen on the proposed enterprise, was preoccupied with the war against Henry of Navarre and the Huguenots, supported by the English and the Dutch and German Protestants, and with the domestic unrest led by his former Secretary of State, Antonio Pérez. Philip was also determined to avoid a repetition of the Armada and any further loss of men and resources. Spanish relations with the Papacy were also strained and the situation was not helped by the numerous changes of pope between 1590 and 1592.[20] After reporting to his superiors in Rome, Crichton and an English Jesuit, William Baldwin, were despatched to Flanders in January 1593. In April he arrived in Douai, via Pont-à-Mousson, to take over the running of the Scots College.[21] Following the failure of his Spanish mission Crichton switched his alleigance back to James, who, despite being a Protestant, appeared to be a more promising champion of the Catholic cause than the indecisive and sickly Philip. Encouraging reports of James's poor relations with his advisers and the Kirk convinced Crichton that his conversion was still possible.[22]

While on the surface Scotland appeared calm the Catholic party remained active, despite the best efforts of the General Assembly to enforce the anti-Catholic legislation of 1587 and 1588. According to Richard Verstegan, an English Catholic agent and publisher in Antwerp: 'In Scotland the Catholique party remaineth strong and more resolute than was supposed; and some of the nobillity have masse publykely said in their countries'.[23] This new found optimism was seriously undermined by the subsequent rapprochement between James and the Kirk following parliament's recognition of the main sections of *The Second Book of Discipline* in the Golden Act of 1592 and the uncovering of the alleged plot which has become known as 'The Affair of the Spanish Blanks'. Despite considerable analysis the plot is still shrouded in a certain amount of controversy, and while it may not have been a complete set up as some have suggested it would appear that the English were aware of it from the outset and, together with the Kirk, manipulated it to discredit the Catholic party and derail any moves towards religious toleration. Gordon and McQuhirrie were at the time engaged in negotiations for freedom of worship and in a petition entitled 'Articles by the Catholic Clergy, Nobles and Commons of Scotland to be answered by the Ministers of the Reformed Kirk' argued the case for religious toleration. The extent of the support for this 'public manifesto' is unclear, though as well as the Catholic community there would appear to have been 'many others of quality' who were 'ready to join in the action to be broched and begun upon sight of fit opportunity... and some so well disposed that it is very strange that such should be thus ensnared'. The Spanish Blanks were in effect the Protestant response to these proposals.[24]

Although Francis Shearman has argued that the plot was concocted by the English there is little doubt that it was originally the work of William Crichton and had been conceived during his time in Spain. A manuscript volume in the Scottish Record Office states that the plot was hatched by 'the Jesuites and chieflie by father Crightoun, who, for some discontentment had, a few yearis before, left Scotland and fled into Spaine: where he endeavoured to insinuate himselfe into King Philip his favour, and publisched a book concerning the genealogie of his daughter, the Infant, maried to the Archduke; wherein he did his best to prove that the two crowns of England and Scotland did apperteine unto her; and, that this cunning Jesuite might rather move King Philip to make warr against the King of Scotland, he wryteth books and pamphlets in the disgrace of his own native prince'.[25] In their confessions two of the alleged conspirators implicated a number of Scottish Jesuits, whose involvement was exploited by the English, in collusion with the Kirk, to embarrass James and the Society. As early as March 1592, around the time when Crichton was advising the Scottish nobles of his negotiations in Madrid, the English became aware of the plot, which was to be implemented in Scotland by Abercrombie and Gordon. James Chisholm of Dundern, a nephew of the Bishop of Dunblane, who had been chosen to act as a messenger and to conduct negotiations with Huntly and Errol, was unable to undertake the mission and was replaced by George Kerr, the brother of Mark Kerr of Newbattle, a royal councillor. George Kerr, who may have previously studied at Pont-à-Mousson, 'considdering that heirby he could have na quyet residence within his native cuntrie, deliberat to pas beyond sea'. Robert Bowes quickly learnt of Kerr's involvement and during the spring of 1592 provided William Cecil, Lord Burghley, with details of the plot. In June Elizabeth instructed Bowes to warn James of the threat of another Spanish invasion of Scotland and to recommend that Huntly be brought to heel and the Jesuits banished. Her advice was ignored by James who showed his annoyance at her meddling by refusing to grant any further audiences to Bowes. However, the ambassador, had other sources of information and Robert Bruce, who was privy to the plot, offered to reveal details in return for a pardon from James for his earlier dealings on behalf of the Society.[26]

The plan hatched by Crichton and communicated to Gordon was undoubtedly naïve, and it is difficult to believe that Philip would have agreed to be party to it. It would appear to have been an attempt by Crichton to kick start the faltering negotiations in Madrid by offering a token of the Scottish nobles commitment to the proposed invasion. This commitment was to take the form of guarantees comprising a number of blank letters bearing their signatures, which were to be completed by Crichton and Tyrie following the successful conclusion of the negotiations with Philip. The proposal was for 30,000 troops to land in Kircudbright or at the mouth of the Clyde, of whom 4,000 or 5,000 would remain in Scotland, while the remainder were to invade England. On receiving the letter from Crichton with details of the enterprise Gordon showed it to Abercrombie, who in turn revealed its contents to Fintry. This much is confirmed by Fintry's confession in which he swore that his first knowledge of the plot had been in the spring of 1592, though he seems undecided whether he met Abercrombie at Abernethy or Linlithgow. This initial meeting was followed by a further one in Stirling Castle, where Fintry was imprisoned and from where he was also in correspondence with Gordon.[27]

Elizabeth's warnings to James of a possible Spanish invasion were unnecessary as he was fully aware of the potential threat. In a memorial entitled 'Certain reasons which may be used to prove it meet, or unmeet, the executing of this enterprise this summer or not. 1592', drafted for use by John Ogilvie of Pourie to promote James's claim to the English throne, he had already weighed up the pros and cons of a Spanish invasion. The various reasons for and against show clearly James's concerns regarding the foreign policies of England and Spain. As the Spanish were not in a position to launch another Armada, and as the inevitable delay would play into the hands of the English, who it was clear knew all about the invasion plans, James was more inclined not to antagonise Elizabeth and to avoid the use of force. He correctly gambled on her eventually favouring his claim: 'I will deal with the Queen of England fair and pleasantly for my title to the Crown of England after her decease, which thing, if she grant to me (as it is not impossible, howbeit unlikely), we have then attained our design without stroke of sword'.[28] He was also astute enough to realise that, despite the manoeuvrings of Crichton and the claims of the Scottish Catholic nobles, there was very little evidence of widespread support for a Spanish invasion, though this did not prevent him continuing to play the Catholic card when it suited him.

During the course of the summer Abercrombie was supported in Scotland by Gordon, William Ogilvie and McQhuirrie, later described by Bowes as the 'four terrible plagues'. Abercrombie spent much of his time on the move being the 'cheiffest man quha travellit to obtene blankis'.[29] McQuhirrie, now a member of the Society, had returned to Scotland via Antwerp and arrived home some time in the early summer.[30] English intelligence reported that 'Mr. William Macwherye, Scottishman and Jesuit – who being long a prisoner was delivered by means of the Master of Gray – has lately come to Montrose out of Flanders in a French ship, which put him on land with a boat near to Montrose, and thereon returned and made sail for Flanders'.[31] Soon after landing McQuhirrie headed north to meet Gordon and then worked his way south to the Lothians and the Borders, where he was sheltered by Alexander, Lord Home, the Warden of the East March, whose servant, Thomas Tyrie, was a nephew of James Tyrie. In October Abercrombie, Gordon, McQuhirrie and other principal Catholics were in Edinburgh awaiting the arrival of Adam Simpson, a priest from Brussels. Simpson, described by a contemporary as 'a verie craftie, cruel, and pestiferous papist, but unlearned', never arrived in the capital and was arrested in Fife carrying a packet of letters 'stuffed with riddles ... [and] full of suspicion'. There was in fact nothing of any substance in the correspondence, which dealt mainly with the affairs of the Scots College at Pont-à-Mousson, where Simpson had been a student.[32] While in Edinburgh the fathers also took the opportunity to canvass support from James and a number of leading nobles, including Home, Lennox, Huntly and Errol. Bowes reported that he had received intelligence from an informant, probably the Edinburgh doctor, James MacCartney, who enjoyed the misplaced confidence of Abercrombie, that Gordon and others had resolved to stay in Scotland and had recently been in Edinburgh. At the same time there were also a number of ministers in the city 'to recover the revolted, to strengthen the weak, to confirm the constant, and to undermine and cast down the mud walls pitched up by the Jesuits and papists'.[33] Errol and others were cited to appear before the ministers, whilst Home was specifically ordered to hand over McQuhirrie and Thomas Tyrie.[34]

The English authorities waited until December before making their move by which stage the blanks had been collected by Abercrombie and Kerr and arrangements made for their delivery to Spain. Details were passed to Bowes by MacCartney, who appears to have had a vested interest in ensuring that they never reached their destination. As well as the blank letters Kerr was also carrying a blank charter to be signed by Crichton authorising the sale of a small area of land in East Lothian in respect of which MacCartney had been acting in some fiduciary capacity. As a result of the proposed sale MacCartney stood to lose out financially.[35] The information regarding the blanks was in turn passed on to the Kirk, who instructed Andrew Knox, the minister of Paisley and later bishop of the Isles, to apprehend Kerr. Knox, with the assistance of a large posse, including a number of students from Glasgow University, arrested Kerr on 27 December as he was preparing to set sail from the Fairlie Road on the Isle of Cumbrae, near Largs. Kerr's luggage was searched and in the sleeves of a shirt his captors found the blanks and a number of other letters addressed to various Jesuits and other Catholic exiles. Kerr was taken to Calder, in West Lothian, by Lord Ross, where he was detained until the Edinburgh magistrates were able to assemble an escort to take him to the capital. On 31 December a troop of 60 horsemen and 200 foot soldiers ensured that he was safely ensconced in the Tolbooth.[36] On New Year's day Angus, one of the signatories of the blanks, unaware of the discovery of the plot, arrived in Edinburgh from Alloa where he had been meeting with James to discuss his recent success as Lieutenant of the North in settling the feud between Atholl and Huntly.[37] Angus was immediately placed under house arrest and the following day was transferred to the castle. Graham of Fintry, who was also implicated in the plot, was already incarcerated in Stirling Castle for his persistent refusal to conform.[38] Hew Barclay of Ladylands, who had been arrested a few days earlier, was interrogated, but escaped before the authorities had the opportunity to extract any incriminating evidence. Meanwhile Huntly and Errol met in Aberdeen to agree upon a response, though none was reached. While Errol favoured military action Huntly urged caution. Despite the discovery of the plot and his recent dealings with Angus, James remained in Alloa celebrating the New Year with the Earl of Mar and it was 5 January before details were made public by the privy council.

Although the aim of the English may have been to implicate both James and the Society, James's advisers portrayed the affair as a Jesuit conspiracy to overthrow the crown and the Kirk, and named Gordon and Abercrombie as the principal movers. The privy council's version of events referred to 'the dangerous effectis of the coverit and bissy travellis of Jesuitis, seminarie preistis, borne subjectis of this realme, and sum utheris strangearis tane occasioun and lasour to perswade sindrie if his Hienes subjectis to apostacie frome that religioun quharin thay wer fosterit, weill instructit and groundit... it hes bene the gude plesour of Almichtie God to mak the pruffe heirof certane and without all doubt, be detecting of the simple treuth of the intentioun and finall caus of all the craftie practizes of thir pernicious trafficquing papists, jesuits and seminarie preistis againis God, trew religioun, his Majestie and libertie of this cuntrey, namelie Maister James Gordoun, fader bruthir to the Erll of Huntlie, Maister Robert Abircrumby, fader bruther to the laird of Murthley'.[39]

The documents which caused such consternation comprised eight blank letters, seventeen other rather mundane letters, Pourie's memorial and the property charter. The blank letters were 'eight clean sheets of fair and gilded paper whereupon nothing is seen written' except the signatures of Angus, Huntly, Errol and Patrick Gordon of Auchindoun, the sheriff depute of Aberdeen and Huntly's uncle and principal adviser. Of the eight blanks two were signed by Angus and Errol in French, a further two by them in Latin, two by Huntly in Latin and two more by all three and Gordon of Auchindoun. Although not addressed to anyone in particular the wording of the docquets on the blanks suggested that they were to be delivered to someone of rank. The earls' seals were also enclosed for appending to each of the blanks.[40] Kerr's explanation that he was planning to remain on the continent for some time and that the blanks were to be used as letters of credit is not totally implausible, though it is somewhat unlikely given the circumstances surrounding the plot. The remaining letters were much more banal and included letters of recommendation for Kerr addressed to a number of Jesuit superiors. There was also correspondence between various Scottish Jesuits, couched in business style language, including a rather transparent letter from Gordon to Crichton calling on him to arrange for Spanish military aid for the following summer: 'use all expeditioun in tyme comming, against the nixt sommer, otherwise yee will tyne credite heere with your factours. If yee come, yee will find more freinds nor ever yee had; but, otherwise, yee will find fewer, becaus the nixt sommer many abound to other countreis, and will not abide on you no longer. Haste home heere; send a word to your freinds that we putt them in good hope of you, and they will tarie the longer... Ye have gottin all yee desired, (relative to the blanks) therefore make haste... We will abide heere yourself shortlie; and I would yee brought the rest of your freinds with you that are beyond sea, (the Spanish armie)... Your wife (the Catholick Romans and their confederats) and your bairnes commend them to you, and looke to see you shortlie'. Abercrombie also wrote to Crichton with snippets of gossip, including news of Crichton and Tyrie's families: 'Camnay is come in the Constable's hands, and your nephew is privy to it, 'by the moyen, I trow, of Abraham, your brother. Bot your maich [kinsman] is little better than begging.' Drumkill (Drumkilbo) is dead, and Thomas Tyrie is tutor.' Abercrombie also advised Crichton that Stephen Wilson was on the make, having obtained payment of an obligation due to him by Lord Livingston. There was also a letter written by John Cecil, the English seminary priest, who was wrongly thought to be a member of the Society. Cecil appears later in this story in opposition to the Jesuits, and in particular William Crichton, though it is interesting to note that at this stage he describes himself as being beholden to the Society. Cecil had considered becoming a Jesuit and despite his subsequent acrimonious relationship with the Society many secular clergy still considered him too pro-Jesuit.[40]

In the weeks following the discovery of the plot James was put under considerable pressure by Elizabeth and the Kirk to respond appropriately, and his reluctance to do so and his eventual lukewarm response were roundly denounced by his critics. Although James agreed to allow Angus, Fintry and Kerr to stand trial and summoned Huntly, Errol and Gordon of Auchindoun to appear in St Andrews to explain their actions the Kirk was indignant at his failure to effectively censure those implicated in the plot. While the main conspirators got off lightly Kerr, the messenger, was not so fortunate. Neither the initial questioning nor the documents he was carrying produced anything of substance, so by the end of January it was decided to subject him to 'a small taste of torture'. He was tortured on a number of occasions, perhaps on the direct instructions of James, by the end of which his interrogators had obtained a confession which was largely fabricated to suit their purposes. Kerr had also been persuaded by his friends to confess to a Spanish plot for the invasion of Scotland and the overthrow of Protestantism throughout Britain, though he refused to implicate Fintry and other leading Catholics. In fact he made every effort to clear their names and to minimise the role of the Catholic earls, while at the same time implicating the Society, and in particular James Gordon.[41] In order to provide corroboration a similar confession was required from Fintry who was transferred to Edinburgh Castle from Stirling Castle, where he had been held since August for his persistent refusal to conform. Fintry, while aware of the background surrounding the plot, was not a prime mover, and his implication was based purely on the fact that Kerr had been found in possession of two letters of a personal nature written by him under an assumed name. Despite Fintry's lack of involvement and the efforts of his friends to keep him in an alcoholic stupor his interrogators managed to extract a confession. In mid February their written confessions were passed to James, and it soon became clear that Fintry's confidence in his king was misplaced. He was executed on 15 February having turned down the opportunity to save himself, claiming that it would be a bad bargain to prefer earth to heaven. His decision to die for his faith may have been made easier by the fact that he was terminally ill with tuberculosis.[42] His execution, as well as appeasing Elizabeth and the pro-English faction at court, also benefited James who acquired an escheat of his property. On this occasion Kerr was more fortunate and was spared by James, who it would appear had a hand in allowing him to 'escape' from Edinburgh Castle. His flight in late June, following the recantation of his confession, which was later confirmed before a judge and notary in Lanark, together with the earlier escape of Angus in mid February, enraged the Kirk. Walter Balcanquhal, the outspoken minister of St Giles in Edinburgh, preached a sermon highly critical of 'suche mockerie'. Bowes was equally indignant, and was undoubtedly justified in his opinion that the escapes had been permitted to prevent any further enquiry into the matter, and in particular into James's involvement.[43] In a later letter to Elizabeth James tried to deny any involvement by blaming the prisoners' guards: 'if they hadd bene in the toure of London, and hadd als false knaves to thair keiparis (quhom thay bribbit and maid to flee with thaime), thay hadd playid the lyke, for since that tyme souir experience hath taucht to my self that the thickness of no wallis can hold out treason'.[44] The real irony of the whole affair was that once the dust had settled and James had taken the necessary steps to convince his critics of his Protestant credentials Crichton had switched his allegiance from Philip to James.

Chapter 8

Glenlivet and the Gowk's Storm

Having sacrificed Fintry and allowed two of the other plotters to escape James was clearly reluctant to permit further investigation into The Affair of the Spanish Blanks, and his subsequent actions did little to convince his critics that his sympathies did not lie with his Catholic subjects. His royal progress through the north east of Scotland and the commissions appointing the Earl Marischal and Atholl to deal with the Catholic earls and their Jesuit advisers did not impress Elizabeth or the Kirk. She sent her ambassador, Lord Burgh, to urge James to punish the earls and to rally the pro-English faction at court. She was also unhappy with the conduct of her co-conspirator, the Kirk, which had withheld details of the plot until it had prepared a version of events suitable for public circulation. The General Assembly, when it met in Dundee in late April 1593, also appealed to James to act decisively. Nevertheless, Huntly managed to persuade James that he had had no contact with Spain since the events at Brig o'Dee in 1589 and that although he had signed the blanks he had been unaware of their true purpose. He had thought that they were required by his uncle, James Gordon, to forward to his superiors in the Society in the event of him being expelled from Scotland. Angus and Errol claimed that they thought they were to be used to pay off debts advanced to various Scottish Jesuits.[1] James was more than willing to accept these explanations and tried to defuse the situation and shield the earls from Elizabeth by switching attention to Bothwell, who he knew had been receiving assistance from the English. James made it clear to her that he was unwilling to deal with the Catholic issue until the threat of Bothwell had been removed. As well as being suspected of witchcraft, Bothwell had on a number of occasions tried to abduct James.[2]

The political implications of The Affair of the Spanish Blanks left James in a quandary: 'tossed as a tennis ball between the precise ministers and the treacherous papists'. Although he disliked the Presbyterians, he was equally wary of Spain and the Papacy.[3] The prospect of excommunication by the pope was a potential threat to his claim to the English throne, and although a Spanish alliance might have helped him achieve his goal he was, quite rightly, unsure of Philip's motives. As a result his policy was to try to maintain a balance between the Catholic earls, the Kirk and the English, with the first acting as a check on the other two. Although he was unwilling to upset this delicate balance by being too heavy handed with the Catholic earls, and was able to convince them that he was sympathetic to their cause, his support amongst them, and within the Society and the wider Catholic community, was beginning to wane. In early 1593 Crichton's hopes of converting James had been temporarily raised by news from his Scottish informants that the king was feeling betrayed by his family and advisers and was looking to his Catholic nobles for support. According to a report by Richard Verstegan in December of that year James had become a Catholic and had published an edict in favour of freedom of conscience. He also reported that James had met with the leading rebels to give them an opportunity to clear their names, provoking a number of ministers to preach from their pulpits that he had become 'a very Papist, and that he heard Masse every day'.[4] Queen Anne, who was unsettled in her religion, was also relying more and more on her Catholic ladies in waiting. However, while the signs looked promising, Crichton and his colleagues were to be disappointed on numerous occasions over the next few years as James continued to maintain the political balance between his Protestant and Catholic subjects.

Despite the Catholic earls' excommunication in September 1593 by the Synod of Fife, which claimed jurisdiction on the dubious ground that they had all been students at St Andrews University, James managed to avoid taking any further action until November when an Act of Abolition or Oblivion was passed pardoning them on condition that they behaved themselves and dismissed their Jesuit advisers.[5] They were given the option of remaining in Scotland as Protestants or going into exile, and had until 1 January 1594 to make their decision. The Act, regarded by many as an unsatisfactory compromise, was rejected by the earls as they were unable to pay the caution demanded and was eventually repealed. They managed to avoid any further censure until May when parliament ratified the sentence of excommunication passed by the Synod of Fife.[6]

* * *

While James and his critics were at loggerheads a number of Jesuits and secular priests took advantage of the confused situation to return to Scotland.[7] The term 'Jesuit' was always used very loosely by the Society's opponents, who were often unable to distinguish between Jesuits and seculars. As a result a number of secular priests involved with the Jesuit mission around this time were mistakenly identified as members of the Society. These included James Cheyne, the first rector of the Scots College at Pont-à-Mousson, and John Scot who was active in the north east during the 1580s and may subsequently have joined the Society. Due to the more lenient regime north of the border there were also a number of English seminary priests serving in Catholic households in Scotland. In the winter of 1593–4 there was great excitement following the capture of one of them who was mistakenly thought to be a Jesuit. When interrogated the prisoner refused to give his name and was wrongly identified as William Ogilvie or Alexander McQuhirrie. Bowes sent his congratulations to John Carey, the deputy governor of Berwick, but it was soon discovered that the prisoner was in fact an English seminary priest, John Ingram from Hertfordshire, who had been ordained at the English College in Rome in 1589. Ingram was well acquainted with a number of the Scottish fathers, including Gordon and Crichton, who had previously tried to persuade him to accompany them to Scotland, but 'this examinate would not be ruled by them'.[8] This comment would suggest a slight antipathy between Ingram and the Society; nevertheless Gordon and Crichton offered to write him a letter of recommendation to Gilbert Brown, Abbot of Dumfries. Ingram preferred to make his own travel arrangements and having landed somewhere between Leith and Dunbar, following an arduous journey from Rome, he found employment as a chaplain to Walter Linsday of Balgavies, a son of David, 9th Earl of Crawford. In a report by Bowes to Burghley in May 1593 he mentioned that Angus, Huntly and Errol had met at Lindsay's house where they heard Mass said by an unknown Englishman, presumably Ingram.[9] Despite the protection of a prominent patron life was by no means peaceful, and at his trial he testified that 'he was pursued in Scotland and constrained to avoid the same for fear of his life'. Following James's demolition of Balgavies' castle near Forfar Ingram fled to England in November 1593 and was arrested crossing the River Tweed at Berwick. Although he initially managed to deceive his captors he was eventually identified by another member of Balgavies' household and following his examination at York by the Earl of Huntingdon was executed at Gateshead in July 1594.[10]

Shortly after Ingram's arrest another secular priest, John Cecil, mistakenly identified by the presbyterian historian David Calderwood, as a Jesuit, returned to Scotland. Originally from Worcester Cecil had been educated at Trinity College, Oxford, Rheims and the English College at Rome, where he was ordained.[11] As early as 1584, a few years after his graduation from Oxford, there were doubts about his health and, more importantly, his character. Despite these doubts he was still admitted to the English College in April 1584 and ordained in December of the same year. He was singled out as a troublemaker by the authorities in Rome, who arranged for him to be transferred to the newly established college at Valladolid in Spain. He subsequently appeared in England in November 1590, and a report written shortly after suggested there had been no change in his demeanour: 'a priest indeed, but a suspicious and dishonest character'.[12] In 1591–2 Persons sent him to England on business for the English mission. He was arrested *en route* from Amsterdam to England following Burghley's interception of a letter from Persons requesting that arrangements be made for Cecil's arrival. Cecil had, in fact, tried to contact Burghley before his departure from Amsterdam to assure him of his loyalty to Elizabeth. He maintained that it was possible to be a good Catholic and a loyal subject and claimed to be opposed to Persons' pro-Spanish policies. In return for his freedom Cecil agreed to act as an English agent, but when details of this deal were discovered he offered his services in Italy or Spain, where he was less well known. Over the course of the next year he appears to have travelled between France, Italy and Spain, and in October 1592, on the instructions of Cardinal Allen, arrived in Scotland where, despite his earlier dealings with the English, his work as a missionary appears to have been exemplary.[13] In August 1593 Cecil was back in Spain, purportedly acting as an emissary of the Catholic earls, and, despite his lack of credentials, was able to persuade Persons to vouch for him and to help advance his plans for a Spanish invasion of south west Scotland. The earls' real representative was, in fact, James Gordon, who at the time was *en route* to Rome to negotiate a deal with the Papacy rather than Spain. In early January 1594 Cecil, using the alias Fitzjames, left Spain bound for Scotland carrying a subsidy from Philip. He was accompanied by William Randall, an elderly English seaman, and a Spanish officer, Porres, who was to act as an adviser to Philip on the military capabilities of the Catholic earls. Their ship was almost wrecked off the English coast and was forced to berth in Plymouth, where Cecil revealed himself to Sir Francis Drake as an English agent and handed over the Jesuit correspondence which he was carrying. In the following month he wrote to Sir Robert Cecil explaining that he had spent the previous year and a half trying to regain the confidence of the Scottish Catholics and now that this had been achieved he was returning to Scotland to report on their activities. He promised that 'not a leaf shall wag in Scotland, but you shall know'.[14] Having convinced the English authorities of his trustworthiness Cecil and his party were allowed to proceed and arrived in Scotland in late April 1594, having taken a further detour via the Low Countries. Their ship ran aground off Montrose and was seized by the authorities and sent to Leith. It was widely suspected that the subsidy he was carrying was destined for James, but a search of the ship revealed nothing. The 'budgett or little masle [trunk] stuffed with gold, silver or other metal weighing an estimated 5 stone' had already been loaded onto a horse and taken to Aberdeen.[15] Cecil's arrival was welcomed by some of the Catholic community, including Angus, but was resented by many, especially James Gordon, whose efforts on behalf of the Catholic earls were clearly at odds with Cecil's.[16]

While Cecil was being welcomed by the Catholic earls Gordon was still in Rome negotiating on their behalf. In early July 1594 Robert Bruce reported from Antwerp that Gordon had returned there from Rome with a Spanish subsidy and was preparing to depart for Calais or Dunkirk to find a ship sailing north to Scotland. It was thought he was proposing to land somewhere in the north near Dunrobin in Sutherland or between Aberdeen and Buchan Ness. Safe in the knowledge that his nephew controlled the north east Gordon disembarked at Aberdeen on 16 July accompanied by the papal nuncio, George Sampiretti, who was to distribute the subsidy from Clement VIII to the Catholic earls.[17] The party was also alleged to include four other Jesuits, including William Murdoch, a priest named Morgan, and a number of Englishmen, including Sir William Stanley and the Earl of Westmorland. Westmorland was identified by some townsfolk in Aberdeen, who when asked by Bowes whether the stranger knew him, told him that the man had said he knew him very well, but would not speak to him.[18] Gordon also brought a letter from the pope to James offering financial incentives for his conversion. Ironically Sampiretti's subsidy was not a bribe for James, but was to be used by Huntly and his confederates to finance their military operations against the king. The receipt to the papal treasury dated 5 August 1594 states clearly that the subsidy was 'for the levying of men against the heretics'.[19]

On disembarking from his ship, *The Esperance,* Gordon was recognised by a local invalid taking a constitutional who reported his arrival to the town council. Despite the influence of Gordon's uncle, the Earl of Huntly, the town council felt obliged to act, and although it was afraid to arrest Gordon, Sampiretti and the English priests were imprisoned in the Tolbooth, the latter on the ground that English subjects were not allowed to enter Scotland without a passport from their own government.[20] A plan to take the ship and the gold on board to Leith was abandoned as the winds were unfavourable. Gordon was allowed to go free and 'him selff with twa or thrie start out of the schip in the nicht, with theare packettis and utheris thingis they brocht with thame'. Sampiretti and his fellow prisoners were imprisoned for three days before Huntly, Errol, and Angus at the head of a large force threatened to ransack Aberdeen. The council soon released their prisoners when the attackers started to torch the town.[21] James, who was never keen to use force against his nobles, could not ignore this open show of aggression and in late July he appealed to the clergy for help, not directly against the nobles, but their Jesuit advisers who had led them astray and whom he referred to as 'the pernitious springis and instrumentis of ther evillis... returnit, not simplie, bot accumpanyit with strangearis and furnist with money, to steir up and prosequite a publict wear'.[22] Gordon and Crichton were criticised for their rôle in procuring the subsidy and for allowing it to be squandered by the earls to the discredit of James and the Society: 'The credit of the company has decayed by reason of the tumults which his [Gordon's] ill-advised proceedings have aroused. His nephew and confederates have, through him and Creyton, lost their goods and lands and very nearly their lives. Creyton has endeavoured to supply Bruscio here, as did Colonel Simple in Spain, as can be proved by letters of his and of other fathers in the Company. His grey hairs and his coat have alone won him credit'.[23]

It is unclear exactly how the subsidy was squandered, but while part was undoubtedly appropriated by the earls for their personal use the remainder was used to finance their summer campaign, which culminated in the resounding Catholic victory at Glenlivet in Banffshire on 3 October. Calderwood, writing for a Protestant readership, referred to it as an 'uncertane victorie', while a modern military historian has described the battle as 'all sound and fury, signifying nothing'.[24] Although it was in some ways a pyrrhic victory it was hugely significant in the wider political context of the period, marking the end of Catholic militancy and the eclipse of the power of the Catholic earls. With the removal of the Catholic threat James was then able to concentrate on bringing the Kirk into line with a series of measures undermining the power of the ministers within the General Assembly and reintroducing episcopacy.[25]

At the end of August, in response to Huntly and his confederates, James assembled a royal army and issued commissions to Argyll, Atholl and Forbes. The latter two refused theirs, but Argyll, still only a youth of eighteen, was persuaded to accept. Elizabeth was highly critical of James's choice of commander: 'You may see, my deare brother, what danger it bredes a king to glorifie to hie and to soudanly a boy of yeres and conduict, whos untimely age for discretion bredes rasche consent to undesent actions… The waight of a kingly state is of more poix than the shalownis of a rasche yonge mans hed can waigh'. There was also a suggestion that treachery within the ranks of the royal army contributed to its defeat.[26]

There are a number of descriptions of the battle, including a report by William Crichton and a first hand account by Alexander McQuhirrie. Crichton's report was based on information received from a Scottish Jesuit lay brother, William Martin, and two other Scots who had fought in the battle.[27] Martin, later described as 'ane litill blak fellow of mid age, a Scottis man and compaynon of Mr Wm Crichton quhen he went abrode', was a seasoned missionary and made a number of visits to Scotland, including one in 1599 when he accompanied James Gordon on his final visit.[28] Crichton, who was always keen to promote the order, attributed the victory to the 'prayers of the Fathers of the Society, who continued on their knees all the time of the engagement'.[29] McQuhirrie's accurate and objective account, of which there are a number of versions, is the more reliable, and despite his involvement in the battle as a chaplain to the Catholic army, he makes little reference to the Society, simply stating that those present 'partook the holy sacrament of penitence, to expiate their sins, and this to the joy of many, but me in particular, who saw the ardour of the Primitive Church, renewed in a beautiful offspring'.[30] Whether or not the victory was attributable to the prayers of the Jesuits may be debatable, but there is no doubt that the Catholic army was highly motivated and achieved an impressive victory against a much larger force.

After a number of preliminary skirmishes the two forces met at Glenlivet on the slopes of Ben Rinnes. Although numerically superior Argyll's force of 8,000 men, comprising a mixture of Campbells, Macleans, Grants and other highland clansmen, included a large number of 'raskalls and poke bearers' [beggars]. The Catholic force was a quarter of the size, but had the benefit of artillery and cavalry: 'all weall borne gentlemen'. It also had the advantage of an experienced commander in Huntly, who was able to use the papal subsidy to pay for the services of experienced officers and mercenaries, such as James Wood of Boniton, a well-known recusant, who during the course of the battle displayed 'eminent valour'. Although numerically inferior and occupying the lower ground the Catholic army was able to rout its disorganised opponents; though for some time the battle hung in the balance until Huntly and Errol had sorted out their differences and rallied their forces. As chaplain to the Catholic army McQuhirrie was involved in the thick of the battle and gave absolution to Sir Patrick Gordon of Auchindoun, who was mortally wounded and then beheaded during the decisive cavalry charge up the slopes of the mountain. The other important factor in the battle was the use of artillery and while the firepower on display was not great its psychological effect was devastating. The decapitation of one of the royal army commanders, the 'noted plunderer', MacNeill of Barra, by a piece of shot left his troops leaderless and disorganised. When the gunsmoke cleared it became clear that the royal army had suffered considerable losses, whereas by comparison there were only a handful of Catholic casualties, though these included a number of the commanding officers.[31]

After the battle James raised another army, but neither side had the stomach for a further fight. An unattributed report of the following year, 'The Establishing of Catholicism in Scotland', confirmed the Catholics' reluctance to take to the field again: 'In wishing to induce the King of Scotland to declare himself a Catholic, or at least to make the conditions of Catholics in that realm better, every other way seems preferable to that of force of arms'.[32] Although James was riled by Huntly's jibe in a letter to Angus that his military response was nothing more than a 'Gowk's [cuckoo's] storm', he was prepared to swallow his pride and allow a peace settlement to be brokered by the Duke of Lennox, Huntly's brother in law, who had been appointed Lieutenant of the North.[33] Despite being the crown's representative, Lennox would appear to have been somewhat lenient towards the rebels, and other than the demolition of Strathbogie and a number of other castles, little effort was made to punish them. Both Huntly and Errol lingered in Scotland in the hope of receiving further aid from Spain or Rome, but any plans they had of resurrecting the rebellion were blighted by the capture of the Jesuit, John Myrton.

Myrton, who was born in St Andrews sometime around 1555, was the brother of the Laird of Cambo. He entered the Society in 1584 and was ordained in the early 1590s. In 1594 he was sent to Scotland by Philip and the pope, but was recognised during the course of the passage by a fellow traveller, a son of the Protestant reformer, John Erskine of Dun, who passed on the information to David Lindsay, the minister of Leith. Myrton was arrested on 24 March 1595 and, like Crichton before him, tried to destroy his instructions, fragments of which were retrieved and deciphered. At a secret meeting in the Tolbooth Myrton was examined by the king to whom he confessed that he was a Jesuit, had served as a confessor at the seminary in Rome and had been sent to Scotland by the pope with messages from Cardinal Cajetan, Crichton and Tyrie to James Gordon and instructions to reprimand the Catholic earls for their misuse of the papal subsidy. Amongst Myrton's possessions was a carved ivory minature of the Crucifixion which was a gift from Cajetan to Queen Anne. When asked by James about its significance Myrton allegedly replied: 'To remind me when I gaze on it and kiss it, of my Lord's Passion. Look, my liege, how lively the Saviour is here seen, hanging between the two thieves, whilst below, the Roman soldier is piercing His sacred side with the lance. Ah, that I could prevail on my sovereign but once to kiss it before he lays it down'. James in response declined to kiss it: 'No, the Word of God is enough to remind me of the crucifixion; and besides this carving of yours is so exceedingly small, that I could not kiss Christ without kissing both the thieves and the executioners'. Under examination Myrton also confirmed that more Jesuits were to be sent to Scotland. Although Myrton was prepared to talk the ministers demanded more information and called for the use of torture. This was refused by James on account of Myrton's earlier openness, and following the examination he was sent packing to Flanders.[34]

With no immediate prospect of aid from the pope or from Spain Huntly and Errol decided to remove themselves to the continent, having negotiated a suitable deal through the good offices of Lennox, which was accepted by the privy council in an Act of Approbation. After a final Mass at Elgin Cathedral Gordon made one last unsuccessful attempt to persuade the earls to remain in Scotland. Despite having to leave their families behind to administer their estates the earls departed for the continent in high spirits. Gordon and Crichton also decided to disappear for a while leaving Murdoch to work alone in the north east. He had not been involved in the fighting at Glenlivet, but shortly before the battle had said Mass for Gordon of Auchindoun at Gartly. He had also been entrusted with the Huntly family papers which he transferred by sea from Strathbogie to Caithness. There he comforted the widow of the recently deceased Earl of Sutherland and acted as tutor to her children. In late March 1595 he was recalled to Moray by Gordon prior to his departure to the continent. During the course of his travels Murdoch also visited the Woods of Boniton and Auchindoun's widow, Agnes Beaton, who was Gordon's sister-in-law.[35]

* * *

On arriving on the continent Huntly, accompanied by Crichton, travelled to Germany, and for a period was resident at Trier, which had once been the temporary home of the Scots College. At some stage in June Crichton met up with Gordon in Brussels and thereafter returned to the college at Douai.[36] Cecil also left Scotland in the aftermath of Glenlivet and reappeared in Spain in December 1594 where he again claimed to be acting on behalf of the Catholic earls in their efforts to secure joint Spanish and papal intervention in Scotland. There was a suggestion that he and Gordon should join forces, and correspondence by Crichton and Gordon to Tyrie, the assistant for France and Germany, suggests that despite their differences the Jesuits were not averse to the proposal.[37]

While in Flanders Crichton learnt of John Ogilvie of Pourie's petition on behalf of James claiming that he was prepared to reconcile himself and the kingdom to Catholicism, which together with Cecil's response are contained in a document known as the 'Summary of the Memorials'. The 'Summary' listed a number of reasons why James was prepared to consider reconciling himself to the Catholic church, including revenge against Elizabeth for the deaths of his parents and her meddling in Scottish affairs. It also suggested that he would be prepared to stamp out heresy in Britain, form a league with Spain, declare war on England and make peace with his Catholic earls. In return he expected Philip to renounce his claims to the English, Scottish and Irish crowns and openly support his own claim.[38] Although Pourie claimed to be engaged with Spain and the Papacy on behalf of James there is no evidence of any formal commission, though he may have acted as a royal messenger on a earlier mission to Spain in 1592. What is clear is that he had been involved in recusant activity in Scotland and in late September 1594 he was denounced as a rebel for failing to appear before the privy council to answer charges of treason and papistry.[39] In June 1595 Pourie was in the Low Countries, where he met with Stephan d'Ibarra, Philip's secretary in Flanders, Charles Paget and other leaders of the Scottish factions amongst the continental exiles. In October he reached Rome where he presented petitions to the pope seeking confirmation of James's right to succeed Elizabeth and a further subsidy to finance another military campaign. These requests must have been received with some scepticism given that the previous year James had been involved, albeit reluctantly, in a war with his Catholic earls. John Cecil in responding to the petition pointed out that few of the Scottish Catholics had any confidence in Pourie as he was friendly with a number of Elizabeth's advisers and his family were Protestants. His dealings on behalf of James were criticised as being 'very shifty, sharp and open to suspicion' and left Cecil in no doubt that 'this negotiation of John Ogilvy hath not much foundation except to pass the time, and to stir up the humours of the world'. He argued that James had never shown any real inclination to become a Catholic and was regarded by his Catholic subjects as a heretic who had conspired with Elizabeth against them.[40] James Tyrie also made it known to Cardinal Cajetan that in his opinion James's approaches were 'all invention and deceit'. Anticipating such criticism Pourie was able to produce further evidence of James's good intentions and in a paper entitled 'Considerations to show the good disposition of the King of Scotland towards Catholics' claimed that James had never persecuted his Catholic subjects, but had in fact maintained them in office and had always looked favourably on the activities of the Scottish missionaries.[41] Malvasia, the papal agent in Brussels, in a report to the Cardinal Secretary, Aldobrandini, commented on James's lax enforcement of the penal laws and his leniency towards Holt and Myrton.[42] Pourie also took the opportunity to take a swipe at his critics, describing Cecil as being of middling abilities and dishonest and Robert Persons as an enemy of the king.[43]

Contrary to Elizabeth's expectations Mary's execution had not simplified the succession question, which became a matter of debate throughout Europe. Persons' view on the matter, outlined in a book *A Conference About the Next Succession to the Crown of England and divided into two parts* published in 1594, rejected James's claim in favour of that of Philip and his daughter Isabella. The 'Conference' takes the form of a dialogue amongst a group of exiles in Amsterdam in 1593 and discusses the background to the activities of the militant Catholics and the claims of the various candidates. Although it held itself out to be impartial the book clearly favoured the claim of the Infanta Isabel who was a descendant of the Lancastrian line of John of Gaunt, a son of Edward III, and was also eligible on her mother's side through the Dukes of Brittany. Other Catholic candidates included the Dukes of

Parma and Savoy, who were also descended from John of Gaunt. Protestant candidates included Lady Arabella Stuart, Lady Catherine Grey and Lady Mary Grey.[44] Although the book was intended to undermine James's claim Crichton felt that it actually served to strengthen it. He was also critical of the timing of its publication and in a letter to Persons reminded him of the French proverb that hares are not caught by beating drums. In response Persons pointed out that the drum was not being beaten to catch the hare, but to scare off the wolf. He also argued that the publication of the book had achieved some good as a number of Jesuits had been released from jail and others were being treated more leniently by the English authorities.[45]

During his stay in Rome Pourie also had an audience with the Duke of Sessa, the Spanish ambassador, as did Walter Lindsay of Balgavies and Hew Barclay of Ladylands, who were acting on behalf of the Catholic earls. Not surprisingly, Sessa was thoroughly confused by the conflicting accounts of Scottish affairs, and like most others who met him appears to have had little faith in Pourie: 'this man cometh hither furnished with inventions and cunning'. Between them Sessa and Cecil managed to persuade Pourie to travel to Spain for further negotiations, where he was imprisoned and interrogated. In August 1598 Pourie was still in jail, but by 1600 was back in Scotland working for Sir Robert Cecil. He was soon arrested and imprisoned in Edinburgh, but while James was contemplating what should be done with him Pourie escaped. From hiding he wrote to James denying having misrepresented him in his negotiations with the pope.[46]

Crichton's response to John Cecil's criticism of James was his 'Apologie and Defence' published in 1598, to which John Cecil responded with his 'Discoverye of the Errors'.[47] While Crichton was named as the author it was allegedly written by Robert More, a student at Louvain. The 'Apologie and Defence' was a systematic refutation of all Cecil's allegations and a tribute to James's moderation, courtesy and integrity, especially towards James Gordon and other fathers of the Society. It also put forward the case in favour of James as the Catholics' preferred candidate to succeed Elizabeth: 'He is wise, he is learned, he is a Mecenas, and with his royall penne hath added immortall honor unto the Muses. I passe over his moderation, his ingenuytie, his morall vertues, which in hopes and blossomes are flowers of fruits to come, when it shall please God to temper his humane perfection with true pietie and religion'. In defence of James's religious views Crichton argued that Gordon had not found him to be a heretic, that any anti-Catholic books had been written in his name and that

Catholics had been banished rather than executed. On the issue of the Spanish Blanks Crichton appears to have conveniently forgotten his own role in the affair and in support of James's reaction to the plot argued that 'No lawe could be found to defend them [the Catholic earls] from the appearance and show of treason'. Not surprisingly this about turn was seized on by Cecil in his 'Discoverye' as one of a number of 'falsehoodes' and 'follyes' in the 'Apologie and Defence', which he denounced as a 'perverse and paltrye pamphlet, or rather a childish and ridiculous declamation'. Cecil's response lists a number of truths and corrections and makes various recommendations as to how James should conduct himself in relation to the succession issue.[48] Following publication of the 'Apologie and Defence' Crichton was banished from Flanders, which can have come as no great surprise to him as it had been threatened for some time. In a letter to Philip, Lorenzo, Duke of Feria suggested that the Acquaviva should be ordered to remove Crichton: 'a man ... of vehement temperament, religious however in his principles, and esteemed by many for his exemplary demeanour, his influence is capable of producing the most injurious consequences in Flanders; and his place there would be advantageously supplied by Father Gordon, a Scotsman, and uncle of the Earl of Huntly, a quiet and dispassionate person divested of possession in favour of his own sovereign, and agreed with those among the English who are proceeding in the right road'. To pacify the Spanish Crichton was transferred to Avignon from where his requests to be reappointed to the Scottish mission were rejected by Acquaviva. Permission would only be granted if it was safe for him to return to Scotland and if he could guarantee not to meddle in politics.[49]

The dispute between Crichton and Cecil was one of the most obvious examples of the ongoing feud between Jesuits and seculars which caused such controversy within the English mission. However, other than their exchanges there is little other evidence of any rift in Scotland where the relationship between Scottish Jesuits and Scottish seculars was relatively harmonious. Any friction appears to have been caused by English priests determined not to be dictated to by Scottish Jesuits or to accept Scottish practices. By contrast the English mission had been rocked by dissension amongst the students at the English College in Rome which later spread to the recusant priests held by the English authorities at Wisbech in Cambridgeshire. The main grievance of the students and the Appellant priests, as they became known, was the growing influence of the Society and the political activities of the likes of Persons and Crichton. Amongst their demands was the appointment of a bishop, which was finally granted after a number of years of mismanagement by a succession of archpriests starting with the appointment of George Blackwell. The reason why this conflict had less impact in Scotland is unclear. Although most accounts of the survival of Catholicism in Scotland suggest that there were relatively few priests of any kind in the post-Reformation period, there were clearly more than some contemporary reports suggest and those who continued to serve in Scotland appear to have been prepared to work with the Society. A report on Scottish affairs written in 1596 by the papal agent, Malvasia, a known opponent of the Society, suggests otherwise and attributes the conflict to a difference in policy, with the Jesuits favouring, and the seculars opposing, the use of force and the imposition of a foreign sovereign. Malvasia produced no evidence to support his views, and there is little other contemporary evidence to substantiate them. A decade later William Murdoch, when he was examined by the Scottish privy council, denied that there was any conflict: '... in uthir partis [England] thar is a grite differ and discord betuix the Jesuitis and utheris commoun preistis' but 'thair wes no suche discord amang thame in this cuntrey'. Thomas Innes, another critic of the Society, in his account of Catholicism in Scotland in the century following the Reformation, made no reference to the conflict, nor any particular criticism of the Society.[50]

Following the departure of Crichton and Gordon in spring 1595 there were still a number of fathers left in Scotland. Murdoch divided his time amongst a number of Catholic families in the north east, while Alexander McQuhirrie appears to have travelled back and forth between Scotland and Flanders acting as a courier for Huntly, Gordon and Abercrombie, who had been appointed as superior in Gordon's absence.[51] In June 1596 Abercrombie reported that he was being assisted in Scotland by McQuhirrie, Murdoch and George Elphinstone.[52] The latter, who had arrived in mid January 1596 was the brother of James Elpinstone, Earl of Innernochtie, and later Lord Balmerino. Through the Elphinstones, McQuhirrie and Thomas Tyrie, James Tyrie's nephew, became involved with the Octavians, a committee of eight members appointed to rationalise the royal finances. The committee was viewed with a great deal of suspicion, partly as its members were suspected of being 'papists knowen, or inclyning to Poperie or malignancie' and partly because its specific role was to reduce court expenditure, and in particular handouts to the nobility.[53] As well as the possibility that McQuhirrie was acting as a messenger for James and the Octavians there is also a suggestion in the 'Scottish

Advices' of June 1596 that the Elphinstones were involved with John Lindsay of Menmuir, the secretary to the privy council and another of the Octavians. The nature of the relationship is unclear, but in a letter from the Master of Gray to James Tyrie in spring 1597 there is reference to an earlier letter from Lindsay to Gray in which he advised that the papal subsidy from Tyrie had been well received.[54] The doubts about the Octavians were further fuelled by the fact that its chairman was the lord president, Alexander Seton, later 1st Earl of Dunfermline, whose previous involvement with Huntly had almost led to his downfall. As a young man Seton had studied at the German College in Rome, and although he outwardly conformed and sought to 'inculcate the belief that he is indifferent' doubts still existed about his religious beliefs.[55] In December 1596 in response to James's refusal to listen to the concerns of the nobles there were riots in Edinburgh instigated by the Kirk and directed against the Octavians, and Seton in particular; 'that Romanist president, a shaveling and a preest, more meete to say masse in Salamanca, nor to beare office in Christian and reformed commounweales'.[56] As a result of the immediate success of the committee in sorting out the royal finances and objections from the hangers-on at court, James was forced to disband it in January 1597.

In late 1596 or early 1597 Huntly returned to Scotland, having negotiated the return of his lands in return for abandoning the Catholic faith. His view that the militant Catholic cause was doomed was no doubt reinforced by the failure of another Spanish armada and the prospect of little foreign assistance in the foreseeable future. James had also made it clear that if he stepped out of line again he would be sent abroad and could 'never look to be a Scotsman again'.[57] He conformed, outwardly at least, at a ceremony at the cross at the Castlegate in Aberdeen on 26 June 1597, and in the following year was relaxed from the horn and restored to his lands. 'This miserable example', as Gordon referred to it, was followed by Angus and Errol, and it was left to Gordon to rally the Catholics by issuing a public challenge to the ministers in which he claimed he would prove that the basis of Protestantism was 'nothing but mere inventions of men contrarie to the express word of God'. He also wrote openly to James asking for support. Gordon, who had been unaware of his nephew's decision, was understandably taken aback by the turn of events and in a letter to Acquaviva noted that:

> The Catholic barons and nobles of inferior rank were thrown into great perturbation by this desertion of their leaders. Almost all have wavered, and most of them have trod in the footsteps of the two

> earls, and have either renounced their religion, or at least consented to attend heretical worship. Catholics everywhere yielded to grief and terror; every day we heard of some deserting their faith either by interior defection, or at any rate in outward profession. The ministers triumphed openly. Such was the state of things in Scotland when we arrived, and it is very little, if at all, improved now. The few of our Fathers who were left (three in all) had to fly for their lives, and conceal themselves wherever they could. Up to this time they had found themselves secure in the north of Scotland, under the protection of the Earls of Huntly and Errol, but henceforth they were obliged to go elsewhere.[58]

Gordon made every effort to dissuade his nephew and it was widely believed that he had come 'into the country of intention to divert him from giving obedience' and 'to recover from the jaws of the Devil, and restore to their true master, the prey which their lies and flaterries had not long before torn from us, or rather from Christ'.[59]

Meanwhile William Murdoch was active in Edinburgh, and not for the first time deceived the magistrates into providing him with alms while he ministered to the needs of the Catholic community. Later in the year he travelled north to visit Gordon and Abercrombie and to deliver correspondence to be forwarded to Rome. Following this visit Gordon was again forced to retire from Scotland, but not before preaching a rousing sermon in Aberdeen in August 1597 and promising to return in the autumn for the disputation with the ministers. With Gordon's departure to Denmark Abercrombie, McQuhirrie and Murdoch, assisted by a secular priest and Jesuit aspirant, James Seton, were left ministering in what Abercrombie referred to as a 'barren vineyard'. Abercrombie had been in Scotland for ten years and understandably for a man in his early sixties was struggling to cope. Despite a more liberal regime than in England life for the missionaries was still tough: 'We live in caves in secret and infrequent places, perpetually moving from place to place, like the gypsies, and we never lodge two nights in the same locality, for fear of falling into the hands of the enemy. Spies and officers are posted at all the inns, and in every parish to discover our whereabouts, and give us up to the authorities... A hot meal would be a luxury to me, even though I am uncertain of my life every mile I go'. A wanted poster showing his face was circulated and a reward of £10,000 offered for his arrest. In spring 1598 Abercrombie retired to Poland to rest, but by the autumn was back in Scotland.[60]

The Scottish mission suffered a number of further setbacks in 1597, not least the death of James Tyrie, one of its most influential supporters. After spells as rector of Clermont College in Paris and the Scots College at Pont-à-Mousson Tyrie was summoned to Rome and appointed as the Assistant for Germany, in which capacity he was responsible for overseeing the Scottish mission. Despite criticism from Persons of his political naïvity Tyrie was highly regarded within the Society. He was a scholar of some note and in 1585 served as the French representative on the Committee of Six which drew up the first edition of the *Ratio Studiorum*, the Society's educational system. Even religious opponents, such as David Buchanan, praised him for his 'singular modesty, gentleness and charity', though at his death Persons noted that he was 'a good and godly mann, yet in many pointes the factiouse had deceived him upon the difference of Nations, and indirectly his authoritie stood them greately in steade, for which it seemeth God tooke him so sodanely away to the admiration of all men'. While Persons was critical of Tyrie's failure to act decisively in the political in-fighting amongst the Jesuits and seculars others commended him for his refusal to become involved and for his part in securing the passage of the decree of the Fifth Congregation of the Society prohibiting its members from interfering in political matters.[61]

By 1598 the tone of the Scottish fathers' correspondence was becoming more upbeat, though there was still great concern about the plight of the Catholic minority. John Hay in a letter to James was very pessimistic about the state of the nation, and in particular the ineffectiveness of the legal system. However, in October McQuhirrie reported to the general that a number of restrictions against the Society had been eased and that it was easier to travel within Scotland to visit the increasing number of Catholics. Although he was under considerable pressure from the ministers and had been advised to retire to a remoter part of the country he was determined to remain in Edinburgh. A lack of funds and ill health over the winter added to his problems, though his spirits were given a boost by the return of Gordon and the lay brother, William Martin, in December of that year. Gordon, who was keen to refute the Kirk's claim that he had backed down from their proposed public debate, alleged that it was in fact the ministers who had been unwilling to meet him. Shortly after his return he presented himself to James for an audience, but was refused access and arrested. According to Gordon, James made every effort to ensure that he was well treated and his identity kept secret. Nevertheless, rumours circulated that a number of Jesuits had entered the country, though it transpired that the suspects were two English soldiers from Berwick in

Edinburgh for a spree with friends. While in Edinburgh Castle Gordon wrote a refutation of an attack on the *Controversies* of Robert Bellarmine, SJ, but the debate fizzled out with the death of the author of the attack. His subsequent release was secured by Huntly who arranged accommodation for him in Edinburgh, from where he continued to press the ministers to agree to a public debate. On James's orders he was transferred to Seton from where the ministers tried to have him removed. Their threats to excommunicate Seton if he did not evict Gordon were dropped at James's insistence. Calls for Gordon's execution were also dismissed and in May 1599 he was again sent into exile. His return to Denmark was a considerable disappointment and McQuhirrie expressed concern that the minor upsurge in Catholic fortunes would not survive his departure as 'the people are not affected as they once were'. Nevertheless, the remaining fathers did not let up and those left in Scotland travelled and ministered even more than before, though Abercrombie and Murdoch were both in their sixties and could not be expected to cope with such demanding workloads.[62]

Chapter 9

Fresh Tumults and Severer Persecution

Despite numerous setbacks a number of the Scottish Jesuits remained optimistic about the prospects of converting James. In April 1600 Crichton was in Rome trying to persuade the pope and the College of Cardinals 'that his King is no heretic, but promises to be a Catholic, and meanwhile will grant toleration in religion'.[1] The following year, McQuhirrie, in a letter to Acquaviva, urged him to support James's representations to the pope: 'he is an easy tempered prince, very desirous of peace, and, what perhaps your Paternity will be surprised to hear, is extremely well acquainted with the affairs of our mission, and with ourselves personally. He is disposed to wink at our proceedings, but he urges our friends to act with great caution lest his ministers should compel him, by solicitation, or by threats, which they do not shrink from using, to take some violent measure against us; and this he would greatly regret'. However, within a few months the position was less clear. A memorial, *The State of Scotland, 1601*, written by Abercrombie and McQuhirrie at some stage during the course of that or the following year spoke of an increasing disillusionment with James: 'The King and the members of the Council are overawed and corrupted by the power and the gold of England... His language consists almost entirely of blasphemy or heresy. The single object of his ambition is the crown of England, which he would gladly take, to all appearance from the hand of the Devil himself, though Catholics and heretic ministers were all ruined alike, so great is his longing for this regal dignity... He is a determined enemy of the Fathers of the Society, thinking that they are unfriendly to him, and that they oppose his claim to the crown of England. He considers them also causes of discord, sedition and civil war'. The memorial continued with a summary of the obstacles encountered by the mission entitled *Of our Fathers*:

> All our annoyances proceed from the causes abovementioned, and we are constantly being excommunicated, outlawed, ordered

abroad, and publicly proclaimed traitors to our King and country. No one is allowed to receive us under his roof on pain of death, loss of all his goods, and outlawry. The royal order requires everyone to apprehend us or kill us, wherever he finds us. The laws are so strict and rigorous that we are often obliged to travel at night, and we have very great difficulty in finding shelter in the daytime. Those who receive us rarely do so except for some consideration, either a share of the pittance which God has given us, or the hope of our obtaining some payment for them from his Holiness, which they consider us bound to do, because they risk their lives and property for us, which is no doubt actually the case. The remuneration of these persons we have left entirely to the wisdom of your Paternity, since we can neither perform nor promise anything without the express knowledge, advice, and direction of your Paternity, as obedient children.

The extent of our field of labour, our mode of operation, and the results which are to be expected, will be sufficiently described by the bearer of this letter, who has passed through almost the whole district in the course of his travels, and has visited and conversed with each of us.

In my opinion the harvest is not so great but that the workers, at present engaged in it, are sufficient for the task; and, whatever others of our brethren may have written as to sending more labourers, I think, on the contrary, that there is no immediate hurry about sending any until the condition of public affairs becomes more peaceful, and our Lord sends us greater freedom. Whereas, if only one single additional Father landed in Scotland, we should only suffer from fresh tumults and severer persecution, and the ministers would, in their addresses from the pulpit, multiply that one into twenty.

The memorial also mentioned a secular priest and Jesuit aspirant, David Law, from Kirkcaldy, who had been at Pont-à-Mousson in the mid 1580s and was active with Murdoch in north east Scotland. He was apparently accepted into the Society by Abercrombie, but never entered the novitiate and returned to Scotland as a secular priest. The memorial, together with copies of a number of Scottish statutes as corroboration of its accuracy, was probably taken to Rome by George Strachan, another former student of Pont-à-Mousson.[2]

The deterioration in the Society's position came about despite its closer links with the royal family, which had developed during the late 1590s when Queen Anne began to take an active interest in

Catholicism. The queen, a daughter of King Frederick II and Queen Sophia of Denmark, had been brought up as a Lutheran, but never became a Presbyterian. In fact, soon after arriving in Scotland she and her chaplain, John Sering, deserted the Lutheran faith, which had been guaranteed to her in terms of the marriage treaty. Her interest in Catholicism has been attributed to fond memories of her childhood in Germany and the influence of one of Charles V's granddaughters. While Anne sought refuge in the Catholic church Sering became a Presbyterian, at which stage she dispensed with his services.[3] Robert Persons, who described Anne as 'a new born lamb set down among so many ravening wolves', and a number of Scottish Catholic nobles at court, expressed concern for her safety. She had made enemies within the Kirk by her outspoken criticism of the ministers and her refusal to attend Protestant services.[4] Sometime in or around 1598 Abercrombie was recommended to the queen as her confessor and was smuggled into Holyrood where he remained hidden for a number of days. During this time Anne was instructed in the Catholic faith and offered holy communion.[5] Over the next few years she celebrated communion on approximately nine or ten occasions and in 1603 refused to leave for England without first receiving it. She also confided in Abercrombie that she wanted to convert James and to have their son Charles, born on 19 November 1600, brought up as a Catholic. James was, of course, aware of his wife's activities, but was prepared to tolerate them: 'Well wife, if you cannot live without this sort of thing, do your best to keep things as quiet as possible; for if you don't, our crown is in danger'.[6] In fact, James was prepared to do more than simply tolerate his wife's Catholicism and the appointment of Abercrombie as Keeper of His Majesty's Hawks was a very public acceptance of the situation. Despite such gestures there was no prospect of James converting to Catholicism and after he had succeeded to the English throne he apparently joked with his courtiers that he had little further use for his Catholic subjects. Although James may have exploited his Catholic subjects in order to secure the English throne, such comments have to be treated with caution given his later attempts to achieve religious stability in his three kingdoms.[7]

In time even Crichton despaired of James's tactics and in 1605 he was highly critical of James Gordon's overly optimistic assessment of him, which he had based on his attitude towards the Puritans at the Hampton Court Conference, first convened in 1604, to address various religious issues, including the Puritan's Millenary Petition of 1603. James, although brought up as a Presbyterian, rejected most of the

Puritans' demands, with the exception of their call for a revised Prayer Book and a new translation of the Bible, the authorised version of 1611. The traditional view of James's attitude towards the Conference has recently been challenged by W. Brown Patterson who has suggested that far from being intransigent, James was, in fact, seeking a compromise between the various religious factions. He maintains that the Conference must be seen as part of a wider political strategy in terms of which James was seeking to reform and unify the churches in Britain.[8] Crichton and Gordon also disagreed over the significance of the Conference, which Gordon believed strengthened the Catholic cause. Crichton's view that James's adherence to Anglicanism was an even greater blow to the Catholic cause than to the Presbyterian. His dismissal of the significance of the Conference indicates a failure on his part to recognise the subtleties of James's strategy and, despite his apparent coolness towards the Catholic community, the continuing role to be played by it.[9]

The efforts of those fathers left in Scotland were not exclusively directed towards the conversion of the royal family. A report on the state of Scottish Catholicism written in 1600 by Gasparo Sungardi, Bishop of Modena, noted that there was a steady stream of Scottish converts arriving daily in Paris and that there were Catholics in almost every family in Scotland and England.[10] While this may have been a slight exaggeration those fathers still working in Scotland were in great demand. While Abercrombie was busy at Holyrood McQuhirrie was active elsewhere in Edinburgh celebrating Mass at various houses within the city. Among those present at one such service was James Wood of Boniton, the veteran of the Battle of Glenlivet, who was arrested and later executed. Wood's Catholicism was at the centre of a family feud, and in response to a threat by his mother to disinherit him he had stolen the title deeds and other papers relating to the family estate. Wood, like Graham of Fintry a decade earlier, was an unfortunate victim of the political situation and his execution on 27 April 1601, apparently for treason and theft, was intended to appease the ministers and refute any allegations of James's involvement with Rome. Calderwood denied that the execution was religiously motivated and described Wood as an 'obstinat Papist, ever looking for pardoun till the last gaspe. He pretended he suffered for the Catholick Roman religioun, but it was not point of his dittay [charge]'.[11] To make matters worse Wood had been about to set out for Rome with letters from the queen to the pope, which were retrieved by James, who, sensitive to the dangers inherent in his wife's new found Catholicism, arranged for

Abercrombie and McQuhirrie to return them to her.[12]

Following Wood's arrest and execution McQuhirrie went to ground in Dunblane, where he lodged with William Blackwood, the pre-Reformation vicar of Duddingston, who had fled there to continue his recusant activities. In Dunblane McQuhirrie wrote an account of Wood's life and execution; however, its publication was blocked by Acquaviva, who along with Crichton, was concerned about the authorities' reaction. In the aftermath of Wood's execution the Kirk, which was in a stronger position than it had been for some time, put pressure on James to authorise a further clamp down on recusant activity. A subsequent report by McQuhirrie made reference to this increased persecution and to a history of the mission, which was being compiled by Abercrombie, but was never completed. Murdoch was also in Edinburgh around this time, and inscribed George Strachan's *Album Amicorum* and also wrote him a letter of recommendation prior to his departure for Rome to deliver the memorial prepared by McQuhirrie and Abercrombie.[13]

The renewed persecution continued during 1602, and despite the obvious dangers McQuhirrie returned to Edinburgh. In a report to Acquaviva he mentioned the good work being done in the city by an unnamed Dominican brother and how he and Eleanor Hay, Countess of Linlithgow, for whom he acted as chaplain, had been involved in the recovery of an important holy relic, the Arm of St Ninian, one of the first missionaries to Scotland. After the relic had been acquired from a group of unidentified English Catholics it remained in Scotland for a number of years before being delivered to the Scots College at Douai by Alexander Seton of Meldrum. Seton was a student of the college, who later joined the Society, but died before he could be appointed to the Scottish Mission.[14] McQuhirrie's movements during the following year are unclear, but he appears to have either accompanied or followed the royal family to England following the union of the crowns in 1603. He certainly spent a large part of that year in London with the English Jesuit, Henry Garnet, awaiting the arrival of Crichton, who it was hoped would be able help them gain access to James. Acquaviva deliberated for some time before allowing Crichton to return to Scotland. James's accession to the English throne forced Crichton to reconsider his position and despite applying for a passport from James he never crossed the channel.[15] By January 1604 McQuhirrie was back in Scotland and his regular reports to Rome painted a somewhat gloomy picture of the mission. Of his colleagues he reported that Abercrombie, now seventy, was starting to feel the pace, while Murdoch, although only six years his junior, was still very active and was widely respected for his sound judgement and medical skills. He also confirmed that despite the persecution, significant numbers were still being converted to Catholicism.[16]

Reports around this time indicate that the issue of attendance at Protestant services was still a matter of debate. There were clearly differences of opinion within the Catholic community and it was not uncommon for fathers to submit questions of conscience to colleagues on the continent for their guidance. In response to one query about whether attendance at a Protestant service at the invitation of the king was permissible it was advised that this should be avoided, but if it was for the common good and there were no prayers it would be permitted. Much to the disgust of a number of English priests travelling through Scotland the practice was to permit attendance; however their hard-line approach indicated a lack of understanding of the position north of the border. In England non-attendance was punishable by a fine, while in Scotland it could result in excommunication with its serious social, legal and financial ramifications. English influence and the abuse of this relaxed approach by a number of leading Catholics led to a hardening in attitude amongst the Scottish fathers and within the Catholic community in general. However, many Catholics in both countries felt that this uncompromising attitude would make their situation more difficult than it already was. McQuhirrie, who complained that he and other liberals were being criticised for their approach, hoped that the union of the crowns might lead to the introduction of the English system of fines and that this relaxation of the recusancy laws might result in an increase in the number of Catholics. Abercrombie, although in favour of a strict approach, continued to advocate that attendance should be permitted as it was already common practice. He identified three types of Catholics: those prepared to profess their faith openly, those who were Catholics at heart but attended Protestant services to preserve their wealth and status and those who were secret Catholics, whose identities were known only to their priests. He was also concerned that if he and his colleagues insisted on non-attendance the number of practising Catholics would decline. In April 1604 Gordon wrote to Acquaviva regarding Abercrombie's and McQuhirrie's concerns, though he himself continued to advocate non-attendance and on earlier visits to Scotland had refused to give absolution to anyone who persistently attended Protestant services. Despite his colleagues' concerns he remained adamant that as the two countries were united the Society could not adopt different stances in each. He believed that permission to attend Protestant services should only be granted to recent converts from Protestantism who had not yet revealed their new faith. Despite changing attitudes in Scotland the Scottish fathers were still perceived as being too soft. John Southcote, an English secular priest, writing a few years later, noted that three old Jesuits 'of good reckoning', Crichton, Gordon and Hay, 'took another course for converting Scotland than the secular clergy of England had done for England, using more profane and corrupt policy. They gave the Catholicks leave to go to church with heretics and to communicate with them in their heretical service and sermons, teaching that there was no sin but scandal. The drift was to save the Catholicks from the loss of their livings but this brought all Catholicks of Scotland to great dissolution. Father Holt and Father Ogleby, a Scottish Jesuit could never be brought to consent to this impiety, but they were either commanded silence or borne down by authority insomuch that few followed them'.[17]

By the end of 1604 McQuhirrie's health was also failing, due partly to the increased pressure of being the only priest working in and around Edinburgh, where there had been a fresh outbreak of the plague. Abercrombie had fled north after narrowly escaping capture in Perth, where he had been celebrating Mass at the houses of Archibald McBreck, the father of two future Jesuits, and of some ladies of the Drummond family. Attempts by the Kirk to tarnish his reputation by suggesting that he was involved in a sexual relationship with a woman were undermined when she retracted her allegation.[18] In the north he took refuge with Huntly at Bog of Gight from where he reported in March 1605 that McQuhirrie was active in the south of Scotland and in England. Although he was having problems contacting him he was sure that he would not break off communication. Soon after Abercrombie advised Acquaviva that he had had enough: 'I am seventy years old, and afflicted by several maladies; my head is never at rest, except when asleep; my hands tremble, my legs swell, my feet are pained with gout, my thighs with sciatica; my whole body is racked now with fever, now with other complaints'; symptoms which suggest he was suffering from Parkinson's Disease. A report later in the year by Crichton confirmed that Abercrombie was very ill and of little use to the mission.[19]

There was considerable concern in Rome for Abercrombie and McQuhirrie's safety given the heightened tension north and south of the border following the discovery of the Gunpowder Plot in November 1605. None of the Scottish Jesuits appear to have been involved, though eight years after the event George Gledstanes, Archbishop of St Andrews, advised James that he had heard that Patrick Anderson, a nephew of Bishop John Leslie of Ross and the first Scottish rector of the Scots College in Rome, had been implicated. There was no evidence to support this claim and Anderson, who was probably in France at the time, always denied the charge. Despite James's initially paranoid reaction and the wave of public relief at the failure of the plot there was no widespread backlash against the Catholic community in either country. James's political response was moderate and measured and acknowledged that the plot was neither a reaction against his religious policy, nor an expression of English xenophobia against him personally. Its origins pre-date the union of the crowns and are to be found in the Catholic militancy of Elizabeth's reign. Although it was acknowledged that the actions of the plotters did not reflect the views of the majority of the Catholic community, two new acts were passed tightening the existing recusancy laws and introducing an Oath of Allegiance. Rather than being an exclusively oppressive measure the Oath was introduced as a basis for religious toleration, and in return for acceptance James intended granting his Catholic subjects a limited form of freedom of worship. Pope Paul V's failure to appreciate the significance of the Oath and his outright rejection of it were a blow to James and heralded an acrimonious debate with Cardinal Robert Bellarmine, SJ, in which James argued, not particularly successfully, that the Oath was a matter of civil rather than spiritual obedience. While James continued to seek a compromise the entrenched views of others on both sides made this impossible and effectively ended any prospects for his proposed ecumenical council.[20]

North of the border extra efforts were made to apprehend Abercrombie and with the strain of many years in Scotland finally taking its toll he began to make preparations to return to Braunsberg and to hand over the running of the mission to McQuhirrie. Prior to his departure to Poland in May 1606 Abercrombie met up with Murdoch at Michrie where he had been sheltering with Gordon of Gight. Murdoch then accompanied Abercrombie to Dundee and after his departure headed back to familiar territory around Dunkeld to deliver Abercrombie's farewell messages to his family.[21] Plans for a smooth hand over to McQuhirrie were disrupted by his death in August 1606, confirmation of which was sent to Rome by Crichton: 'Father Alexander McQuhirrie laboured with good effect, covering in the course of his travels every part of the kingdom, but in particular he comforted and confirmed in the Catholic faith the Countess of

Linlithgow, who was always a benefactrix of the Society. In her house Father Alex. died'.[22] Murdoch then headed south to Linlithgow to collect McQuhirrie's books, which according to his later testimony to the privy council he was unable to retrieve. He then returned to Moray, where he was arrested in late April 1607 by Alexander Douglas, Bishop of Moray. His life appears to have been in no immediate danger and even his captors pleaded for clemency on his behalf.[23] During his initial interrogation in Edinburgh in late June he refused to co-operate with his captors, but was soon more forthcoming, though careful not to implicate anyone who was not already a known Catholic. The information he provided about Gordon and Abercrombie was of little use to the authorities, though, details concerning William Paterson, a soldier turned Augustinian friar, and John Hamilton, a former rector of Paris University, may have led to their arrests. Murdoch denied having had much contact with Hamilton, who was 'a doctor of theologie and of great giftis and qualitiyis', whereas he was 'bot a simple preist'. His confession and the correspondence he was carrying left the privy council in no doubt of his guilt, though it confirmed to them that Murdoch was 'ane simpill, ignorant man, constant in his awne errour, but no practizair nor busy body'. His claim that 'the cause of his stay in Scotland was for the intertenyment of helth, seeing his awne naturall ayre aggreis best with him' did not convince the privy council and in late September he was tried for treason, sentenced to be humiliated at the market cross in Edinburgh and banished from Scotland on pain of death.[24] His humiliation involved the burning of his 'Popish baggage', including his Mass clothes, a particularly significant act given the lack of vestments, which were an essential part of the celebration of the Mass. Calderwood narrates that: 'a preest who had beene a certane tyme in waird before in the Tolbuith of Edinburgh, was brought doun on the mercat day, to the Mercat Croce, with all his messe clothes upon him, wherewith he was taikin, with his chalice in his hand. He stayed at the Croce from ten houres till twelve. Then all his messe clothes and chalice were burnt in a fire beside the Croce, and himself carried backe to waird'.[25] Interestingly among his effects was a note referring to John Knox's ordination as a Catholic priest in 1536, perhaps written by Abercrombie or McQuhirrie.[26]

With Murdoch's departure to Pont-à-Mousson in late September 1607 the active involvement of the first generation of Jesuit fathers in Scotland came to an end. Four of them, Abercrombie, Murdoch, Crichton and Gordon continued to play a role in various Jesuit provinces and missions well into the second decade of the seventeenth century, outliving many younger colleagues, such as John Myrton and John Hay.[27] After fleeing from Scotland Abercrombie spent his final years at Braunsberg College where he resumed his teaching and pastoral duties. The college, which he had helped to establish, remained popular with young Scots for many years and the student roll included many familiar names, including Abercrombies, Hays, Leslies and Setons. In 1610, much to his embarrassment, Abercrombie was accused of being the author of an anonymous pamphlet criticising James – a charge which he strongly denied. He died a few years later on 5 October 1613 at the age of seventy.[28] After many years of active service in Scotland Murdoch enjoyed a long retirement at Pont-à-Mousson where he died on 21 August 1616.[29] Crichton, despite his lengthy imprisonment during the 1580s and his apparent poor health, lived on into his eighties. In his later years he worked in various houses in France before returning to Lyons where he died on 9 July 1617.[30] James Gordon outlived all his contemporaries and after withdrawing from active duty on the Scottish Mission travelled extensively throughout northern Europe. When not travelling he resided mainly in Bordeaux from where he helped direct the affairs of the Scottish and Canadian Missions. In 1613 he asked permission to return to Scotland to take control of the mission, but for various reasons his request was denied by Acquaviva, who appointed John Ogilvie instead. As well as old age the general may have been concerned about criticism of Gordon in the latter years of his superiorship. Andrew Crichton, a secular priest and former Jesuit novice, and John Myrton had both criticised him for being overly cautious (an 'auld feartie'), and the latter had called for him to be replaced by his name-sake, James Gordon of Lesmoir. Gordon's last years were spent in Paris where he died on 17 April 1620.[31]

The first Scottish fathers were inevitably followed by a generation of young men whose perception of the Catholic church was different. As John Durkan has pointed out the religious experiences of the next generation of Scottish recruits were totally post-Reformation and 'were conditioned as much by the Melvillian 'anti-seminary' as by the Jesuit seminary'.[32] Unlike their predecessors none had any first hand experience of service in the pre-Reformation Catholic church in Scotland and in many cases were converts from Protestantism. Despite James's determination to broker a religious settlement conditions for the Jesuit missionaries remained tough, and with his departure to England became tougher still. Although Crichton, Gordon, Myrton and Murdoch were arrested and imprisoned by the authorities north and south of the border they suffered relatively little physical abuse and all escaped with their lives. John Ogilvie, executed in 1615, did not enjoy the sort of clemency which James showed towards Gordon or Myrton. John McBreck, a Scottish Jesuit in the seventeenth century, alluded to these tougher conditions when describing the mission as 'almost the most arduous and difficult one in the charge of our Society'.[33]

It is unclear exactly how many other fathers were operating in Scotland during the first years of the seventeenth century as the reports of their activities are somewhat contradictory. In 1609 Guido Bentivoglio, the papal nuncio in Brussels, reported that as a result of the lack of interest amongst the Scottish Catholics there were only six or seven priests working in Scotland. In contrast Archbishop Spottiswoode of Glasgow, who was responsible for the arrest and execution of Ogilvie in Glasgow on 10 March 1615, had 'sure information' of twenty seven Jesuits operating throughout Scotland.[34] Although the intention behind Ogilvie's execution had been to discourage other Catholic missionaries one historian has suggested that it had the opposite effect: 'Scotland was never so infested by prowling Jesuits and traffickers as after the martyrdom of Father Ogilvie'. However, Jesuit records seem to indicate that during this period there were never more than one or two fathers in Scotland at any one time, including Patrick Anderson, who made a number of visits during the first two decades of the century before being arrested and banished in 1620. James Moffat was arrested in 1615 and eventually banished, having turned down offers of preferment in the Scottish church.[35] In fact, there were so few Scottish fathers Acquaviva was forced to ask the Irish superior, Christopher Holywood, whether he could spare any of his. When it became clear that the Irish mission was unwilling or unable to help Anderson turned to the Franciscans for assistance. The combined missions to Colonsay and the other Western Isles are well documented, and from the papers collected by Cathaldus Giblin, OFM, it is clear that they achieved considerable success. By the 1620s the situation in Scotland had improved, though there were still only a handful of Jesuits operating there compared with thirty or so in Ireland and over one hundred in England.[36]

10

Leaders of a Forlorn Hope

The limited success of the early missions and, until the excution of John Ogilvie in 1615, the absence of a Scottish martyr to inspire future generations, has meant that relatively little attention has been paid to the early activities of the Society in Scotland. In the absence of any detailed studies one is left wandering in what Thomas McCoog refers to as as the 'chartless seas of sixteenth-century Scottish Jesuit history'. Although our understanding of this neglected subject has developed little over the last fifty years, the conclusion of this study confirms the findings of such earlier analysis as exists; that the Society, despite the persistence of individual fathers over a period of almost forty years, failed in its primary aim, the restoration of Scotland to the Catholic faith through the conversion of James and his nobles. With hindsight it is easy to suggest that the failure of the Society's 'way of proceeding' was inevitable, but to contemporaries the Society and its Papal and Spanish backers appeared to pose a very real threat. In the early 1580s when the political situation appeared to be swinging in favour of Lennox and the other Catholic *politiques* it was less obvious than it is now that the Reformation was 'utterly secure', and had been since 1572.[1]

Despite the widespread support for a Scottish mission various factors, within and outwith the Society, contributed towards its lack of success. Limited resources, concerns about safety and a widely held belief that Protestantism was well entrenched in Scotland meant that service on the continent was often given priority. It is difficult to disagree with the observation by the Catholic historian, William Anderson, that the Scottish Jesuits' main contribution to the Society was made outwith Scotland and that Scotland would still be Catholic and Poland Protestant had the Society's deployment of its personnel followed national lines. This comment by a Protestant convert who was known to be antipathetic towards the Society may have been slightly tongue in cheek, but it does reflect the Society's general attitude towards Scotland. During the 1570s and 1580s when the political situation in Scotland was still unstable Edmund Hay and William Crichton were able to arrange for the majority of Scottish fathers to be based in France in order to serve on the Scottish Mission. However, by the turn of the century when it became clear that attempts to woo James had failed resources were directed away from the mission and used to fund the education of Scottish exiles. Scotland became part of the Flemish province and novices were assigned to colleges elsewhere in Europe. Even though Thomas McCoog's research shows that there were more Scottish Jesuits than previous studies have identified, there were rarely enough to man the Scottish Mission or, despite Anderson's comments, to make anything more than a relatively modest contribution to the Society elsewhere within Europe.[2]

The belief that James was staunchly Protestant was not one shared by a number of the Scottish Jesuits, whose reports to Rome continued to suggest that he was a potential ally. However, in time his policy of compromise and reconciliation wore down even his most loyal supporters within the Society, who were hard pressed to convince their superiors in Rome that their continued efforts to convert him were justified. Until the mid 1590s, when political Catholicism and Melvillian Presbyterianism were finally subdued, James asserted royal control by wooing both sides and playing one off against the other. His more lenient treatment, by English standards, of Catholics and individual Jesuits, has to be seen in the context of his political and religious aims; a smooth succession to the English throne and a religious settlement acceptable to all his subjects. Although his conversion was never more than a delusion in the minds of a number of Catholic exiles, James appears to have enjoyed and valued the company of Catholics and at various times his household and government included significant numbers. His continued attempts after 1603 to portray himself as a 'universal king' and to fashion a religious settlement suggest that there was a place for them as long as they remained loyal to the crown.

As John Durkan has suggested the Jesuits' 'awareness of international horizons were exactly what Scots Catholicism needed, not to speak of their new spirit of self-discipline and their sublime confidence in the scholarship of their famous Society'.[3] Although the Scottish Mission was always small the authorities' concern about the influence of the Scottish fathers was understandable. However, in reality the threat they posed was more apparent than real. Nevertheless, a number of them were able adversaries, who, while not of noble birth (with the exception of James Gordon), were kinsmen of a number of powerful and politically active Catholic nobles. One criticism of the Scottish fathers was their failure to operate outwith the protective zone of these Catholic kinsmen, though in fairness to them their principal 'way of proceeding' in Scotland was never to minister to the spiritual needs of the wider Catholic community. The three senior Scottish Jesuits of the period, Edmund Hay, William Crichton and James Tyrie, were appointed to prominent posts within the Society and would have pursued equally successful ecclesiastical careers in Scotland had they chosen to switch sides. Hay and Moffat, and no doubt others, were offered positions in the Kirk, and as Thomas Smeaton found out a spell in the Society did one's job prospects no harm. Although Hay, Crichton and Tyrie were appointed to high office, John Hay was perhaps the most intellectually gifted Scottish Jesuit of his generation. He was a scholar of international standing, though something of a loose cannon. His temperament made him a liability to the Scottish Mission and resulted in his withdrawal from active service. Abercrombie, Durie, Gordon and McQuhirrie never achieved the same prominence within the Society, but displayed an impressive combination of academic excellence and missionary zeal, and along with Murdoch, served for long periods in Scotland. There were also many who failed to make their mark and were refused entry to or dismissed from the Society. A significant number simply disappear from the records and it must be assumed that they died or were dismissed.

The connections between the majority of the early Scottish fathers have been touched on by John Durkan, though the extent of these links and the influence of Bishop Robert Crichton have not been fully explored. The common family and academic backgrounds of the Scottish fathers suggest a pattern of recruitment, which appears to have been co-ordinated by William Crichton and Edmund Hay with the assistance of Robert Crichton. As a result of these earlier relationships there was a certain *esprit de corps* within the Scottish Mission which was not always apparent elsewhere within the Society. While there were tensions amongst Jesuits of various nationalities, including between English and Scottish fathers, there is little evidence of any amongst the Scots. There were inevitably disagreements and clashes of personality, but not the same factionalism as was sometimes prevalent elsewhere within the Society. Similarily, there does not appear to have been much animosity between Scottish Jesuits and other clergy operating in Scotland, and while this may be a reflection of the weakness of the other orders, there is little evidence to suggest that the relationship was anything other than harmonious.

While the aim of this study has been to focus on the activities of the Society it should be borne in mind that the Jesuit mission was simply one strand, albeit an important one, of a much wider movement, involving the secular, monastic and mendicant clergy. Although the Society's 'way of proceeding' concentrated too much on the upper echelons of Scottish society and failed to produce tangible short-term results its efforts were instrumental in helping to preserve Scottish Catholicism at a time when the spiritual and political opposition to the Kirk was disorganised and ineffectual. The Society did not step into a religious vacuum, but built on foundations laid by others, such as Bishop Crichton, Abbot Gilbert Brown and the Franciscan friars, Leitch and Veitch. John Hay, Abercrombie and McQuhirrie in their reports to the Society all acknowledged that there were other priests operating in Scotland, though by the time of the establishment of the Scottish Mission their numbers were dwindling. A number of pre-Reformation secular clergy who expressed an interest in joining the Society were turned down on account of their age.

Whatever its shortcomings the Society can rightfully claim to have played a prominent rôle in the survival of Scottish Catholicism as, unlike the other clergy operating in Scotland, it was present throughout the decline, reorganisation, consolidation and expansion of the Catholic church. As William Anderson has suggested the shipwreck of Scottish Catholicism was unsalvageable and a new vessel was required, rather than a replica of the old one which had proved unseaworthy. The main legacy of the Society was that it provided leadership and continuity during the unsuccessful salvage of the pre-Reformation church and the relaunch of a new brand of Scottish Catholicism.[4]

Appendix 1

Eulogy to James Tyrie

We read in Drew's Fasti S.J., where he [James Tyrie] is called Assistant for Germany, that, when yet a boy, rays of light were seen to shine round his head, foreboders of his future sanctity. When studying logic at the Roman College, being over-much addicted to his books, St. Ignatius appeared to him in a vision, chided him for langour in the study of virtues, and for filching a portion of his time from prayer to give to his studies, an unworthy and dangerous theft, concluding his correction by the following, 'James more virtue; less of learning'. James therefore recovered himself again, and giving to God and virtue the things of God entirely, he became a man eminent both for virtue and learning.

A short eulogy, preserved in the archives of the Society, states that when a youth in his native country of Scotland, before he was acquainted with any member of the Society, he would often imagine in his mind some Order totally devoted to the service of God and the help of one's neighbour, of which he longed some day to become a member, and such in fact as he afterwards experienced the Society of Jesus to be. Hence it would appear that from this early time, before he had so much as heard of the name of the Society, Divine Providence, with its accustomed sweetness had efficaciously disposed him for a vocation to His service. At this time a certain priest well known for his sanctity of life, on once beholding the youth and closely regarding him, divinely inspired (as we may well believe), ordered him to apply himself diligently and with good courage to study, for that he would become religious in a certain holy Society, and would seriously apply himself to the conversion of his country from heresy to the Catholic religion. In the meantime Father Edmund Hay, who afterwards entered the Society and died Assistant of France and Germany, when he came to know the youth in Scotland, and had frequently heard of the excellency of his talent by the letters of his friends, began to reflect how he could get him away from Scotland, where heresy was then rampant, into France or Flanders. Many letters having passed between him and the mother and eldest brother of James to no effect, he resolved to cross over to Scotland himself for the purpose, which he accordingly did, and succeeded in accomplishing his object, getting their permission to take James to Louvain. Having arrived there, and becoming familiarly acquainted with our Fathers, he recognised in them the members of such a Society as he had so often depicted to his own mind. Discovering herein the call of God, he determined to follow it and go to Rome, and there beg the accomplishment of his desires. On passing through Trent, where the Council was at that time sitting, he fell in with Father James Laynez, who at once recognised him and addressed him by his proper name, to his great astonishment, and also received him with singular marks of kindness. Lastly, having been admitted to the Society in Rome and having passed through a shorter noviceship than customary, he was ordered to apply himself to his studies, and entered upon them with such avidity that one night Saint Ignatius appeared to him and gave him the admonition we have before mentioned. He was so affected by the vision, that he never forgot his correction from the best of Fathers, and after that time grave and dangerous troubles and perturbations of mind, which had for some time afflicted him, entirely vanished….

(Quoted from H. Foley, *Records of the English Province of the Society of Jesus* (Roehampton, London, 1877–84), iii, 726–8)

Appendix 2

Father de Gouda to Father Laynez

30 September 1562

Very Reverend Father in Christ. Pax Christi.

1 While I was in Holland at Easter-tide I received, on Tuesday in Holy Week [March 24] a letter from Father Everard [Mercurian], the Provincial, calling me to Louvain. On my arrival he showed me a letter from the Reverend Father Salmeron, the vicar-general, along with an apostolic brief and a letter from Cardinal Amulio, enjoining me to proceed to Scotland to deliver to the queen, the bishops, and to some of the chief men of that realm the apostolic letters which had been sent me. I did not set off at once, but waited till June, for reasons already explained more than once in my letters, and in those of the Reverend Father Provincial addressed to the cardinal and to the Father Vicar-General, so that it would be [a] waste of time to repeat them here. I will therefore now confine myself to the particulars of my mission, and my transactions with the persons to whom I was accredited; finally, I shall add a few words about their state and that of the whole kingdom. From all which you will easily understand amongst other things why I could not write sooner either to the cardinal or to yourself to report my proceedings.

2 In the first place, then, by a singular favour of God, who sweetly disposes all things, while I was preparing to start from Louvain, I felt a wonderful increase in my strength, beyond what I or any other expected. Next, a Scottish priest, named Edmund [Hay], a bachelor of theology, presented himself, and offered to accompany and guide me all the way to Scotland. Nor was this all, for with marvellous charity and zeal he remained with me all the time I was there. Indeed, I should not have been able to accomplish what I came for had I not had his aid or its equivalent. Guided by this man, as by the angel Raphael, we first reached Zealand on the tenth of June, where, through God's good providence, we found directly a Scottish vessel, which was weighing anchor at the very moment we arrived. Thus the Scottish heretics on shore and on board, though somewhat suspicious, had no time to ask many questions or stay our journey, as they

would certainly have done, had they but known the cause of our going.

3 Christ thus leading us onward we got aboard, and put to sea with a favourable breeze that same tenth of June. Next day, however, so great a storm arose, that we were nearly swamped, but such was the goodness of the Lord Jesus in our regard, that, moved by the prayers of your reverence, and those of the Society, He freed us from danger, and brought us safe and sound to Scotland within the space of nine days. The day before we disembarked the heretical Scots, of whom there were many on board, began to grow very suspicious, and curiously to question Master Edmund who we were, and on what errand we had come. He answered curtly, 'What are they to me? They are of age, let them answer for themselves.' And so we passed undiscovered.

4 On reaching land, Master Edmund took us privately to a house in the harbour town, belonging to a kinswoman of his. Here, almost at the same hour and very opportunely, the Lord Jesus sent us a certain faithful servant of the queen, Master Stephen, a Scotsman, through whom I immediately sent word to her Majesty of my arrival, and inquired where I could see her, and in what dress, whether as a cleric or as a traveller; but I had to wait there a whole month or more for a definite answer. The queen, as so happened, was hindered all that while by various occupations, but for me the delay seems to have occurred by a Divine dispensation, as I had time to recover from a pain in my feet, which had troubled me many days, and an accidental injury to one of my shins due to the violence of the storm on board ship. Meanwhile, I did my best to procure an audience, partly by letters, partly by messengers, but principally by Master Edmund, who saw her in person, and obtained her leave for an interview. They discussed the manner in which the conference should be conducted; as it appeared out of the question to have the Pontiff's letter read, or any of the messages commended to me delivered in public before the council, which consists entirely of heretics and deadly enemies of the Apostolic See, the queen resolved to treat with me in private. For this purpose she commanded Master Edmund and Master Stephen to bring me secretly to Edinburgh, the capital of the kingdom, which she expected to reach in a few days.

5 Meanwhile, the arrival of a nuncio from the Supreme Pontiff had been bruited all over the kingdom, throwing the heretics and the congregation into confusion and indignation. So much so that their leader, and most famous preacher in the royal city, John Knox, a Scot by birth, raged wonderfully in almost every sermon against the Pope as antichrist, and against me whom he called an emissary of Satan, and a nuncio of Baal and Beelzebub. He strove to stir the whole populace and the chief men of the realm, who solemnly attend all his sermons in great numbers, and to excite them, not against me only, but against the queen as well, for admitting such a man as myself into her realm, and giving audience to

those who were bent on corrupting the pure Gospel, the light of which had now at length dawned upon them. We were consequently often threatened with extremities, and could not now with safety be seen abroad. On this account Master Edmund took us to his parents' house [at Megginch]. They welcomed us most kindly, and concealed us for nearly two months. When at last we were to go to the queen, they sent three horsemen to bring us safely to Edinburgh, lest we should be surprised or attacked on the road, as there was some reason to fear.

6 When we had reached the city and dismissed our guard, we proceeded under the guidance of Master Stephen, but not without risk, across the fields and along the town walls, to the residence of the queen's almoner. Not long before he had not a little scrupled to receive me for fear of the heretics, but he now admitted us out of respect for the queen and the Pope, and immediately announced our arrival to her Majesty. To keep everything secret she sent us word to come to the palace next day, July 24, the Vigil of St. James, in the almoner's company, to a private chamber, at an hour when the aforesaid heretical courtiers were at the sermon, so that no one should know of our interview. I was admitted first by myself, and having respectfully saluted the queen in the name of the Pope, I briefly stated the object of my mission, and delivered his Holiness' letter. She said she understood my Latin, but could not so easily reply to everything in that language. I asked if I might call in my colleague, Master John Rivat, a Frenchman, and Master Edmund, a Scot, who were waiting in readiness outside the door, and who would interpret all her proposals faithfully. She agreed, and they immediately came in. The queen turned at once to Master Edmund as to a subject of her own, whom she had met before, and began her response in the Scottish tongue. The following is a summary of it.

7 She began by excusing herself for not receiving the Pope's nuncio in another way and with greater honour, which she said was owing to the disturbed state of the kingdom. Having read the apostolic brief, she answered that she hoped the Supreme Pontiff would have regard to her ready will rather than to anything she had actually done since her return, and much wished that his Holiness knew what the troubles were in which she found her kingdom. To save a spark of the old faith, and the germs of future Catholicism, to wit, herself and the others who even now adhered to the orthodox religion, she had been obliged unwillingly and perforce to bear many things, which she would not otherwise have borne. The Pope exhorted her in defending the faith to follow the example of Queen Mary of England, now departed in Christ; but the position, and that of the kingdom and of the nobility, of the English queen were very different from hers. To the request that some of her subjects should be sent to the Council of Trent, her reply was, that she would consult with her bishops, to see how it could be done, but under present circumstances with little

hope of success. For herself, she would rather die at once than abandon her faith.

8 Such was her first reply to the main subject of my negotiations, and to the papal brief. I noticed her anxiety about the time, and her fear lest the courtiers should come back from the sermon, and so made no farther proposals about religion for the moment, but mentioned the subject of the papal letters addressed to the bishops, asking advice, as it were, how these could best be delivered. Would she send for some of them and give the letters to them herself, or should I visit each in turn? She said that my delivering them was out of the question, adding, after a moment, that it could not be done without causing disturbance, for she feared their delivery would be a sign for a revolution. I said my orders were to deliver them, but she again replied that it was impossible, except perhaps in the case of one bishop. She alluded to the Bishop of Ross, the president of the council, or of the Parliament, who was then in town. The queen herself sent her secretary to him the same day, requesting him to confer with me, and his answer may be more conveniently related further on.

9 My next proposal was to ask her approval for an interview with her brother, the Lord James, Earl of Mar (who albeit illegitimate, governs almost everything in the realm), as I wanted to lay before him the object of my embassy, lest he should suspect me of any designs against himself or against any of the great nobles. She said she would inquire whether he would admit me to an interview; but I heard no more of it, and learnt afterwards that it would never have done for me to have met him, they are [all] so prejudiced and embittered against the Pope. I then asked for a safe conduct, or security for such time only as I remained in the kingdom. She answered that she thought no one would do me any injury in public, while as for the secret attempts of miscreants she could not hinder them even by the law. 'If I did give you one,' she added, 'I should rather be betraying you, and greater danger would threaten you when known. You are safer unknown. Wherefore do not go abroad, but keep in some secret chamber.'

10 Lastly, I said that I had been anxious to treat with her, had time allowed, on the best means of succouring her people, now so miserably led astray; but as it did not permit further discussion, for it was necessary she should dismiss us before the return of the courtiers, that is her brother and his followers, from the sermon, I said in brief that the most easy and fitting method was that followed by the emperor and most of the Catholic princes, secular and ecclesiastical, including her uncle, the Cardinal of Lorraine, namely, to establish a college where she could always have pious and learned men at hand, who might instruct in Catholicism and piety both the people and the young who were the hope of the commonwealth. She replied, in one word, that this might come in due time, but was impracticable just then, and so dismissed us.

11 A little later that same day she sent her secretary to me to ask what the

points were which I still wished to set before her. I said there were two principal ones, which I then told the secretary verbally, and afterwards set them forth more fully in a letter to the queen. One was, that before I came to Scotland, I had meant to strengthen her adhesion to the true and orthodox religion, by various reasonings, examples, and testimonies taken from the Scriptures; but that, since I had been in Scotland, I had heard so many things on such good authority of her exceptional piety and constancy in the faith that I thought the attempt superfluous. Instead of this I prayed her to reflect on the great benefits (and these I set down in writing) which her perseverance in the faith would occasion, and to rejoice at so singular a gift of grace given her by God, and to persevere therein. The second point, I said, was this. I should have liked to explain at greater length the benevolent feelings of Pope Pius towards her, his good-will and singular affection both for her and for the whole kingdom of Scotland, as well as his very loving endeavours to promote its peace, tranquillity, and good estate, as he did that of all Christendom, and the whole Church Catholic, whose faith, unity, peace, and safety he strove to preserve and promote, as became a true pastor of the Church, who is also the Supreme Vicar of Christ on earth.

12 After this she sent the secretary once more to ask for the Pontiff's letters addressed to the bishops, promising to have them duly delivered. I gave them to him on condition that she should inform the Pope, in her reply, that she had undertaken the responsibility for the letters, and that I could not have delivered them myself. This she willingly did, and gave me her letter to the Pontiff to read unsealed; and when it had been read by Master Hay and Master John, my colleague, she signed and closed it. This, reverend father, is in brief the history of my dealings with the queen. I will now relate summarily what occurred in my negotiations with the bishops and with some peers of that realm.

13 The queen, as I have previously stated, sent her secretary to the Bishop of Ross, requesting him to treat with me. The bishop answered that he would come in person to the queen, and treat with her on the subject. He went that day directly after dinner, and told her he could not possibly venture upon seeing me. 'At whatever time or place, or in whatever dress, the Pope's nuncio should come to me and I should deal with him, I am sure that my house would be sacked within twenty-four hours, and I should expose myself and all mine to the greatest peril'. When this was communicated to me by the queen's almoner I endeavoured to explain to him by letter why I had been sent to him, and begged him to write to me, or better still, to the Pope. Receiving no answer, I wrote again, and sent my second letter by the hand of a Carthusian prior, a good and learned man who was living there in secular dress, petitioning the queen for the restoration of some portion at least of the goods of his monastery, which the heretics had plundered. By this prior then I sent letters to the bishop once more,

but he on receiving them answered, 'I do not thank you at all.' When the prior urged him to reply to my letter, or better still, to write to the Pope, he answered, 'What shall I do? I durst not write. No one would convey the letter and what would happen if it fell into the hands of the heretics? The nuncio will never get away from the country without his letters being opened and read.' So he desired the prior to offer his excuses, alleging that the administration of justice and some other occupations prevented his writing to me. So much for him.

14 There was another prelate in the same city at that time, the Bishop of Dunblane, a kinsman of whose, now his bishop coadjutor, named William Chisholm, wished to join our Society at Rome. I had not yet approached this prelate when I tried to obtain an interview with the Bishop of Ross, but about a week later he left for his episcopal city, and thinking there could be no danger in his seeing me there, I asked one of his relatives to take me to him, as it was about a day's journey. When I got there I completely changed my dress, disguising myself as one of his own servants, so that no one could have suspected me of being the Pope's nuncio, and yet he dared not admit me to a conference for the same reasons which had made the Bishop of Ross refuse.

15 As one might surely hope for something from these two bishops more than from the rest, I began to see from them what would happen if I endeavoured to visit the others. For though the queen had told me that I could not deliver the apostolic briefs, and other good Catholics were of the same opinion, still I should have tried to visit them at least in secret, and treat with them personally about the object of my mission. As this might not be, I endeavoured by letter to inform them of that for which I had come. I therefore wrote to the rest of the bishops, though not quite to all, seeing that two of them are heretics, and that two sees, Galloway and Brechin, are vacant, though bishops have been designated for them. Two out of the number replied, viz. the Archbishop of St. Andrews, who wrote to me, and the Bishop of Dunkeld, who wrote to the Pope as well. These letters I send herewith to your paternity.

16 Among all the bishops, the last named was the only one who dared admit me to speak to him, and this only on the condition that I should pass myself off as a certain banker's clerk, come to request payment of a debt. This was to prevent even his servants finding out who I was, yet he now resides in a certain island, at a considerable distance from others. He entertained me at dinner, but on condition that we talked of nothing except money matters all dinner time. Your reverence will be at no loss to gather from these particulars how little could be done for the cause of religion by negotiation with these good men. So much then for the bishops.

17 As regards the nobles and the queen's councillors, your reverence must know that she has not a single Catholic adviser. Nearly all public business is transacted by heretics, both at court and throughout the kingdom.

Many lords and earls are Catholics, but the violence and tyranny of the heretics is such, that these noblemen keep away from court, and from any share in the administration. When I asked to whom I had best forward the apostolic briefs, three were specially commended, and to them I sent briefs by a safe hand, as I could not go myself. With them I sent letters which I had written, to set forth the benevolent mind of the Pope towards them and the whole realm of Scotland, and I now await the answers which Master Edmund is to bring.

18 The above is a brief narrative of my negotiations with the queen, the bishops, and some of the nobility. I now add a few words on the position of these persons and of the rest of the kingdom, especially in regard to religion. The aspect of things from this point of view would excite any one's pity. The monasteries are nearly all dissolved; some completely destroyed; churches and altars are overthrown; all things holy profaned; the images of Christ and of the saints are broken and cast down. No religious rite is celebrated in any part of the kingdom; no Mass ever said in public, except in the queen's chapel, and none of the sacraments are publicly administered with Catholic ceremonial. Not a baby may be baptized except according to the custom of the heretics, and that at the time they prescribe, viz. on Sundays, so that many infants die unbaptized. The ministers, as they call them, are either apostate monks, or laymen of low ranks, and are quite unlearned, being tailors, shoemakers, tanners, or the like, who in every sermon rage with revolting temerity against the Pope, and the most holy sacrifice of the Mass, the invocation of saints, and the veneration of images. The Mass, they call idolatry, and they cease not teaching the simple, uncultured people these and other impious dogmas of a like nature, which it were over long to repeat here. Such is the insane fury of these men that they have not only cast away the images of the saints, but also burnt the writings of the holy fathers of the Church, so that no standing ground is left for the general councils and apostolic tradition. They reverence nothing but Holy Scripture, and this they pervert according to their private judgments, and wrest into a sense as opposite as possible to the teaching of the Church. They have superintendents, who diligently visit the churches, which they seize with unrestrained violence, and eject the legitimate pastors.

19 Thus they not only confirm in their errors the poor people who have already lost the faith, but they draw away from the Church almost all the rest, and even priests, from the true religion. One day, and close to the place where I was then lodged, three priests publicly abjured the Catholic faith. At another time while I was there, one of these superintendents, a leading man amongst them, a doctor of theology and a monk, then about seventy years of age, was openly married. This was done to enforce by example, as he had often done by word, their doctrine of the unlawfulness of the vow of chastity, which they are perpetually trumpeting from

the pulpit. They also use wonderful cunning in their attempts to lead the poor people astray.

20 As for the magistrates, they so abuse their office, that even in judicial proceedings they ask the parties if they are Catholics, or 'Papists', as they say, or whether they belong to their congregation. Should they find them to be Catholics, their cause is either entirely neglected or very tardily expedited.

21 The leading men in the government acknowledge the queen's title, but do not let her use her rights. They have many ways of acting in opposition to her, and they set themselves to draw her over to their way of thinking. They often impose upon her with falsehoods, and sometimes influence her with threats of an English invasion, especially when she would attempt to execute any measure in support of her faith, reminding her that the English did really invade Scotland three years ago, at the time when her mother, of pious memory, tried to expel the heretics by means of the French, whom she had called in. What, I would here ask, should a young lady do in such circumstances? She is devout, has been nurtured in princely luxury, and numbers scarce twenty years of age. She is alone, and has not a single protector or good counsellor. Her very confessor left her just before I went away, and returned to France with some of her Catholic attendants, and she now remains almost alone among heretics, whose machinations, nevertheless, she continues to counteract to the best of her power. There is no mistaking the imminent peril of this good lady's situation. In the mean time, the men of power are taking unfair advantage of her gentleness, and do what they like. They keep a strict watch to prevent any access to the queen, except about unimportant matters, unless the reason is told them. Otherwise the closest secrecy must be used, as we had to do.

22 The bishops indeed perceive the unholy aims and endeavours of these men, but, Catholics though they be for the most part, things have now gone so far that they can do nothing against the heretics, however much they may desire it. The Bishop of Dunkeld is a case in point. Last Easter he desired to administer the sacraments according to the Catholic rite, and that a Catholic preacher should teach his people. Thereupon he was so vehemently impeached before the queen for offending the public decree, that he was compelled to desist by the queen's command; for when she first came to Scotland, those lords by some cunning put forth a public proclamation, which has now been in force for a year, that she would sanction no change in matters of religion until the assembling of Parliament, and that till then all was to remain in the state it was at the time of her arrival. The bishops therefore are silent and live but for themselves. I say nothing of most of them being destitute of the resisting powers requisite for meeting the foe and standing firm in the day of battle.

23 The only exception is the coadjutor Bishop of Dunblane, whom I have

already mentioned. Though but a coadjutor while his bishop lives, he has nevertheless shown himself a man of mark both in public speech and in private exhortation, and has confirmed many in the faith, and shown himself altogether a man whom all good men can justly love and be proud of. There are some Catholic preachers, but they are few in number, and such as venture not to moot the questions which are now controverted, or are unable to explain them fittingly. Some monks too there are, but very few, and they either wander about without any fixed abode, or wear secular clothes and live among their friends. There are some priests also, but one would hardly distinguish them from laymen by their dress and appearance. Some of the nobles and men of means are also Catholics. They hear Mass occasionally, but secretly, in the privacy of their own houses, so that they too are not free to make public profession of the true orthodox religion unless they want to risk exposing themselves and all their belongings to extreme danger. A large number of the ordinary common people indeed are still Catholics, but they are so oppressed by the tyranny of their opponents that they constantly sigh and groan, waiting for the deliverance of Israel. Yet, when they see their sovereign's firmness in the Catholic faith, and pious zeal for the orthodox religion, they are sustained by a strong hope that one day or other they will be set free. Those of the common people who have been led astray by the heretics are gradually perceiving that they have been fed on false hopes, and ensnared with hollow promises of liberty. In time, one may well entertain the hope that it might be easy to bring the whole people back to the Catholic faith. I will immediately explain how this might be done, but must first indicate what good Catholics think is the cause of the great misfortunes mentioned above.

24 Their opinion is that they are owing to the suspension of the ordinary election in conferring abbacies and other dignities. Benefices are constantly bestowed on children, and on absolutely unworthy persons, who care for nothing so little as for God's honour and the service of the Church. One and the same person holds many benefices, sometimes even in the same church. For instance, the son of one prelate has been appointed to the archdeaconry and two canonries in his father's church. The second cause is the lives of priests and clerics, which are extremely licentious and scandalous; and a third cause is the absolutely supine negligence of the bishops, who are now reduced to such misery that they cannot venture to discharge their duties, however much they may desire it, on account of the fury and audacity of the heretics. I will not describe the way in which these prelates live, the example they set, or the sort of men they choose as their successors. It is no wonder that, with such shepherds, the wolves invade the flock of the Lord, and ruin all.

25 Leaving this subject, I will briefly explain how, in the opinion of good men, that kingdom might be relieved and restored to the old religion.

First, they think it is absolutely necessary that the queen should marry a strong Catholic prince – one powerful enough to restrain by his authority and power the enemies of the faith, who will not let themselves be moved by any reason or argument. Secondly, care must be taken that the queen may have Catholics and prudent men as councillors. Thirdly, that men be instituted as bishops and prelates who will be truly such, who will care for the office of the Church and the salvation of their people. Moreover, the Apostolic See should send men of weight, invested with power and authority to examine into the lives of prelates and pastors, to reform them, or, if necessary, to remove them from office. Fourthly, some college should be established where good and learned men would be ready to give pious and Catholic instruction to the people and to the young, who are the hope of the commonwealth. Finally, they think that, through King Philip of Spain, precautions should be taken to prevent English enterprises against the Queen of Scotland. By this one threat, her councillors and the leading nobles of the kingdom, who are heretics, frighten her from acting in opposition to the congregation of the heretics or promoting the interests of the orthodox religion. Although religion is most dear to her, yet, as I said before, she cannot execute the holy desires of her heart, because she is alone and is well-nigh destitute of human aid. If she were supported, without a doubt this kingdom would soon be restored to the orthodox faith, as there are still large numbers of Catholics, not only among the people, but even amongst the nobility and men of power; whereas our adversaries are not so very numerous, nor so very strong. They greatly fear a powerful Catholic prince, and can hardly help seeing that their rule, maintained with so much fanaticism and impiety, cannot last for long.

26 The trouble undergone on our account by Master Edmund's parents and the history of our return to Flanders must now be noticed, and then I will conclude. Such bitter threats were uttered against Master Edmund for bringing us to Scotland, and against his parents for receiving us into their house, that I was obliged to write to the queen entreating her not to give easy credence to lies and calumnies which might reach her against them. I will only mention that I was credibly informed that almost all the ports were watched to prevent my escaping in safety with my letters, and it was only by the great skill and industry of Master Edmund and his kinsman, Master William (who have both now joined the Society), that we departed thence in safety. They dressed me as a sailor, and bargained with the seamen that we should be taken on board from a boat some miles out from the port, and separate ourselves from Master Edmund. Thus the guide of our voyage stayed behind for a while, thereby to ensure our getting off in safety, and to gather together and bring with him a band of young men whom he had collected together to be educated as Catholics in these countries, no contemptible result of our foray into Scotland. His kinsman, Master William, however, accompanied us as our guide on our return,

and showed us so much charity that I can hardly describe it.

27 Everything then being prepared, with Christ as our leader, we left Scotland, and embarked on a Flemish vessel on the 3rd of September, and we reached Antwerp, safe and sound, by God's grace, on the 13th of the same month. We went on immediately that very day to Louvain, and not finding the Father Provincial there, proceeded straightaway to Cologne, and thence to Mayence, where we met Father Nadal and the Father Provincial to our great contentment.

So much for our expedition to Scotland and return hence. Other particulars will be more easily communicated by word of mouth than by letter. These points Master Edmund and Master William, whom we daily expect, will be able to set before you more fully. For the rest, I pray Christ our Lord to complete the work. He has begun through His Supreme Vicar on earth, for the consolation of the queen and her kingdom, by the hands of the same holy Pontiff, to the honour of His Holy Name and the salvation of His people. And may the same most loving Jesus long keep your reverend paternity in health for us and His Church. Farewell.

Mayence, 30 September 1562

Your reverend paternity's unworthy son, NICHOLAS DE GOUDA

(Quoted from *Papal Negotiations with Mary Queen of Scots during her Reign in Scotland, 1561–67*, ed. J.H. Pollen, SJ (SHS, 1901), 129–39)

Appendix 3

Excerpt from Edmund Campion's *Brag*

Moreover I doubt not but you, her Highness' Council, being of such wisdom and discreet in cases most important, when you shall have heard these questions of religion opened faithfully, which many times by our adversaries are huddled up and confounded, will see upon what substantial grounds our Catholic Faith is builded, how feeble that side is which by sway of time prevails against us, and so at last for your own souls, and for many thousand souls that depend upon your government, will discountenance error when it is betrayed, and hearken to those who would spend the best blood in their bodies for your salvation. Many innocent hands are lifted up to heaven for you daily by those English students, whose posterity shall never die, which beyond seas gathering virtue and sufficient knowledge for the purpose, are determined never to give you over but either to win you heaven or to die upon your pikes. And touching our Society be it known to you that we have made a league – all the Jesuits of the world, whose succession and multitude must overreach all the practices of England – cheerfully to carry the cross you shall lay upon us and never to despair your recovery, while we have a man left to enjoy your Tyburn, or to be racked with your torments or consumed with your prisons. The expense is reckoned, the enterprise is begun, it is of God, it cannot be withstood. So the faith is planted, so it must be restored.

(Quoted from B. Basset, SJ, *The English Jesuits: From Campion to Martindale* (London, 1967), 456)

Appendix 4

Excerpts from John Hay's *Certaine Demandes concerning the Christian religion and discipline*

I.

I DEMAND in the first of the Ministers of Scotland, that thay schaw the confession of faith vsed in the Inglishe congregation at Geneua, receaued and approued be thame in thair new erected kirk of Scotland, and prefixit and set furth in the beginning of thair psalme buik, to haue bene acknauledged be ony christian people, at any tyme before Ihone Caluin.

14.

Quhy esteme ye that ye have ane infallibill mark of the trew religion, becaus ye cite onlie the wretin wourd? Sen that hes bene commoun to all heretiks from the beginning: Or quhat have ye mair for you nor thay had in this point.

26.

Quhat is the cause that in your kirk ye wil haue na bischops being from the Apostles dayes to this present, the bischops hes had the cheif place and administration of the kirk of God: and ar so cleirlie recommendit be saincts Petir and Paul.

29.

Quhether is the generall assemblie subiect to the king, and sould be called in his authorite, or nocht, Gyf it be subject quhy refuse ye your status to be examined be his counsell? Gyf ye say it is not subiect, Quhy deny ye that to the king of Scotland, quhilk your brethrene of Ingland grantes wnto thair Quene.

44.

Quhether aucht we to beleif rather our lord Iesus Christ quhen he said in the latter supper, tak eat, this is my body, quhilk salbe gevin for yow: or Caluin your maister, quha sayes that he gewe onlie ane signe or figure of his body? Or quhair reid ye that thir wourdes, this is my body, sould be vnderstand, this is ane figure of my body.

123.

Quhether gyf your reformation, quhilk ye have maid in the realme of Scotland, in pulling doune of the kirkes, is lykar to the reformation of Turkes and Paganes, nor to ane reformation maid be Christian men.

134.

Quhy have ye given the patrimonie of the kirk in few to your wyfes and bairnes, and quhether do ye any preiudice or nocht to your successours in this poinct.

166.

Quether gyf this your doings tendes to the abolition of all memorie of our lord Iesus Christ or nocht? sen alreddy some of yow doutes in quhat tyme of the yeir he was borne, quhether in winter or in sommer, sua that appearandlie your nixt dout salbe quhether he was borne or nocht, quhilk appeares to be the end and conclusion of your new Evangell.

Conclusion.

Christien reader sen be thir demandes thow perceaves alradie that the religion quhilk at this present is professed in the realme of Scotland, is nocht so soleid and trew as perchance afoir thow beleawed, and therfoir wald be glaid to vnderstand be quhat way thow mycht estableis thy conscience in this maist dangerous days: I can gewe the na better consell nor that quhilk sainct Augustin gewes in the leik cas wreatand to Honoratus in this matter. Sell we feir to repois our selfes in the bosoome of that kirk quhilk hes obteaned the swpreme authoritie be the succession of bischops from the cheare of Petir, nochtwithstanding the barking of heretiks againis it, quha partlie hes bean condamned ewin be the iwgeament of the people, paertlie be the authoritie of coonselles, and paertlie throw the strenthe and force of miracles. Of the quhilk succession of bischops he makes mention in his epistle ane hundrethe sextie fyve wreatand, Our lord said to Petir, vpon this roik I wil bwylde my kirk, and the yettes of hell sell nocht owrcome it...

(Quoted from *Catholic Tractates of the Sixteenth Century (1573–1600)* ed. T.G. Law (STS, 1901), 31ff)

Appendix 5

Excerpts from the Register of Novices in Rome

Robert Abercrombie the Scot
He came to the house on the 19th day of August 1563. He was examined as an indifferent and since he displayed no impediment he showed himself prepared to obey all instructions put to him during examination. He brought with him the Meditations of Augustine, a Gerson, the catechism of Canisius in Latin and Italian, letters of Sadoletus, a leather money bag, a leather pouch and a sword.

(An indifferent was a recruit, who after entry to the Society, left it to his superiors to decide whether he became a priest or a lay brother.)

Master William the Scot (William Crichton)
He came to the house on 5th December 1562, sent by the Father General in Trent, was examined and no impediment being found, was admitted as an indifferent. He brought with him thirty seven gold Italian scudi, four bronze scudi, two silver julii also and eight gold Scottish coins. He brought books with him: a history of Scotland in Latin, a breviary and book of daily services (Roman), a small New Testament in Latin and French, a compendium of Theology, biblical prayers in three languages, an exposition on symbolism by Joannes Hessels, the psalms in Hebrew, Marcus Aurelius in Scots, discourses by Machiavelli in contemporary Italian, the History by Machiavelli, Petrarch on the rule [ms. illegible], prayers of the Fathers; also a sword, a primal, a leather pouch with a drawstring, four smocks – two of them well worn, a cloth shirt to cover the whole body from Holland, another prayer gown made of black satin, a dozen handkerchiefs, four plaids, six pairs of slippers, a case and a leather bag, a pair of boots, a flask, a bag made of skin, a pair of black-clothed sandals, two [ms. illegible], a small brush, a dart made of [ms illegible], an iron press, a sheath with a knife and a cooking pot.

James Gordon the Scot
He came to the house on the 11th day of October 1564 from the city of Mainz where he had already been staying for eight months in the college of the Society, and for three months also at Cologne.

Father Edmund the Scot (Edmund Hay)
He came to the house on the 5th day of December 1562, sent by the Father General in Trent, was examined and, no impediment being found, was admitted as an indifferent. He brought with him some books: one bible in four volumes, though one volume has some text missing, two volumes from the works of Augustine, the New Testament in Latin and Greek, Joannes Hessels on symbolism with other works by the same author, the letters of Paul in their larger form; and some summer clothing, a belt with a sword, two smocks, a hat, a tabard and two pairs of sandals.

John Hay the Scot
He came to the house on the 24th day of January 1566. He was examined as an indifferent and, as he had no impediment, showed himself ready to carry out all instructions put to him during examination. He brought with him a cloak with a collar made of good quality velvet.

Walter Hay the Scot, from Perth
He came from Cologne where he had been admitted into the Society a year and a half previously and had already taken simple vows. He came as I state on the 14th day of April 1564.

Peter Livius the Scot
I Peter Livius the Scot from Edinburgh came to this house of the Society of Jesus in Rome on the 26th day of February 1562. I was examined as an indifferent and was accepted on the condition that no impediment be found in me; and I showed myself prepared to obey all instructions from the superior of the Society. And I brought with me the following: a used black cloak, boots only, silk breeches, a book entitled 'Method of Confession', a book containing four languages, a dictionary of eight languages, a Latin grammar, a French map, a bread bag.

Robert Methven
I Robert Methven came to the house on 9th November 1558, was examined as an indifferent and, no impediment being found, showed myself ready to carry out any instructions from the superiors. I brought with me a good monk's cloak from Florence, three used surplices of white cloth, four pairs of slippers,one pair of used silk socks, a used tunic of Spanish linen, a habit of the same material as the cloak, a cassock of good Flemish material, a used hat, a pair of old velvet shoes, another pair made of worn hide, a pair of old breeches, a wooden crucifix, a small 'Our Lady of Loreto', a new Calepina, a book entitled 'Letters of Various Illustrious Men', Letters from India, Cicero on Duties, Joannes Gerson, Letters of Cicero, Terence, the New Testament, Letters to Atticus Brutus and his brother Quintus, Rules of Perottus, the anthology of

various writings by Saint Gregory, Ortulus on souls, an inkwell, seal, scissors and a small knife.

William Murdoch the Scot
He came to the house on the 29th day of August 1563. He was examined as an indifferent and as he had no impediment he showed himself prepared to obey all instructions put to him during examination. He brought with him the Meditations of Augustine, and a Canisius.

Thomas Oswald the Scot
He came to the house on the 7th of October 1569. He was examined as an indifferent and was found without impediment. He showed himself ready to undertake all instructions put to him during examination.

Thomas Rouye the Scot
I Thomas came to the house on 8th February 1560. I was examined as an indifferent and, as no impediment was found, showed myself ready to carry out any instructions from the superiors. I brought with me a used cloak and a Gerson.

Thomas Smeaton the Scot
He came to the house on 22nd September 1566 and was examined as an indifferent and as he had no impediment, showed himself ready to carry out all instructions put to him during examination. He brought with him one black cloak, a French dictionary, a comparison of French and Greek languages, an alphabet in Latin and Greek, Aesop's Fables in Latin and Greek, Cicero's Letters to his Friends in French and Latin, eighteen tragic histories in French, a sword, a skin hat, a belt and a pair of old black sandals.

James Tyrie the Scot
He came to the house on the 19th day of August 1563. He was examined as an indifferent and as he had no impediment he showed himself prepared to obey all instructions put to him during examination. He brought with him the Cathechism of Canisius and a worn, black cloak.

Appendix 6

Transcript of Father Crichton's Map, 1595

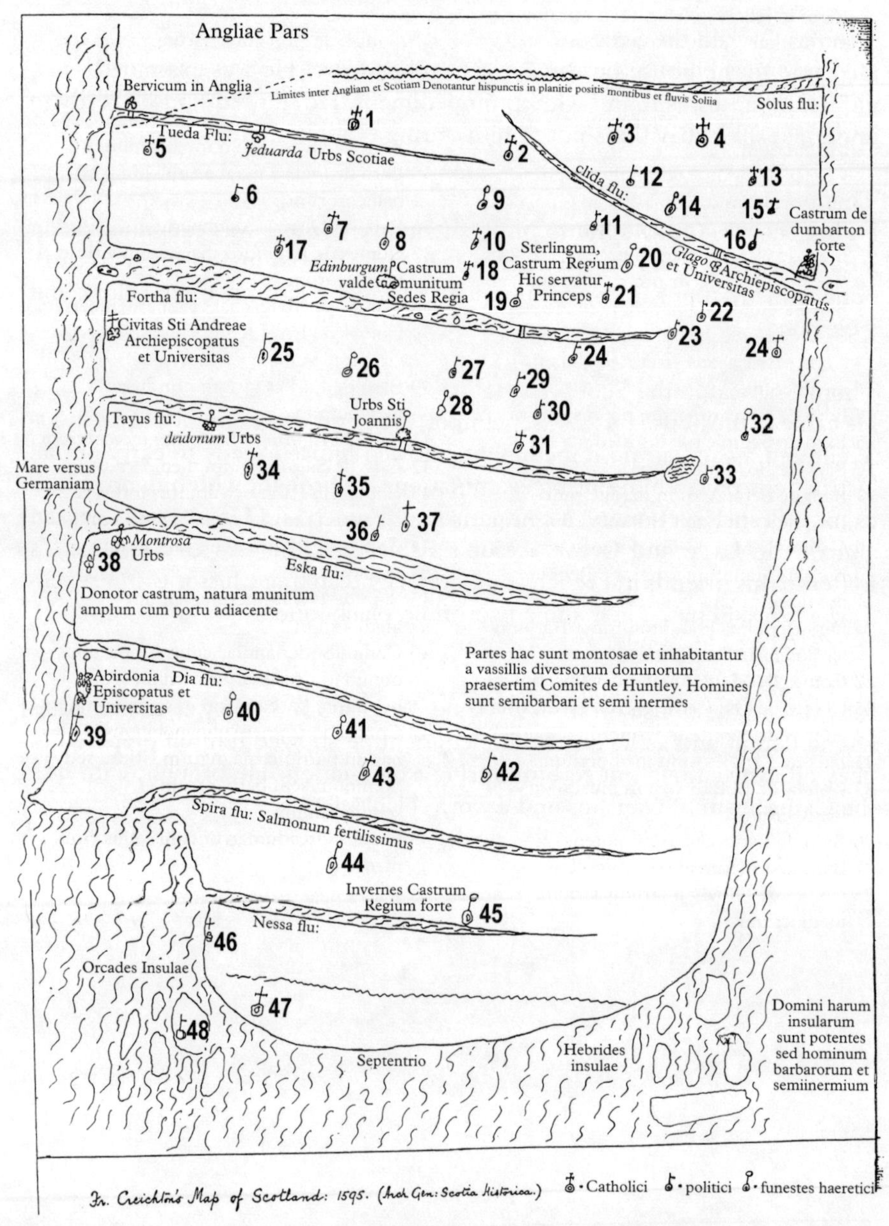

KEY

1 Comes Angusiae primus inter nobiles magnarum virium
2 Baro de Creyton virium mediocrium
3 Baro de Herys virium plusquam mediocrium
4 Comes de Morton Maxuel, gubernator limitum occidentalium multorum virium bellicosorum
5 Baro de Hume gubernator Limitum orientalium. Capitanus custodiae regis, vir magnarum virium hominum bellicosorum
6 Baro de Yester puerulus virium mediocrium
7 Comes de Boduel admiralius regni magnarum virium
8 Baro de Borthok parum potens
9 Baro de Ochiltry parum potens
10 Baro de Fleming virium mediocrium
11 Baro de Somervel parum potens
12 Baro de Rosse parum potens
13 Comes de Cassels virium plusquam mediocrium
14 Baro de Carcart parum potens
15 Baro de Semple potens mediocriter
16 Baro de Boyd mediocris
17 Baro de Seton virium mediocrium
18 Baro de Levingston virium mediocrium
19 Comes de Mar parum potens
20 Baro de Hamilton sanguine Regi proximus potens bellicosorum
21 Dno Claudius Hamilton frater Baronus vir potens bellicosorum
22 Comes de Mongomery puerulus, potens
23 Comes de Glencarne virium mediocrium
24 Comes de Monteith virium mediocrium
24 Dux de Lenox virum mediocrium
25 Comes de Rothes virium plusquam mediocrium
26 Baro de Lyndsay parum potens
27 Baro de Innermeid parum potens
28 Comes de Gowry puerulus virium mediocrium
29 Comes de Montrose virium plusquam mediocrium
30 Baro de Drummond, gubernator Stratherniae virium mediocrium sed bellicosorum: eius loco omnia gubernat eius frater, Baro ab Inchefray, quia surdus est
31 Baro de Inchefray virium plusquam mediocrium, quia eum sequuntur et sui et omnes Baronis de Drommond sui fratris
32 Comes de Argyl magnarum virium sed hominum barbarorum et inermium
33 Comes de Athol virium mediocrium semibarbarorum et semiinermium
34 Baro de Gray virium mediocrium
35 Baro de Ogilvy magnarum virium et bellicosorum
36 Baro de Glames, mediocrium
37 Comes de Crauford magnarum virium et bellicosorum
38 Comes de Mareschal virium mediocrium
39 Comes de Errol Regni Conestablius virium plusquam mediocrium
40 Baro de Forbes virium plusquam mediocrium
41 Baro de Elphingston virium mediocrium
42 Baro de Salton virium mediocrium
43 Comes de Huntley subditus totius regni potentissimus sed ab aula regia remotus
44 Comes de Murray puerulus virium mediocrium
45 Baro de Lovat puerulus virium mediocrium
46 Comes Soderlandiae solus his partibus dominatur magnarum virium, sed hominum barbarorum et semiinermium
47 Comes de Catnes solus nobilibus et aliis harum partium magnarum virium sed hominum semibarbarorum et semiinermium
48 Comes Orcadum avunculus regis virium med:

Endnotes

Introduction: Devils and Dissemblers, Saints and Savants

1 The title to the introduction is taken from J.W. O'Malley's essay 'The Historiography of the Society of Jesus: Where Does It Stand Today?', in *The Jesuits: Cultures, Sciences and the Arts, 1540–1773*, edd. J.W. O'Malley, SJ, and others (Toronto, 1999); F. Edwards, SJ, *The Jesuits in England from 1580 to the present day* (Tunbridge Wells, 1985), 11 and *Robert Persons: The Biography of an Elizabethan Jesuit, 1546–1610* (St Louis, 1995), ix [Edwards, *Robert Persons*]; T.J. Campbell, SJ, *The Jesuits 1534–1921* (New York, 1921), 2 [Campbell, *Jesuits*]; J.C.H. Aveling, *The Jesuits* (New York, 1982), 18–48 [Aveling, *Jesuits*]; J. Lacouture, *Jesuits: A Multibiography* (Washington DC, 1995), 348, 350–1 [Lacouture, *Jesuits*]; see also A. Pritchard, *Catholic Loyalism in Elizabethan England* (London, 1979), Chapter X, 'The Myth of the Evil Jesuit', 175ff [Pritchard, *Catholic Loyalism*]; H. MacPherson, *The Jesuits in History* (Edinburgh, 1914), 149

2 T.M. McCoog, SJ, *The Society of Jesus in Ireland, Scotland and England, 1541–1558: 'Our Way of Proceeding?'* (Leiden, 1996), 265 [McCoog, *Our Way of Proceeding*]; others take a different view of historical objectivity with 'its esoteric language, its impartial dryness and objectivity, for the sake of which the stupid and the wise, the sublime and the ridiculous are treated with equal respect... incomparably deeper insight into the being and the meaning of Jesuitism is afforded by all the hate-filled pamphlets, the highly coloured apologies, distorted representations, doctored reports, the slanderings and glorification of the order's history', R. Fülöp-Miller, *The Power and Secret of the Jesuits* (New York, 1930), vii–viii

3 T.M. McCoog, SJ, '"Pray to the Lord of the Harvest": Jesuit Missions to Scotland in the Sixteenth Century', *IR*, 53 (2002), 127–88 [McCoog, Jesuit Missions to Scotland]; McCoog, *Our Way of Proceeding*, 7; On John Ogilvie see T. Collins, *Martyr in Scotland, The Life and Times of John Ogilvie* (London, 1955); W.E. Brown, *John Ogilvie: An Account of his Life and Death* (London, 1925) and F.A. Forbes and M. Cahill, *A Scottish Knight-Errant: A Sketch of the Life and Times of John Ogilvie, Jesuit* (New York, 1920)

4 See *Narratives of Scottish Catholics under Mary Stuart and James VI* , ed. W. Forbes-Leith, SJ (London, 1889) [Forbes-Leith, *Narratives*]; *Collected Essays and Reviews of Thomas Graves Law, LLD*, ed. P. Hume Brown (Edinburgh, 1904) [Law, *Essays*]; *Papal Negotiations with Mary Queen of Scots during her Reign in Scotland, 1561–67*, ed. J.H. Pollen, SJ (SHS, 1901) [Pollen, *Papal Negotiations*]; *Letters and Memorials of Father Robert Persons, S.J., vol.1 1578 to 1588*, ed. L. Hicks, SJ, (CRS, vol.39, 1942) [*Persons Letters*]; Edwards, *Robert Persons*; A. L. Martin, *Henry III and the Jesuit Politicians* (Geneva, 1973) [Martin, *Jesuit Politicians*]; H. Chadwick, SJ, began, but never completed, a history of the Scottish Mission, see 'Beginning of H. Chadwick's History of the Society of Jesus in Scotland 1542– ', ABSI 46/4/7/68–77; the recently published *The Oxford Companion to Scottish History*, ed. M.Lynch (Oxford, 2001) [Lynch, *Oxford Companion to Scottish History*] and *The New Penguin History of Scotland from the Earliest Times to the Present Day*, edd. R.A. Houston and W.W.J. Knox

(London, 2001) make only passing reference to the Society in Scotland.

5 See H. O. Evennett, *The Spirit of the Counter-Reformation*, ed. J. Bossy (Notre Dame, 1970); M.A. Mullett, *The Catholic Reformation* (London, 1999), 29ff [Mullett, *Catholic Reformation*]; M.D.W. Jones, *The Counter Reformation: Religion and Society in Early Modern Europe* (Cambridge, 1995); J. W. O'Malley, SJ, *Trent and All That: Renaming Catholicism in the early modern era* (Cambridge, Massachusetts, 2000), 2, 5, 140; J. Wormald, *Court, Kirk and Community, Scotland 1470–1625* (London, 1981), 120 [Wormald, *Court, Kirk and Community*]; on internal reform in Scotland see also I.B. Cowan, *The Scottish Reformation* (London, 1982), 72ff [Cowan, *Scottish Reformation*], G. Donaldson, *The Scottish Reformation* (Cambridge, 1960) and *Statutes of the Scottish Church 1225–1559*, ed. D. Patrick (SHS, 1907), 84ff; J. H. Pollen, SJ, *The Counter-Reformation in Scotland* (London, 1921), 31ff [Pollen, *Counter-Reformation*]; D. MacLean, *The Counter-Reformation in Scotland, 1560–1930* (London, 1931), 19ff [MacLean, *Counter-Reformation*]

6 B. Moore, *Black Robe* (London, 1994); R. Bolt, *The Mission* (Harmondsworth, 1986); Silvio Back, the Brazilian producer of a documentary on the Paraguayan missions, described the film of *The Mission* as an aquatic western, see Lacouture, *Jesuits*, 258–9; other general studies of the Society include D. Letson and M. Higgins, *The Jesuit Mystique* (Toronto, 1995) and A. Wodrow, *The Jesuits: A Story of Power* (London, 1995)

7 U. Eco, *Foucault's Pendulum* (London, 1990), 470: 'Templarism is Jesuitism'; Eco's main character, Casaubon, claims that the secret knowledge of the Templars was passed to the Jesuits and that the Society built the forerunners of computers

8 J. Anderson, *The Winter Night* (Glasgow, 1713), 16; the poem was dedicated to the Protestant reformer, John Erskine of Dun

9 See the entry for James Anderson at Bendochy in the appendix to M. J. Yellowlees, 'Dunkeld and the Reformation' (unpublished thesis, Edinburgh University, 1990), 312 [Yellowlees, Dunkeld]

10 J. Brodrick, SJ, *The Progress of the Jesuits (1556–79)* (repr. Chicago 1986), 312 [Brodrick, *Jesuits*]; for biographies of the first generation of Scottish Jesuits see *DNB*, the new edition of which will be published shortly; H. Foley, SJ, *Records of the English Province of the Society of Jesus* (Roehampton-London, 1877–84) [Foley, *Records*]; G. Oliver, *Collections Towards Illustrating the Biography of the Scotch, English and Irish Members, S.J.* (Exeter, 1838) [Oliver, *Collections*]; *Dictionary of Scottish Church History and Theology*, edd. N.M. de S. Cameron and others (Edinburgh, 1993); McCoog, Jesuit Missions to Scotland, 159–88

11 Aveling refers to 'the ecclesiastical "ordinariness" and earthiness of Jesuit life and history', Aveling, *Jesuits*, 32

12 On Nadal and his view of the Ignatian Way see W.V. Bangert, SJ, ed. T.M.McCoog, SJ, *Jerome Nadal, S.J., 1507–1580: Tracking the First Generation of Jesuits* (Chicago, 1992) 27ff; Brodrick, *Jesuits*, 278; J.W. Donohue, *Jesuit Education: An Essay on the Foundations of its Idea* (New York, 1963), 3–4

13 The superior generals during the period covered by this study were Ignatius Loyola (1541–1556), Diego Laínez (1558–1565), Francis Borgia (1565–1572), Everard Mercurian (1573–1580) and Claudio Acquaviva (1581–1615)

14 Brodrick, *Jesuits*, 278ff

15 A. L. Martin, *The Jesuit Mind: The Mentality of an Elite in Early Modern France* (Ithaca, New York, 1988), 30 [Martin, *The Jesuit Mind*]; see also J.C. Futrell, *Making an Apostolic Community of Love: the Role of the Superior according to St. Ignatius of Loyola* (St Louis, 1970)

16 *The Constitutions of the Society of Jesus*, trans. G. E. Ganss, SJ (St Louis, 1970), 286 [Ganss, *Constitutions*]

17 Pollen, *Papal Negotiations*, 490–1

18 Ibid., 151

19 Martin, *The Jesuit Mind*, 31–2

20 *Documents of the Thirty First and Thirty Second General Congregations of the Society of Jesus*, ed. J. Padberg, SJ (St Louis, 1977), 32; for introductions to the Constitutions and other documents see Ganss, *Constitutions*, 35ff

21 J. W. O'Malley, SJ, *The First Jesuits,* (Cambridge, Massachussetts, 1995), 37 [O'Malley, *The First Jesuits*]

22 A metaphor suggested by John Moffatt, SJ, Edinburgh, 1999

23 J. Brodrick, SJ, *Saint Peter Canisius* (repr. Chicago, 1998), 455 [Brodrick, *Canisius*]; for general accounts of Scottish Catholicism since the sixteenth century see P.F. Anson, *The Catholic Church in Modern Scotland 1560–1937* (London, 1937) and *Underground Catholicism in Scotland 1622–1878* (Montrose, 1970); G. Scott-Moncrieff, *The Mirror and the Cross: Scotland and the Catholic Faith* (London, 1960); M. Dilworth, 'Roman Catholic Worship', in *Studies in the History of Worship in Scotland* edd. D. Forrester and D. Murray (Edinburgh, 1996), 127–48 [Forrester and Murray, *Worship in Scotland*]

Chapter 1: The First Jesuit Mission to Ireland and Scotland

1 Pollen, *Papal Negotiations*,142; the Papal bull confirmed Loyola's *Formula Instituti* of 1540; on Methven and Rouye see *Angliae*, III, 568–9

2 W.A. McNeill, 'Scottish Entries in the *Acta Rectoria Universitatis Parisiensis* 1519 to c.1633', *SHR*, 43 (1964), 70ff [McNeill, Scottish Entries]; on the foundation of the Society see O'Malley, *The First Jesuits*, 23ff; Lacouture, *Jesuits*, 56–7, quoting from Pierre Favre's memoirs describes the events: 'On Saint Mary's day in the month of August, in this year of 1534, already united by a like determination and all (with the exception of Master Francis [Xavier] who had not yet performed them but shared in our designs) well versed in the *Exercises*, we betook us to Our Lady of Montmatre near Paris, where each of us swore the vow to leave for Jerusalem at the appointed day and to place ourselves upon our return under the authority of the Pontiff of Rome, and also, at the appropriate hour, to leave our families and our nets'.

3 The legislation included The Act of Supremacy 1534, The Ten Articles 1536, Cromwell's Injunction to the Clergy 1536 and The New Injunction 1538; see W.V. Bangert, SJ, *Claude Jay and Alfonso Salmerón* (Chicago, 1985), 167 [Bangert, *Jay and Salmerón*] and McCoog, *Our Way of Proceeding*, 18

4 A. Gwynn, SJ, *The Medieval Province of Armagh 1470–1545* (Dundalk, 1946), 248ff [Gwynn, *Armagh*]; *Angliae*, III, 5

5 Gwynn, *Armagh*, 249; *Angliae*, III, 5; G. Schurhammer, SJ, *Francis Xavier: His Life, His Times* (Rome, 1973–82), I, 499, 548, 551 [Schurhammer, *Francis Xavier*]; Bangert, *Jay and Salmerón*, 167

6 J. Durkan, 'Robert Wauchope, Archbishop of Armagh', *IR*, 1 (1950), 64–5 [Durkan, Robert Wauchope]

7 *Rentale Dunkeldense*, ed. R.K. Hannay (SHS, 1915), 289, 325, 338 [*Dunkeld Rentale*]

8 W. M. Brady, *The Episcopal Succession in England, Scotland and Ireland A.D. 1400–1875* (repr. Rome, 1971), I, 130–2 [Brady, *Episcopal Succession*]; D.E.R.Watt, ed., *Fasti Ecclesiae Scoticanae Medii Aevi ad annum 1638* (Edinburgh, 1969), 99–100,109 [Watt, *Fasti*]; J. Dowden, *The Bishops of Scotland* (Glasgow,1912), 91–4 [Dowden, *Bishops*]

9 Durkan, Robert Wauchope, 48, 49, 50, 52; McNeill, Scottish Entries, 78, 82; J. Durkan, 'The Cultural Background in Sixteenth Century Scotland' in *Essays on the Scottish Reformation, 1513–1625*, ed. D. McRoberts, (Glasgow, 1962), 290, 315, 338 [McRoberts, *Essays*]

10 J. Cameron, *James V: The Personal Rule 1528–1542* (East Linton, 1998), 236

11 McCoog, *Our Way of Proceeding*, 14; Campbell, *Jesuits*, 38, 41

12 On Salmerón see Bangert, *Jay and Salmerón*, 166–7; *Epistolae P.P. Paschasii Broët, Claudii Jayi, Joannis Codurii et Simonis Rodericii*, ed. F. Cervós, SJ (MHSI, Madrid, 1903), 421–7 [*Broët*]; *Angliae*, III, 4–7

13 *Letters of St. Ignatius of Loyola*, ed. W.J. Young, SJ (Chicago, 1959), 42 [Young, *Letters of St. Ignatius*]; *Angliae*, III, 3

14 *Angliae*, III, 3–4

15 *The Heads of Religious Houses in Scotland from Twelfth to Sixteenth Centuries*, edd. D.E.R.Watt and N.F. Shead. (Edinburgh, 2001), 61–2 [Watt and Shead, *Heads of Religious Houses*]; *The Letters of James V*, edd. R.K. Hannay and D. Hay (Edinburgh, 1954), 380, 392–3 [*James V Letters*]; *Angliae*, III, 8–12

16 *Angliae*, III, 19–26

17 Young, *Letters of St. Ignatius*, 51–2

18 *Angliae*, III, 17–19, 29; M. Colpo, SJ, 'Paschase Broët c1500–1562', *AHSI*, 59 (1990), 244; On Zapata see also Schurhammer, *Francis Xavier*, 500, 721

19 *Letters and Instructions of St. Ignatius Loyola*, ed. A. Goodier, SJ (London, 1914), 50–64; *Angliae*, III, 30ff

20 *Angliae*, III, 12–13

21 Bangert, *Jay and Salmerón*, 168; *Angliae*, III, 50ff

22 For Broët's and Salmerón's accounts of the mission see *Broët*, 23–31 and *Epistolae P. Alphonsi Salmerónis Societatis Iesu*, edd. R. Vidaurre, SJ, and F. Cervós, SJ (MHSI, Madrid, 1906–7), I, 2–10

23 *Angliae*, III, 50–9

24 Durkan, Robert Wauchope, 51–2; *Angliae*, III, 53

25 Watt, *Fasti*, 99–100, 109; *James V Letters*, 251, 260; Dowden, *Bishops*, 88, 91ff; *Angliae*, III, 57

26 Bangert, *Jay and Salmerón*, 168–9; *Angliae*, III, 55–6

27 *James V Letters*, 435–6; *Angliae*, III, 53, 59–60;

28 *James V Letters*, 435–6; *Angliae*, III, 57–8; the first three Scottish recruits to enter the Society were Robert Methven (entered 9 November 1558), Thomas Rouye (entered 8 February 1560) and Peter Livius (entered 26 February 1562); James Kirk suggests that the Protestant reformer, John Row, was a Jesuit prior to the Reformation, though there is nothing in the Jesuit archives to substantiate this, J. Kirk, P*atterns of Reform: Continuity and Change in the Reformation Kirk* (Edinburgh, 1989), 77 [Kirk, *Patterns of Reform*]

29 F. Thompson, *Saint Ignatius Loyola* (London, 1962), 110 [Thompson, *Loyola*]

30 Bangert, *Jay and Salmerón*, 170; The English Jesuit, Edmund Campion, in his *Histories of Ireland* described the Irish as 'religious, frank, amorous, ireful, sufferable, of pains infinite, very glorious; many sorcerers, excellent horsemen, delighted with wars, great almsgivers, passing in hospitality', quoted in Evelyn Waugh, S*aint Edmund Campion, Priest and Martyr* (Manchester, 1996), 41 [Wauchope, *Saint Edmund Campion*]; for a fuller analysis of Campion in Ireland see C. Lennon, 'Edmund Campion's *Histories of Ireland* and Reform in Tudor Ireland' in *The Reckoned Expense: Edmund Campion and the Early English Jesuits. Essays in Celebration of the First Centenary of Campion Hall, Oxford (1896–1996)*, ed. T.M. McCoog, SJ (Woodbridge, 1996), 67–83 [McCoog, *Essays*]

31 C. Lennon, *Sixteenth Century Ireland: The Incomplete Conquest* (Dublin, 1994), 138 [Lennon, *Sixteenth Century Ireland*]; M.V. Ronan, *The Reformation in Dublin 1536–1558* (London, 1926), 303–9

32 *Angliae*, III, 68; McCoog, *Our Way of Proceeding*, 20–1

33 Bangert, *Jay and Salmerón*, 226

34 *Angliae*, III, 60–1

35 *The Elizabethan Jesuits: Historia Missionis Anglicanae Societatis Jesu (1660) of Henry*

More, ed. F. Edwards, SJ (London, 1981), 11 [More, *Historia*]
36 Bangert, *Jay and Salmerón,* 172–3; *Angliae*, III, 81
37 On Broët and Salmerón's activities in the aftermath of the mission see Bangert, *Jay and Salmerón*, 173ff; on Zapata see Schurhammer, *Francis Xavier*, 500
38 Thompson, *Loyola*, 110; Lennon, *Sixteenth Century Ireland*, 324
39 F.M. O'Donoghue, SJ, 'The Jesuit Mission in Ireland 1598–1651' (Unpublished PhD thesis, Catholic University of America, Washington, 1981), 16
40 C. Giblin, *Irish Franciscan Missions to Scotland 1619–1646* (Dublin, 1964), 6, 20, 21

Chapter 2: Nicholas de Gouda's Mission of 1562

1 W.J. Anderson, 'Rome and Scotland, 1513–1625', in McRoberts, *Essays*, 476–7; Jenny Wormald takes a rather different line and argues that the pre-Reformation Papacy was largely irrelevant in Scotland except in its bureaucratic and legal capacity, Wormald, *Court, Kirk and Community*, 120
2 Pollen, *Papal Negotiations*, 45–6; The Golden Rose was 'Une roze dor qui fut presente de la parte du Pappe, a laquelle y a huit blanches et ung petit saphis au bout', Ibid., 48–9. On de Gouda's mission see Pollen, *Papal Negotiations*, 113–61 and Forbes-Leith, *Narratives*, 63–79
3 Brodrick, *Canisius*, 455
4 G Sommervogel and A. de Backer, *Biblotheque de la Compagnie de Jésus* (Paris and Louvain, 1890–1960), 3 (2), 1635
5 *Saint Ignatius Loyola; Letters to Women*, ed. H. Rahner, SJ (Freiburg, 1960), 156–66 [Rahner, *Loyola Letters to Women*]
6 *DHGE*, XXI, col. 928; Rahner, *Loyola Letters to Women*, 164
7 O. Braunsberger, SJ, *Beati Petri Canisii Epistulae et Acta* (Freiburg, 1896–1923), I, 337–41 [Braunsberger, *Canisius*]; Brodrick, *Canisius*, 155; Rahner, *Loyola Letters to Women*, 164
8 *DHGE*, XXI, col. 929
9 P.J. Begheyn, SJ, 'Nik Goudanus en het Godsdienstgesprek van Worms in 1557' in *Archief voor de Geschiedenis van de Katholieke Kerk in Nederland*, XI (1969), 12–53; Brodrick, *Canisius*, 388–9
10 Brodrick, *Canisius*, 394
11 *Rheinische Akten zur Geschichte des Jesuitenordens 1542–82*, ed. J. Hansen (Bonn, 1896), 769–71; *DHGE*, XXI, col. 929
12 Pollen, *Papal Negotiations*,77–8
13 Ibid., 75
14 Ibid., 77–8
15 Ibid., 79–80, 102; *Angliae*, III, 399–400, 568–9
16 Pollen, *Papal Negotiations*, 92
17 Ibid., 92
18 A.W.K. Stevenson, 'Notes of an early sixteenth-century Scottish colony at Bergen-Op-Zoom and an altar there once dedicated to St. Ninian' *IR*, 26 (1975), 50–2
19 Pollen, *Papal Negotiations*, 102; *Angliae*, III, 399–400
20 Brodrick, *Canisius*, 456; Pollen, *Papal Negotiations*, 100–2
21 Pollen, *Papal Negotiations*, 104–5
22 Ibid., 108–10
23 Ibid., 103, 105–6, 154; the Society's records indicate that Hay and Crichton were admitted to the novitiate in December 1562, *Angliae*, III, 560, 564 and see Appendix 5
24 Pollen, *Papal Negotiations*, 105–6
25 Ibid., 130; the Angel Raphael was revered as a guide, companion and watcher, G.

Davidson, *A Dictionary of Angels*, (New York, 1967), 240
26 Foley, *Records*, III, 726–8 and see Appendix 1
27 *The Historie of Scotland wrytten First in Latin by the most reverend and worthy Jhone Leslie, Bishop of Rosse*, edd. E.G. Cody and W. Murison (STS, 1888,1895), II, 470
28 Watt, *Fasti*, 118; *Dunkeld Rentale*, 358–9, 361
29 *CSP Scot.*, I, nos. 797, 812, 918; *John Knox's History of the Reformation in Scotland*, ed. W.C. Dickinson (Edinburgh, 1949), I, 373 [Knox, *History*]
30 Pollen, *Papal Negotiations*, 114, 130, 147
31 The success of Sir Francis Walsingham and the English intelligence service is well-documented, for recent studies see A.Plowden, *The Elizabethan Secret Service* (Hemel Hempstead, 1991); A. Haynes, *The Elizabethan Secret Services* (Stroud, 2000); J. Bossy, *Under the Molehill: An Elizabethan Spy Story* (New Haven, 2001) [Bossy, *Under the Molehill*]; less well-known are the activities of Hugh Owen and the Catholic intelligencers, see A.J. Loomie, SJ, *The Spanish Elizabethans: The English Exiles at the Court of Philip II* (London, 1963), 52ff [Loomie, *Spanish Elizabethans*]; Pollen, *Papal Negotiations*, 131
32 *The Works of John Knox*, ed. D. Laing (Wodrow Society, 1846–64), II, 342 [Knox, *Works*]; for recent studies of John Knox see R.K. Marshall, *John Knox* (Edinburgh, 2000) and R. Graham, *John Knox: Democrat* (London, 2001)
33 Pollen, *Papal Negotiations*, 140–1
34 *CSP Scot.*, II, no.161
35 Pollen, *Papal Negotiations*, 142; David Riccio was Mary's Savoyard singer turned secretary, described by a contemporary as 'a man of no beautie or outwarde shape, for he was mishapen, evil favoured, and in visage very black, but for his fidelity, wisdom and virtue and his other good parts and qualities he was richly adorned', *History of Mary Queen of Scots, A Fragment, translated from the original French of Adam Blackwood*, ed. A. MacDonald (Maitland Club, 1834), 9–10
36 Pollen, *Papal Negotiations*, 131; on Crawford see J. Durkan, 'Education in the Century of the Reformation' and 'The Cultural Background in Sixteenth Century Scotland' in McRoberts, *Essays*, 165, 315; For an impression of the layout of Edinburgh around this period see Georg Braun and Franz Hogenberg's map of Edinburgh, *Edenburgum, Scotiae Metropolis*, c.1582 (National Library of Scotland) and the plans of the Canongate and the lower section of the Royal Mile in M. Lynch, *Edinburgh and the Reformation* (Edinburgh, 1981), 4, 12, 13, 27
37 Pollen, *Papal Negotiations*, 131–2; M. Philippson, *Histoire du règne de Marie Stuart* (Paris, 1891), II, 40–1
38 *Accounts of the Collectors of Thirds of Benefices 1561–1572*, ed. G. Donaldson (SHS, 1949), ixff [*TB*]
39 *CSP Foreign*, 1562, no.170
40 I. B. Cowan, 'The Roman Connection: Prospects for Counter Reformation during the Personal Reign of Mary, Queen of Scots', in *Mary Stewart, Queen in Three Kingdoms*, ed. M. Lynch, (Edinburgh, 1988), 108 [Lynch, *Queen in Three Kingdoms*]; Jenny Wormald in her recent biography of Mary is rather more forceful, accusing her of a religious and political sell-out in which she squandered the opportunities which had existed in 1561 for the preservation of the Catholic faith. She is also highly critical of her deception of de Gouda, describing what she said to him as 'simply dishonest, a pathetic defence of an untenable position', J. Wormald, *Mary, Queen of Scots: Politics, Passion and a Kingdom Lost* (London, 2001) , 126, 129 [Wormald, *Mary*]; David Starkey in his much acclaimed biography of Elizabeth I also questions Mary's loyalty to Rome and refers to her reinvention of herself as a Roman Catholic devóte following her flight to England, D. Starkey, *Elizabeth: Apprenticeship* (London, 2000), 321–2
41 Pollen, *Papal Negotiations*, 132; *A Diurnal of Remarkable Occurents that have passed within the country of Scotland, since the death of King James the Fourth till the year 1575*,

ed. T. Thomson (Bannatyne Club, 1833), 77, 79 [*Diurnal of Occurents*]; D. Hamilton, *The Healers: A history of medicine in Scotland* (Edinburgh, 1987), 32; In England, Thomas Bourchier, an English Franciscan, attributed Elizabeth's lack of faith to the failure of her bishops, describing them as 'dumb dogs who cannot bark, worse than Cerberus [the three-headed dog guarding the entrance to Hades], who not only have not barked but have betrayed the house of God to thieves and brigands', P.J. Holmes, *Resistance and Compromise: The Political Thought of the Elizabethan Catholics* (Cambridge, 1982), 55 [Holmes, *Resistance and Compromise*]

42 Pollen, *Papal Negotiations*, 133–4; 142–3

43 Ibid., 134; Dowden, *Bishops*, 207; Watt, *Fasti*, 78; J.H. Cockburn, *The Medieval Bishops of Dunblane and their Church* (Edinburgh, 1959), 215ff [Cockburn, *Dunblane*]

44 Pollen, *Papal Negotiations*, 137, 481, 483; Thomas Randolph was less complimentary about Chisholm and on the death of his uncle described Chisholm junior as 'lyke hym in conditions, savinge thys man hathe but ij childrene, whear thother had x or xij, bysydes that which he begotte upon his owne dawghter'. Chisholm, senior, apparently had eight daughters; *CSP Scot.*, II, nos. 124, 161

45 Pollen, *Papal Negotiations*, 417; Yellowlees, Dunkeld, 103ff; Watt, *Fasti*, 109, 357; Dowden, *Bishops*, 88–9

46 *Diurnal of Occurents*, 61

47 *CSP Scot*, I, no. 881

48 Knox, *History*, I, 335

49 *CSP Scot*, I, nos. 885, 886; M. Mahoney, 'The Scottish Hierarchy, 1513–1565', in McRoberts, *Essays*, 81; *CSP Domestic Elizabeth*, 1560–61, 454–5

50 *Dunkeld Rentale*, 317

51 M.J. Yellowlees, 'The Ecclestistical Establishment of the Diocese of Dunkeld at the Reformation', *IR*, 36, (1985), 78–81 [Yellowlees, Dunkeld at the Reformation]

52 Pollen, *Papal Negotiations*, 135; the lands of Clunie had been held by the bishops of Dunkeld since the fourteenth century. Bishop George Brown (1483–1515) was responsible for the construction of the small L plan castle in the early sixteenth century.

53 Ibid., 148

54 Ibid., 184

55 Ibid., 135

56 The wording of the commission to the Lairds of Arntilly and Kinvaid is quoted in D. McRoberts, 'Material Destruction Caused by the Scottish Reformation' in McRoberts, *Essays*, 442

57 J. Spottiswoode, *An Account of all the Religious Houses that were in Scotland at the time of the Reformation*, (Edinburgh, 1824), 430; Pollen, *Papal Negotiations*, 120n.; Forman left Scotland in 1576 and died in France in 1575, see M.B. Verschuur, 'The Perth Charterhouse in the sixteenth century', *IR*, 39 (1988), 1ff

58 *RMS*, IV, no. 1380

59 D. McRoberts, 'Material destruction caused by the Scottish Reformation' in McRoberts *Essays*, 459; Yellowlees, Dunkeld, 22–5; *Satirical Poems of the Time of the Reformation*, ed. J. Cranstoun (STS, 1891–3), I, 232 [Cranstoun, *Satirical Poems*]

60 Pollen, *Papal Negotiations*, 135; a similar accusation was made of the English clergy by a later English Jesuit, John Rastall, who described them as 'cobblers, weavers, tinkers, tanners, cardmakers, tapsters, fiddlers and gaolers', quoted in McCoog, *Our Way of Proceeding*, 45

61 Yellowlees, Dunkeld, 67ff; D.G. Mullan, *Episcopacy in Scotland: The History of an Idea 1560–1638* (Edinburgh, 1986), 17ff [Mullan, *Episcopacy*]; Kirk, *Patterns of Reform*, 154ff; Pollen, *Papal Negotiations*, 136

62 A. Bellesheim, *The History of the Catholic Church of Scotland* (Edinburgh, 1887–90), III, 58 [Bellesheim, *History*]; Forbes-Leith, *Narratives*, 80

63 Pollen, *Papal Negotiations*, 155; Benoist later became a popular preacher in France

and was known as 'le Pape des Halles'. Henri III of France appointed him as a religious adviser and in 1593 he was responsible for receiving Henri IV back into the Catholic church, see M. Wolfe, *The Conversion of Henri IV: Politics, Power and Religious Belief in Early Modern France* (Cambridge, Massachusetts, 1993), 135ff.

64 *Certane Tractatis for Reformatioun of Doctryne and Maneris in Scotland by Niniane Winzet*, ed. J.K. Hewison (Maitland Club, 1835), xvi-xvii

65 M. Dilworth, *The Scots in Franconia: A Century of Monastic Life* (Edinburgh, 1974), 23–31 [Dilworth, *Scots in Franconia*]; Brodrick, *Jesuits*, 200

66 Pollen, *Papal Negotiations*, 154, 161

67 *DHGE*, XXI, col. 929

68 Durkan identifies William Murdoch as a member of Crichton's faction, however, Robert Abercrombie, Stephen Wilson and, perhaps, William Crichton, were also involved. The faction comprised a number of the leading figures in the chapter, including the dean, James Hepburn, a cousin of James Hepburn, 4th Earl of Bothwell, his successor John Barton and the precentor, William Curll, whose family were leading Edinburgh Catholics. A significant number of canons and chaplains were also involved, along with three Franciscans, Robert Veitch, Father Leitch and Thomas Aitken. Veitch and Leitch were still active in Scotland in the 1580s and are mentioned in Robert Abercrombie's report of his mission of 1580, J. Durkan, 'William Murdoch and the Early Jesuit Mission in Scotland', *IR*, 35 (1984) 3ff [Durkan, Early Jesuit Mission]; Anderson, Narratives, I, 32; see also J.Durkan, 'Sidelights on the Early Jesuit Mission in Scotland', *Scottish Tradition*, XIII (1984–5), 34–45 [Durkan, Sidelights]

69 M.J. Yellowlees, 'Dunkeld and Nicholas de Gouda's Mission to Scotland, 1562', *IR*, 44 (1993) 53; 'Documents Illustrating Catholic Policy 1596–1598', ed. T.G. Law, in *Miscellany of the Scottish History Society First volume* (SHS, 1893), 49–50 [Law, Documents Illustrating Catholic Policy]

70 John Ogilvie was the eldest son of Walter Ogilvie of Drum, near Keith in Morayshire, and Agnes Elphinstone, who was a Catholic. She died when John was three.

71 F. Shearman, 'The Spanish Blanks' *IR*, 3 (1952), 83 [Shearman, Spanish Blanks]

72 *The Scots Peerage*, ed. Sir J.B. Paul (Edinburgh, 1904–14), V, 219–20 [*Scots Peerage*]

73 L. Carrez, *Catalogi Sociorum et Officiarum Provincae Companiae Societatis Jesu* (Châlons sur Marne, 1897–1914), I, 166–7 [Carrez, *Catalogi*]; *Angliae*, III, 564

74 Knox, *Works*, VI, 482, 485–512

75 A. Tyrie, *The Tyries of Drumkilbo, Dunnideer and Lunan* (Glasgow, 1893), 48

76 A.J. Warden, *Angus or Forfarshire, the Land and People* (Dundee, 1882), III, 210; *Rental Book of the Cistercian Abbey of Cupar-Angus*, ed. C. Rogers (Grampian Club, 1879–80), II, 248

77 *Charters of the Abbey of Inchcolm*, edd. D.E. Easson and A. Macdonald (SHS, 1938), 241–3; W.J. Anderson 'Narratives of the Scottish Reformation I. Report of Father Robert Abercrombie, S.J. in the year 1580', *IR*, 7 (1956), 28 [Anderson, Narratives I]; *DHGE*, I, col. 107

78 Knox, *History*, II, 175; Pollen, *Papal Negotiations*, 492, 495; J. Durkan and A. Ross, *Early Scottish Libraries* (Glasgow, 1961), 66, 139; *Dunkeld Rentale*, 347–8

79 Watt, *Fasti*, 118

80 *Bamff Charters 1232–1703* ed. J.H. Ramsay (Oxford, 1915), 100

81 Oliver, *Collections*, 9; Foley, *Records*, VII, 347–8; R. Darowski, 'John Hay, S.J., and the origins of philosophy in Lithuania', *IR*, 31 (1980), 7–15 [Darowski, John Hay]; W. Forbes Leith, SJ, *Pre-Reformation Scholars in Scotland in the XVIth Century* (Glasgow, 1915), 80–2 [Forbes Leith, *Pre-Reformation Scholars*]; *DNB*, IX, 267–8

82 *Dunkeld Rentale*, 358–61

83 *RSS*, v, no. 1638; SRO RH9/2/180 & 284

84 *RMS*, III, no. 1257; Watt, *Fasti*, 115, 257

85 *CSP Scot.*, I, nos. 797, 812, 918; Knox *History*, I, 373
86 *CSP Foreign, 1564–1565*, nos. 1703, 1711
87 *RMS*, III, no.3202; *RPC*, ii, 206; *RSS*, v, nos. 824, 2908, 3093; vi, no.2434; viii, nos. 800, 1677; *TB*, 100;
88 *Early Records of the University of St. Andrews*, ed. J.M. Anderson (SHS, 1926), 150–4, 255, 257, 259, 264 [*Early Records St. Andrews*]; *Acta Facultatis Artium Universitatis Sanctiandree, 1413–1588*, ed. A.I. Dunlop (SHS, 1964), II, 401–14 [*AFA*]
89 *AFA*, I, lxvii; *RMS*, IV, no.1277; *RSS*, iv, no. 1831; v, no. 2653; on Cranston's philosophical innovations see A. Broadie, *The Tradition of Scottish Philosophy* (Edinburgh, 1990), 78–82
90 McNeill, Scottish Entries, 72; J. Durkan, 'The French Connection in the Sixteenth and Early Seventeenth Centuries', in *Scotland and Europe 1200–1850*, ed. T.C. Smout (Edinburgh, 1986), 20
91 *AFA*, I, lxvii; *Register of the Ministers, Elders and Deacons of the Christian Congregation of St. Andrews*, ed. D.H. Fleming (SHS, 1889), I, 169–71
92 Anderson, Narratives I, 3
93 Bellesheim, *History*, III, 302; Yellowlees, Dunkeld, 116–7; Watt, *Fasti*, 100; Dowden, *Bishops*, 93
94 *RPC*, I, 629; *Diurnal of Occurents*, 78; *CSP Scot.*, II, no. 124; Yellowlees, Dunkeld, 115–7; Yellowlees, Dunkeld at the Reformation, 77–8

Chapter 3: Nests of Rats and Tombs for Jesuits

1 Pollen, *Papal Negotiations*, 148; Scottish students at Louvain included William Crichton (1561), Robert Abercrombie and James Gordon (1562), James Tyrie and William Murdoch (1563) and John Hay (1563–4), see J. Durkan, 'The Cultural Background in Sixteenth-Century Scotland', in McRoberts, *Essays*, 324–5; on Laínez and his involvement in the Colloquy of Poissy and the Council of Trent see J.H. Fichter, SJ, *James Laynez, Jesuit* (St Louis, 1944), 195ff
2 Pollen, *Papal Negotiations*, 151
3 Ibid., 479
4 Ibid., cxxxix; *Angliae*, III, 444–5
5 Carrez, *Catalogi*, I, 162, 166–7, 174–5; *DHGE*, I, col. 107; Pollen, *Papal Negotiations*, 486, O'Malley, *The First Jesuits*, 56; *Angliae*, III, 567–8; in 1604 Alexander McQuhirrie reported to Acquaviva that 'Father George Durie, brother of Father John, still survives: he lives among his relatives and friends, as forgetful as his brother was a most observant member of his order. Ours for many years now have had no concern for him'. Thank you to Father McCoog for this quotation which will be cited in his forthcoming *Innes Review* article on the Scottish Jesuits.
6 *Angliae*, III, 455–6, 458–9, 567–9; Ganss, *Constitutions*, 92ff
7 Brodrick, *Jesuits*, 183; on the Jesuit houses in Rome see *Gregory Martin, Roma Sancta 1581*, ed. G.B. Parks (Rome, 1969), 58ff. Gregory Martin was a close friend of Edmund Campion.
8 *Angliae*, III, 567–9; see Ganss, *Constitutions*, 349–56 on the diversity of grades of priests within the Society.
9 *Angliae*, II, 280; *English and Welsh Jesuits 1555–1650, Part II: G-Z*, ed. T.J. McCoog, SJ (CRS, 1995), 205
10 Pollen, *Papal Negotiations*, 510–2; *Records of the Scots Colleges*, (New Spalding Club, 1906), I , 7 [*Records of the Scots Colleges*]
11 *Broët*, 91
12 *Epistolae et Acta patris Iacobi Laínii secundi praepositi generalis Societatis Iesu*, ed. E. Astudillo, SJ, (MHSI, Madrid, 1912–16), VII, 629

13 Martin, *The Jesuit Mind*, 54

14 J. Brodrick, SJ, *The Life and Work of Blessed Robert Francis Cardinal Bellarmine, S.J. 1542–1621* (London, 1928), I, 94 [Brodrick, *Bellarmine*]

15 Martin, *The Jesuit Mind*, 12, 17; H. Fouqueray, SJ, *Histoire de la Compagnie de Jésus en France des origines à la supression (1528–1762)* (Paris, 1910–25), I, 515 [Fouqueray, *Histoire*]

16 Pollen, *Papal Negotiations*, 496; C. Hollis, *A History of the Jesuits* (London, 1968), 22

17 H. Chadwick, SJ, 'The Scots College, Douai, 1580–1613', *English Historical Review*, 56 (1941), 571ff [Chadwick, Scots College]

18 *Dodd's Church History of England*, ed. M.A. Tierney, (London, 1841) IV, 122ff [*Dodd's Church History*]

19 *The First and Second Diaries of the English College , Douay*, ed. T.F. Knox (London, 1878), 157; some idea of life in the Scots College may be gleaned from Anthony Munday's recollections of his time as a student at the English College, *Anthony Munday: The English Romayne Lyfe 1582*, ed. G.B. Harrison (London, 1925). Munday later worked as a spy for the notorious pursuivant, Richard Topcliffe.

20 *Records of the Scots Colleges*, I, 5; *Calendar of the Manuscripts of the Most Hon. The Marquis of Salisbury K.G. preserved at Hatfield House* (HMC, 1883–), V, 126 [HMC, *Salisbury*]

21 On the Scots College in Rome and the politics surrounding its foundation see *The Scots College Rome 1600–2000*, ed. R. McCluskey (Edinburgh, 2000), the papal bull is quoted on pages 151–2; see also W.J. Anderson, 'Abbe Paul MacPherson's History of the Scots College, Rome', *IR*, 12 (1961), 3–172

22 *Records of the Scots Colleges*, I, 5, 9, 10; Chadwick, Scots College, 583–403

23 A.O. Meyer, *England and the Catholic Church under Queen Elizabeth* (London, 1916), 114ff [Meyer, *England and the Catholic Church*]; 'The Antiquity of the Christian Religion of the Scots', ed. H.D.G. Law, in *Miscellany of the Scottish History Society Second volume* (Edinburgh, 1904), 131ff; on Thomson see also Pollen, *Papal Negotiations*, 404–5; Edwards, *Robert Persons*, 170; *Records of the Scots Colleges*, I, 1ff

24 Pollen, *Papal Negotiations*, 479

25 E. Piaget, *Histoire de l'etablissement des Jesuites en France (1540–1640)* (Leiden, 1893), 65; *Les Establissement des Jésuites en France depuis quatres siécles*, ed. P. Delattre, SJ, (Enghien, 1949–57), II, cols. 1508, 1561; D.F. Zapico, SJ, 'La Province d'Aquitaine de la Compagnie de Jésus d'après son plus ancien catalogue (1566)', *AHSI*, 5 (1936), 272, 283; Martin, *The Jesuit Mind*, 217

26 Pollen, *Papal Negotiations*, 495

27 Martin, *The Jesuit Mind*, 55–7, 70, 83, 99, 105–7, 200, 203

28 Ibid., 58–9, 152

29 Ibid., 158, 165

30 Pollen, *Papal Negotiations*, 480; on the Jesuits in Austria and their relations with the Imperial Court see H. Louthan, *The quest for compromise: Peacemakers in Counter-Reformation Vienna* (Cambridge, 1997), 112–3, 129–31 [Louthan, *The quest for compromise*]

31 Pollen, *Papal Negotiations*, 483; Brodrick, *Canisius*, 580

32 Pollen, *Papal Negotiations*, 480, 486

33 Ibid., 486; *Relations politiques de la France et de L'Espagne avec L'Ecosse au XVIème Siecle*, ed. A. Teulet (Paris, 1862), I, 312–7 [Teulet, *Relations*]

34 Pollen, *Papal Negotiations*, 197, 488–96; HMC, *Salisbury*, III, 172–3

35 Pollen, *Papal Negotiations*, 200; C. Bingham, *Darnley* (London, 1997), 108ff; S. Adams, 'The Release of Lord Darnley and the Failure of Amity', in Lynch, *Queen in Three Kingdoms*, 123ff

36 Pollen, *Papal Negotiations*, 489, 491

37 Ibid., 370, 492, 496, 521

38 Ibid., 497; on Chisholm's second mission to Scotland and Laureo's nunciature see sections VII and VIII, ibid., 232ff
39 Ibid., 499
40 On Darbyshire see Foley, *Records*, III, 710; VII, 193–4
41 *Miscellanea Recusant Rolls*, ed. C. Talbot (CRS, vol. 53, 1960), 206–7, Darbyshire was described as being 'About 50 years of adge, leane of bodye and face, his bearde cute shorte of abrowne collor mixed with graye heares, his face full of wrinkles, his nose somewhat flate'.
42 Pollen, *Papal Negotiations*, 501; *Angliae*, II, 286; *Angliae*, III, 564
43 Pollen, *Papal Negotiations*, 497
44 Ibid., 404ff, 497, 500; considerable doubt has been expressed about the authorship of the report which has been wrongly attributed to James Tyrie. It was probably the work of George Thomson, a student of Pont-à-Mousson in 1581 and later principal of the college at Maximin in Provence, *Records of the Scots Colleges*, I, 2; J. Durkan, 'The identity of George Thomson, Catholic contraversialist', *IR*, 31 (1980), 45–6
45 Pollen, *Papal Negotiations*, 274–8
46 Ibid., cxii, 278; Pollen argues that Mondovi's proposals were not as sanguine as they appear. The other *sclerati* named were Argyll, Morton, Lethington, Bellenden and MacGill.
47 Ibid., 351
48 Ibid., 369, 393, 507–8
49 On Mary's defeat and flight into exile see A. Fraser, *Mary Queen of Scots* (London, 1981), 399ff [Fraser, *Mary*]; I.B. Cowan, *The Enigma of Mary Stuart* (London, 1972), 150ff [Cowan, *Mary Stuart*]; P.J. Holmes, 'Mary Stewart in England', in Lynch, *Queen in Three Kingdoms*, 195ff; J. Mackay, *In My End is My Beginning, A Life of Mary Queen of Scots* (Edinburgh, 2000), 191ff [Mackay, *Mary*]; Wormald, *Mary*, 170ff
50 Oliver, *Collections*, 9; Foley, *Records*, VII, 347, 1461; *DNB*, IX, 255; *DHGE*, XXIII, col. 21; *Angliae*, III, 564
51 Pollen, *Papal Negotiations*, 146, 148
52 Ibid., 480, 485; Foley, *Records*, VII, 2
53 Pollen, *Papal Negotiations*, 480–1; Broderick, *Canisius*, 566–7
54 Ibid., 485
55 Anderson, Narratives I, 27ff; M. Murphy, 'Robert Abercromby S.J. (1536–1613) and the Baltic Counter-Reformation', *IR*, 50 (1999), 58ff [Murphy, Robert Abercromby]; Oliver, *Collections*, 1; Foley, *Records*, VII, 2
56 *RPC*, ii, 334; Pollen, *Papal Negotiations*, 506; Watt, *Fasti*, 115
57 Durkan, Early Jesuit Mission, 3ff; Oliver, *Collections*, 19; Foley, *Records*, VII, 533
58 Pollen, *Papal Negotiations*, 148, 485; Oliver, *Collections*, 24; Foley, *Records*, VII, 792
59 M. Taylor, 'The Conflicting Doctrines of the Scottish Reformation', in McRoberts, *Essays*, 271; *Catholic Tractates of the Sixteenth Century 1573–1600* ed. T. G. Law (STS, 1901), 1ff [Law, *Tractates*]; Forbes Leith, *Pre-Reformation Scholars*, 73; on Tyrie and Knox and the latter's doctrine of the Church see T.F. Torrance, *Scottish Theology from John Knox to John McLeod Campbell* (Edinburgh, 1996), 26–34
60 M. Taylor, The Conflicting Doctrines of the Scottish Reformation' in McRoberts, *Essays*, 271; Law, *Tractates*, 33ff
61 T. McCrie, *Life of Andrew Melville* (Edinburgh, 1824), I, 56 [McCrie, *Melville*]; *The Diary of Mr James Melvill, 1556–1601*, ed. G.R. Kinloch (Bannatyne Club, 1829), 34 [Melville, *Diary*]
62 Oliver, *Collections*, 7–8; Foley, *Records*, VII, 309; *DNB*, VIII, 205–6; *Acts and Proceedings of the General Assemblies of the Kirk of Scotland from the year M.D.LX*, ed. T. Thomson (Bannatyne Club, 1839–45), II, 706, 725 [*BUK*]; Forbes Leith, *Pre-Reformation Scholars*, 70–2

63 Pollen, *Papal Negotiations*, 480; *Scots Peerage*, V, 219–20
64 Pollen, *Papal Negotiations*, 500–1; H. Chadwick, SJ, 'A Memoir of Father Hay S.I.', *AHSI*, 8 (1939), 82 [Edmund Hay's Memoir]
65 Darowski, John Hay, 8; *DNB*, IX, 267; Forbes-Leith, *Narratives*, 141; Oliver, *Collections*, 9; Foley, *Records*, VII, 347
66 Darowski, John Hay, 7–9;
67 Foley, *Records*, VII, 347–8; Forbes Leith, *Pre-Reformation Scholars*, 81
68 See the entries for Aquinas and Aristotle in *The Catholic Encyclopedia*, now on-line on www.newadvent.org/cathen
69 Dilworth, *Scots in Franconia*, 24
70 Forbes Leith, *Pre-Reformation Scholars*, 81; Law, *Tractates*, xxxvi
71 *Early Records St. Andrews*, 154, 259; *The History of the Kirk of Scotland by Mr David Calderwood sometime minister of Crailing*, ed. T. Thomson (Wodrow Society, 1842–9), III, 405–6 [Calderwood, *History*]
72 *Thomae Dempsteri Historia Ecclesiastica Gentis Scotorum: sive, De Scriptoribus Scotis*, ed. D. Irving (Bannatyne Club, 1829), II, 586; Smeaton was undoubtedly a man of some ability and was later described by James Melville as one of the 'thrie of the lernedest in Europe', the others being Andrew Melville and Alexander Arbuthnot, the principals of Glasgow and Aberdeen Universities, Melville, *Diary*, 60
73 H. Scott, *Fasti Ecclesiae Scoticanae* (Edinburgh, 1915–50), III, 162, 410; *BUK*, II, 612; J. Durkan and J. Kirk, *The University of Glasgow 1451–1577* (Glasgow, 1977), 334–5; Melville, *Diary*, 57; *DNB*, XVIII, 404–5

Chapter 4: The Establishment of the Scottish Mission

1 For the relationship between Marianism, Catholicism and conservatism see G. Donaldson, *All the Queen's Men: Power and politics in Mary Stewart's Scotland* (London, 1983), 8 [Donaldson, *All the Queen's Men*]
2 J.H. Burns, 'The Political Background of the Reformation, 1513–1625', in McRoberts, *Essays*, 25; Bellesheim, *History*, III, 223
3 Bellesheim, *History*, III, 230; On the conclusion of the civil war see G.R. Hewitt, *Scotland under Morton 1572–80* (Edinburgh, 1982), 19ff [Hewitt, *Morton*]; *CSP Foreign*, 1572–1574, no. 1047; *Diurnal of Occurents*, 341; *The Historie and Life of King James the Sext*, ed. T. Thomson (Bannatyne Club, 1825), 71–2 [*Hist.KJS*]; *RPC*, ii, 334; *Accounts of the Lord High Treasurer of Scotland*, edd. T Dickson and Sir J.B. Paul (Edinburgh, 1877–1916), XII, 379
4 Melville, *Diary*, 47; *CSP Domestic Addenda*, 1566–1579, 523; Hewitt, *Morton*, 83ff; Donaldson, *All the Queen's Men*, 126; Bellesheim, *History*, III, 223
5 Kirk, *Patterns of Reform*, 96ff and 305ff; Yellowlees, Dunkeld, 25–57, 278–80; Hewitt, *Morton*, 83ff
6 M. Lynch, *Scotland: A New History* (London, 1991), 227ff; Hewitt, *Morton*, 103ff; D. Shaw, *The General Assemblies of the Church of Scotland 1560–1600* (Edinburgh, 1964), 51–6; Kirk, *Patterns of Reform*, 344ff
7 W.J. Anderson, 'Narratives of the Scottish Reformation, II. Thomas Innes on Catholicism in Scotland, 1560–1653, *IR*, 7 (1956), 117–8 [Anderson, Narratives II]; there is no study of the role of secular priests within the Scottish Mission, but for an insight into the work of a later secular priest see *A Breiffe Narration of the Services Done to Three Noble Ladyes by Gilbert Blackhal Preist of the Scots Mission in France, in the Low Countries and in Scotland 1631–1649*, ed. J.Stuart (Spalding Club, 1844)
8 Anderson, Narratives II, 119; On the apparent rivalry between Jesuits and seculars see M.V. Hay, *The Blairs Papers (1603–1660)* (London, 1929), 72ff [Hay, *Blairs Papers*]; despite what Blair says there is little evidence to support claims of any rivalry

between Jesuits and seculars in Scotland in the immediate post-Reformation period.

9 Watt, *Fasti*, 100; Dowden, *Bishops*, 93; NLS Adv. MSS 17.1.3 fos. 367, 369; Hewitt, *Morton*, 108; *RSS*, VI, no. 2812; *BUK*, I, 270, 331–2, 340–1, 350–1; Calderwood, *History*, III, 347–8; *RPC*, II, 363–4

10 McCoog, *Our Way of Proceeding*, 34; O'Malley, *The First Jesuits*, 28

11 'Some Correspondence of Cardinal Allen, 1579–1585 from the Jesuit Archives', ed. P. Ryan, SJ, in *Miscellanea VII* (CRS, vol.9, 1911), 45, 62 [Allen Correspondence]; Mullett, *Catholic Reformation*, 99–100; On the early English Jesuits see T.H. Clancy, SJ, 'The First Generation of English Jesuits 1555–1585', *AHSI*, 57 (1988), 137–62; on Pole and his relationship with the Society see McCoog, *Essays*, 21ff

12 Edwards, *Robert Persons*, 11–13

13 *The Letters and Memorials of William Cardinal Allen (1532–1594)* ed. T. F. Knox (London, 1882), 38 [Knox, *Cardinal Allen*]

14 R. Simpson, *Edmund Campion* (London, 1896), 136ff; B. Basset, SJ, *The English Jesuits* (London, 1967), 33–4 [Basset, *English Jesuits*]; Knox, *Cardinal Allen*, 68–9

15 More, *Historia*, 71

16 Teulet, *Relations*, V, 143–8

17 Martin, *Jesuit Politicians*, 63–5; the college was well established by 1584, but declined after 1588 following the assassination of Guise. In 1594 the students were transferred to St Omer.

18 *CSP Spanish*, II, 646–7

19 Teulet, *Relations*, V, 144 ff; *CSP Spanish*, III, 4–7

20 On the Negative Confession see G. Donaldson, *Scottish Historical Documents* (Edinburgh, 1974), 150–3 [Donaldson, *Scottish Historical Documents*]

21 Martin, *Jesuit Politicians*, 68

22 Ibid., 68–9

23 Ibid., 68; Basset, *English Jesuits*, 34

24 Forbes-Leith, *Narratives*, 141–65

25 Ibid., 145–6

26 *RPC*, III, 204

27 Law, *Tractates*, 31–70; Forbes Leith, *Pre-Reformation Scholars*, 79–82

28 Oliver, *Collections*, 1; Foley, *Records*, VII, 2; Anderson, Narratives I, 27–8

29 Anderson, Narratives I, 31–2; *Estimates of the Scottish Nobility during the Minority of James the Sixth*, ed. C. Rogers (Grampian Club, 1873), 32

30 Anderson, Narratives I, 31–2, 34–5, 40

31 As with Mary there is a vast amount of secondary material on James; See D. H Willson, *King James VI and I* (New York, 1967) [Willson, *James VI and I*]; M. Lee, Jr., *John Maitland of Thirlestane and the Foundation of Stewart Despotism in Scotland* (Princeton, New Jersey, 1959) [Lee, *Maitland*]; A. Fraser, *King James VI of Scotland and I of England* (London, 1977) and M. Lee, *Great Britain's Solomon: James VI and I in His Three Kingdoms* (Urbana, Ill., 1990) are excellent studies. For two comprehensive modern studies with extensive bibliographies and notes see *The Reign of James VI*, edd. J. Goodare and M. Lynch (East Linton, 2000) [Goodare and Lynch, *James VI*] and W.B. Patterson, *King James VI and I and the Reunion of Christendom* (Cambridge, 2000) [Patterson, *James VI and I*]

32 Anderson, Narratives I, 36ff

33 Murphy, *Robert Abercromby*, 64–5

34 T. M. McCoog, SJ, 'Playing the Champion: The Role of Disputation in the Jesuit Mission', in McCoog, *Essays*, 139; McCoog, *Our Way of Proceeding*, 177–8

Chapter 5: The Sacred Expedition to Scotland

1 *CSP Spanish*, III, 370; *The Correspondence of Robert Bowes of Aske, Esquire, The Ambassador of Queen Elizabeth in the Court of Scotland*, ed. J. Stevenson (Surtees Society, 1842), 32 [*Bowes, Correspondence*]; Forbes-Leith, *Narratives*, 136
2 *Bowes, Correspondence*, 49, 64, 84
3 A. Ross, 'Reformation and Repression', in McRoberts, *Essays*, 398–9; J.H. Burns, 'Nicol Burne: plane disputation bayth at libertie and in persone', *IR*, 50 (1999), 123–4; Cranstoun, *Satirical Poems*, I, 333–45
4 *BUK*, II, 512, 515ff; Calderwood, *History*, III, 801ff; V, 407ff; Donaldson, *Scottish Historical Documents*, 151
5 Martin, *Jesuit Politicians*, 63–5
6 Ibid., 65; for discussions of the Jesuit way of proceeding see McCoog, *Our Way of Proceeding*, 265ff; O'Malley, *The First Jesuits*, 370ff
7 'The Memoirs of Father Robert Persons, Memoir I, Father Persons Autobiography', ed. J.H. Pollen, SJ in *Miscellanea II* (CRS, vol. 2, 1906), 26 [Persons Autobiography]; Foley, *Records*, III, 117ff; VII, 225–6; on Campion see Waugh, *Saint Edmund Campion*. His companion Emerson was described by John Gerard, SJ, as 'a very little man in build, but in endurance and sturdiness of spirit he was as great as you could wish anybody to be', *John Gerard: The Autobiography of an Elizabethan*, trans. P.Caraman (London, 1951), 78
8 More, *Historia*, 77ff
9 Ibid., 353; Campion's *Brag* is much quoted, but the following section is worth repeating: 'And touching our Society be it known to you that we have made a league-all the Jesuits of the world, whose succession and multitude must overreach all the practices of England-cheerfully to carry the cross you shall lay upon us and never to despair your recovery, while we have a man left to enjoy your Tyburn, or to be racked with your torments or consumed with your prisons. The expense is reckoned, the enterprise is begun, it is of God, it cannot be withstood. So the faith is planted, so it must be restored', Basset, *English Jesuits*, 456. Persons also made a similar mission statement considered by some to be the better of the two: '... you are persecuting a corporation that will never die, and sooner will your hearts and hands, sated with blood fail you, than will there be lacking men, eminent in virtue and learning, who will be sent by this Society and allow their blood to be shed by you for this cause', quoted in full in 'Persons' Confession of Faith for the London Magistrates 19 July 1580' in *Persons Letters*, 35–41, and see McCoog, *Our Way of Proceeding*, 146–8. On the English Catholic community at home and abroad see P. Guilday, *The English Catholic Refugees on the Continent, 1558–1795* (London, 1914); Meyer, *England and the Catholic Church* ; J.H. Pollen, SJ, *The English Catholics in the Reign of Elizabeth: A Study of Their Politics, Civil Life and Government* (London, 1920); Loomie, *The Spanish Elizabethans*; Pritchard, *Catholic Loyalism*; J. Bossy, *The English Catholic Community, 1570–1850* (London, 1975); Holmes, *Resistance and Compromise*; A. Plowden, *Danger to Elizabeth: The Catholics under Elizabeth I* (London, 1974), S. Brigden, *New Worlds, Lost Worlds: The Rule of the Tudors 1485–1603* (London, 2000)
10 *Persons Letters*, 109; Forbes-Leith, *Narratives*, 166
11 *Persons Letters*, xlii, 108–10; Martin, *Jesuit Politicians*, 68; McCoog, *Our Way of Proceeding*, 178ff; *CSP Spanish*, III, 170; Forbes-Leith, *Narratives*, 166; G. Anstruther, OP, *The Seminary Priests, A Dictionary of the Secular Clergy of England and Wales 1558–1850, 1, Elizabethan* (Gateshead, 1968), 374 [Anstruther, *Seminary Priests*]; 'The Memoirs of Robert Persons, Memoir IV, Punti per la Missione d'Inghilterra', ed. J.H. Pollen, SJ, in *Miscellanea* IV (CRS, vol.4, 1907), 21 [Persons Punti]; Edwards, *Robert Persons*, 58–60; Law, *Essays*, 220, 226–8, 234
12 *Persons Letters*, 108ff; Forbes-Leith, *Narratives*, 166ff

13 En route to Edinburgh he also visited the Baron of Grencknols, a Catholic 'in the frigid manner which is customary here', Forbes-Leith, *Narratives*, 170; Law, *Essays*, 225; *Persons Letters*, 110ff: *CSP Spanish*, III, 194

14 *CSP Spanish*, III, 194; On Heywood see Foley, *Records*, VII, 351–2; D. Flynn, 'Out of Step: Six Supplementary Notes on Jasper Heywood', in McCoog, *Essays*, 179ff; *Angliae*, II, 351–2; *Unpublished Documents relating to the English Martyrs, vol.1, 1584–1603*, ed. J.H.Pollen, SJ (CRS, vol.5, 1908), 60 [*English Martyrs*]

15 *CSP Spanish*, III, 235; *Persons Letters*, 112ff; Forbes-Leith, *Narratives*, 172ff

16 Persons Punti, 23; *CSP Spanish*, III, 194, 235

17 *CSP Spanish*, III, 195–6; *Persons Letters*, xlvii-xlviii

18 Allen Correspondence, 93, 101; *Persons Letters*, 239; 'Tower Bills 1575–1589', ed. J.H. Pollen, SJ in *Miscellanea III* (CRS, vol. 3, 1906), 17 [Tower Bills]; *English Martyrs*, 102–3; Persons Punti, 113; Foley, *Records*, VII, 350; More, *Historia*, 172–3

19 Edwards, *Robert Persons*, 170; Anstruther, *Seminary Priests*, 174–5

20 *CSP Spanish*, III, 235, 286; More, *Historia*, 154; Persons Punti, 21, 23, 24; *Persons Letters*, 125–6

21 *CSP Spanish*, III, 265, 276; Persons Punti, 57

22 *CSP Scot.*, VI, no. 86; Forbes-Leith, *Narratives*, 178–9

23 Anderson, Narratives II, 119–20;

24 Persons Punti, 23, 57, 59; Knox, *Cardinal Allen*, 117, 129; *CSP Spanish*, III, 349, 370; McCoog, *Our Way of Proceeding*, 181ff; Martin, *Jesuit Politicians*, 68ff; Persons Autobiography, 30

25 Forbes-Leith, *Narratives*, 177–8; Bellesheim, *History*, III, 261; *Persons Letters*, 114–7; *CSP Spanish*, III, 349

26 Martin, *Jesuit Politicians*, 69

27 *CSP Spanish*, III, 320; Edwards, *Robert Persons*, 64, 68

28 *CSP Spanish*, III, 285–9, 291; Martin, *Jesuit Politicians*, 70

29 On the consolidation of the Kirk in Scotland see Kirk, *Patterns of Reform*, 96ff; Yellowlees, Dunkeld, chapters 2 and 3, 90ff; M. Lynch, 'Preaching to the Converted?: Perspectives on the Scottish Reformation', in *The Renaissance in Scotland: Studies in Literature, Religion, History and Culture*, edd. A.A. MacDonald and others (Leiden, 1994), 323ff; for studies of recusant activity in Scotland see Cowan, *Scottish Reformation*, 159ff and M.B.H. Sanderson, 'Catholic recusancy in Scotland in the sixteenth century', *IR*, 21 (1970), 87–107

30 Forbes-Leith, *Narratives*, 174–5; Bellesheim, *History*, III, 261

31 Persons Punti, 58; J. Kretzschmar, *Die Invasionsprojekte der katolischen Mächte gegen England zur Zeits Elisabeths* (Leipzig, 1892), 123 [Kretzschmar, *Invasionsprojekte*]; Teulet, *Relations*, V, 235–8; Forbes-Leith, *Narratives*, 181; for William Crichton's memoir of this period, 'Of the Scottish Mission: Certain points to be noted to serve for the History of the Society' see *Mary Queen of Scots and the Babington Plot*, ed. J.H. Pollen, SJ (SHS, 1922), 162 [William Crichton's Memoir]

32 William Crichton's Memoir, 162–3; Persons Punti, 61; Teulet, *Relations*, V, 237; Kretzschmar, *Invasionsprojekte*, 123–4, 128,130

33 Kretzschmar, *Invasionsprojekte.*, 123–4, 128, 129–30; Teulet, *Relations*, V, 235–6; *CSP Spanish*, III, 316, 362; William Crichton's Memoir, 163; Persons Punti, 60; Martin, *Jesuit Politicians*, 72

34 Law, *Essays*, 236–7, 239; *Calendar of Letters and Papers relating to the Affairs of the Borders of England and Scotland*, ed. J.Bain (Edinburgh, 1894–6), I, 85 [*Border Papers*]

35 Persons Punti, 59; *CSP Spanish*, III, 322–3, 362; Knox, *Cardinal Allen*, 129; Kretzschmar, *Invasionsprojekte*, 129; Forbes Leith, *Narratives*, 182; William Crichton's Memoir, 163

36 Martin, *Jesuit Politicians*, 73; *CSP Spanish*, III, 330–3, 362, 370–3, 379, 392; Teulet, *Relations*, V, 257–8; Kretzschmar, *Invasionsprojekte*, 131–5

37 Teulet, *Relations*, V, 244ff; Kretzschmar, *Invasionsprojekte*, 131–5; Persons Autobiography, 31; *Persons Letters*, 158–66

38 *Persons Letters*, 146–7, 158–66

39 Teulet, *Relations*, V, 244ff; Knox, *Cardinal Allen*, 405–6; *Persons Letters*, 146–8; McCoog, *Our Way of Proceeding*, 131; *CSP Spanish*, III, 371

40 J.A. Froude, *History of England* (London, 1870), XI, 248 [Froude, *History*]

41 *CSP Spanish*, III, 363, 377; Persons Punti, 61

42 Persons Punti, 61

43 Persons Autobiography, 31; *CSP Spanish*, III, 378; Kretzschmar, *Invasionsprojekte*, 148; *Persons Letters*, 168; Teulet, *Relations*, V, 254–7; Martin, *Jesuit Politicians*, 72

44 Persons Autobiography, 31; Persons Punti, 61, 63; Kretzschmar, *Invasionsprojekte*, 156–8; *Persons Letters*, 170–1

45 Calderwood, *History*, III, 635–6, 637ff; *CSP Spanish*, III, 438–9; *RPC*, III, 506–9

46 *CSP Spanish*, III, 400–1; *RPC*, III, 509–11.; Teulet, *Relations*, III, 142; Calderwood, *History*, III, 693; *The History of the Church of Scotland. By John Spottiswoode, Archbishop of St Andrews*, ed. M. Russell (Bannatyne Club, 1850), II, 297–8 [Spottiswoode, *History*]; *CSP Scot.* VI, no. 545; Martin, *Jesuit Politicians*, 106; Forbes-Leith, *Narratives*, 183

47 *CSP Spanish*, III, 401–2; While in England Lennox met with de la Mothe Fénélon, *Warrender Papers*, ed. A.I. Cameron (SHS, 1931–2), I, 153

48 *CSP Scot.*, VI, no. 334; Kretzschmar, *Invasionsprojekte*, 166; Persons Punti, 23; Calderwood, *History*, III, 702–3; *Bowes Correspondence*, 372–3

49 *Bowes Correspondence.*, 372–3; Calderwood, *History*, III, 702; IV, 394, 430; Forbes-Leith, *Narratives*, 177

50 *Bowes Correspondence*, 375, 382–3, 389, 391, 485

51 Ibid., 399, 416, 508, 513; Persons Punti, 93; *CSP Spanish*, III, 460, 503; Knox, *Cardinal Allen*, 191–2; *Warrender Papers*, I, 162, 247; one account states that Mowbray escaped from Edinburgh Castle but fell and died from his injuries. The next day the corpse was strung up and quartered. His friends claimed that he had been strangled, but there is no evidence to corroborate this, Spottiswoode, *History*, III, 107

52 Teulet, *Relations*, V, 280ff; Kretzschmar, *Invasionsprojekte*, 166, 171

53 Knox, *Cardinal Allen*, 206–7; *Persons Letters*, 185–6; 348–52; Teulet, *Relations*, V, 307–11,316–21

54 Martin, *Jesuit Politicians*, 114

55 *Persons Letters*, 196–7; *CSP Scot.*, VII, no. 247; A. Lang, *A History of Scotland* (Edinburgh, 1902), II, 306

56 *The Acts of the Parliaments of Scotland*, edd. T.Thomson and C.Innes (Edinburgh, 1814–75), III, 292–312 [*APS*]; Calderwood, *History*, IV, 338; see also J. Goodare, *State and Society in Early Modern Scotland* (Oxford, 1999), 186, 201–3 and Lee, *Maitland*, 53ff. Episcopacy in various forms survived until 1638 and was restored in 1660.

57 Forbes-Leith, *Narratives*, 189–92; *Persons Letters*, 213

58 *Persons Letters*, 221–2

59 Edwards, *Robert Persons*, 107, 117ff; McCoog, *Our Way of Proceeding*, 203–4, 208; *Persons Letters*, 218, 222; Forbes-Leith, *Narratives*, 200–1; Persons Punti, 154–7

60 McCoog, *Our Way of Proceeding*, 209

61 *Persons Letters*, 254, 258

62 HMC, *Salisbury*, III, 107, 157, 173; Forbes-Leith, *Narratives*, 206; K. Brown, 'The Making of a *Politique*: The Counter Reformation and the Regional Politics of John, Eighth Lord Maxwell', *SHR*, LXVI (1987), 158–9 [Brown, Maxwell]

63 *Persons Letters*, 307; on Holt's later career see Foley, *Records*, VII, 368–9, 1231–46; Oliver, *Collections*, 102–3; *DNB*, IX, 1102–3

Chapter 6: Shaking off the Yoke of the Heretics

1 Martin, *Jesuit Politicians*, 114; McCoog, *Our Way of Proceeding*, 201–2; Forbes-Leith, *Narratives*, 196–7
2 Edwards, *Robert Persons*, 275; William Crichton's Memoir, 162
3 Persons Punti, 147
4 McCoog, *Our Way of Proceeding*, 205 & n.
5 William Crichton's Memoir, 163; *CSP Scot.*,VII, no. 297; *Persons Letters*, lxiv, 254
6 *DNB*, V, 93–4; P.F. Tytler, *History of Scotland* (Edinburgh, 1841–3), VIII, 216 [Tytler, *History*]; Bellesheim, *History*, III, 337; Froude, *History*, XI, 513–4; Law, *Essays*, 306
7 From an engraving by Cornelius Danckerts in the British Library entitled 'Popish Plots and Treasons from the Beginning of the Reign of Queen Elizabeth', BM PS 318 013 [Popish Plots and Treasons]
8 Law, *Essays*, 305.
9 Bellesheim, *History*, III, 337; Law, *Essays*, 220, where he points out that there is scarcely a paragraph without a mistake in Froude's chapter 'The Jesuits in Scotland', see chapter LXV, 227–334
10 On Waad see *DNB*, XX, 401–4; Law, *Essays*, 306–7; P.W. Hasler, *The History of Parliament, The House of Commons, 1558–1603*, III, Members M–Z (London, 1981), 560–2 [Hasler, *House of Commons*]
11 Knox, *Cardinal Allen*, 425–34; see Hicks, *An Elizabethan Problem: Some Aspects of the Careers of Two Exile Adventurers* (London, 1964), 235–8, which casts doubt on the authenticity of Crichton's confession [Hicks, *An Elizabethan Problem*]; Froude, *History*, XII, 41; *The Ven. Philip Howard Earl of Arundel 1557–1595*, ed. J.H. Pollen, SJ, and W. MacMahon, SJ, (CRS, vol. 21, 1919) , 289ff [*Arundel*]; On Popham see Hasler, *House of Commons*, III, Members M–Z, 234–6
12 *CSP Spanish*, III, 532; Foley, *Records*, VII, 247; William Crichton's Memoir, 164; *Angliae*, I, 80, II, 303; on Nicholas Faunt see Hasler, *House of Commons*, II, Members D–L, 109–10
13 *CSP Foreign,* August 1584–August 1585, 107, 310
14 Tower Bills, 18–24; 'Official Lists of Catholic Prisoners During the Reign of Queen Elizabeth 1581 to 1602', ed. J.H. Pollen, SJ, in *Miscellanea II*, (CRS, vol.2, 1906), 239; for a recent study of life in the Tower and accounts of Addy and Crichton's imprisonment see B.A. Harrison, *A Tudor Journal: The Diary of a Priest in the Tower 1580–1585* (London, 2000) [Harrison, *Tudor Journal*]
15 *Persons Letters*, 254, 262, 268
16 *English Martyrs*, 319–21; Acquaviva was more concerned about Weston and Emerson
17 Forbes-Leith, *Narratives*, 199
18 *Arundel*, 70–1, 175–6; *CSP Foreign,* August 1584– August 1585, 310; William Crichton's Memoir, 166
19 C. Lennon, *An Irish prisoner of conscience of the Tudor era: Archbishop Richard Creagh of Armagh, 1523–1586* (Dublin, 2000), 117–8, 127, 131; Harrison, *Tudor Journal*, 186–7; William Crichton's Memoir, 166
20 William Crichton's Memoir, 156, 165, 171
21 Ibid., 165–6, 171
22 Ibid., 166; Tolomeo Galli, Cardinal of Como, was Pope Gregory's secretary from 1572 to 1585
23 William Crichton's Memoir, 166; The writer of Popish Plots and Treasons confirms that Parry was unable to find an opportune time to carry out the deed:

'The Jesuites vile Doctrines do Convince
Parry, 'Tis Merit for to kill his Prince
The fatal Dagger he prepares with Art

And Means to sheath it in her Royal Heart
Oft he Attempts, and is as oft put by,
By the Majestick Terrors of her Eye
At last his Cursed Intentions he Confest
And So his welcom'd a fit Tyburn Guest'

Bossy dismisses Parry as a theatrical character, though he does acknowledge that, even though relations between him and Elizabeth were quite cordial, he was a potential threat, Bossy, *Under the Molehill*, 96ff, 133–4, 142; on Parry see Hasler, *House of Commons*, III, Members M-Z, 180–4

24 William Crichton's Memoir, 165

25 Ibid., 167–8; *Warrender Papers*, I, 228–9; Anstruther, *Seminary Priests*, 19–20, 361–3; Bossy refutes any notion that the Babington plot was a set-up. The plot was 'short-lived, totally theoretical, riddled with holes, and hamstrung by Babington's own political and theological doubts; but it certainly existed', Bossy, *Under the Molehill*, 140ff

26 William Crichton's Memoir, 168; *CSP Scot.*, XII, no. 217; J.R. Elder, *Spanish Influences in Scottish History* (Glasgow, 1920), 300–1 [Elder, *Spanish Influences*]; on Hatton see Hasler, *House of Commons*, II, Members D-L, 276–9

27 *CSP Domestic Addenda*, 1580–1625, 159; *Arundel*, 82–3

28 Bellesheim, *History*, III, 261

29 *CSP Domestic Addenda*, 1580–1625, 155; Forbes-Leith, *Narratives*, 202–4, 206; Pollen, *Counter-Reformation*, 53, 59–60

30 Pollen, *Papal Negotiations*, 175; Forbes-Leith, *Narratives*, 208; *Arundel*, 81–3

31 *CSP Spanish*, III, 668; *Arundel*, 82–3

32 *CSP Scot.*, VIII, nos. 93, 100; Dowden, *Bishops*, 347, 373–4; Watt, *Fasti*, 132, 308, 336; Watt and Shead, *Heads of Religious Houses*, 72–3; J.M. Webster, *Dunfermline Abbey* (Dunfermline,1948), 76–7

33 Forbes Leith, *Pre-Reformation Scholars*, 85

34 *Arundel*, 74

35 *CSP Foreign*, August 1584 – August 1585, 715; *The Hamilton Papers*, ed. J.Bain (Edinburgh, 1890–2), II, 673; Edmund Hay's Memoir, 74

36 *Arundel*, 78

37 *Warrender Papers*, I, 198

38 *CSP Scot.*, VIII, nos. 93, 100; On Gray see Lee, *Maitland*, 63ff

39 *CSP Scot.*, VIII, no. 91

40 Brown, Maxwell, 161–9; *Warrender Papers*, I, 247; Pollen, *Counter-Reformation*, 56

41 Forbes-Leith, *Narratives*, 204–5; *Border Papers*, I, 220

42 *Arundel*, 84; *Borders Papers*, I, 220, Melville, *Diary*, 51; *BUK*, II, 429, 431, 722; III 832, 876; *RPC*, IV, 20, 233, 773–4; Calderwood, *History*, V, 416–7; *Miscellaneous Papers principally illustrative of events in the reigns of Queen Mary and King James*, ed. W.J. Duncan (Maitland Club, 1834) 26, 42–56 [*Miscellaneous Papers Mary and James*]; Forbes-Leith, *Narratives*, 204–5; M. Dilworth, 'Abbot Gilbert Brown, a sketch of his career', *IR*, 40 (1989), 153–5

43 *Borders Papers*, I, 220; P.J. Shearman, 'Father Alexander McQuhirrie, S.J.', *IR*, 6 (1955), 25–6 [Shearman, McQuhirrie]

44 *Early Records St. Andrews*, 177, 286, 287, 289

45 *Records of the Scots Colleges*, I, 2, 3

46 Shearman, McQuhirrie, 27–9

47 *CSP Foreign*, August 1584 – August 1585, 259; *Record of the Scots Colleges*, I, 2

48 Edmund Hay's Memoir, 74–5

49 *The Burghley State Papers*, ed. W. Murdin (London, 1759), 458–9; Edmund Hay's Memoir, 75

50 *CSP Spanish*, III, 596

51 Ibid., III, 590, 630–1; IV, 27–8

52 *English Martyrs*, 146; Anstruther, *Seminary Priests*, 60–1

53 *Border Papers*, I, 258–9; *CSP Spanish*, IV, 144; Anstruther, *Seminary Priests*, 43–4

54 *Warrender Papers*, I, 226–33, 264ff; Cowan, *Mary Stuart*, 206ff; Lee, *Maitland*, 98ff; Fraser, *Mary*, 590ff; Mackay, *Mary*, 273ff; for a modern account of the mythology surrounding Mary see J.E. Lewis, *Mary Queen of Scots: Romance and Nation* (London, 1998); on the unsuccessful attempts to have Mary canonised see P.Davidson, 'Saint Mary, Queen & Martyr: An Alternative History of Mary Stuart', *History Scotland*, vol.2 no.1 (Jan./Feb. 2002), 32–7

55 L. Hicks, SJ, 'The Strange Case of Dr William Parry', *Studies* (1948), 343–62; on Morgan and Paget see Hicks, *An Elizabethan Problem*

56 *Warrender* Papers, I, 251; on James's reaction to his mother's death see Goodare and Lynch, *James VI*, 123–4, 146–7; Willson, *James VI and I*, 78–80; Lee, *Maitland*, 105ff

57 Cowan, *Mary Stuart*, 212

58 Pollen, *Counter-Reformation*, 62; Cockburn, *Dunblane*, 228–9; McCoog, *Our Way of Proceeding*, 242

59 Watt, *Fasti*, 78; Dowden, *Bishops*, 207–8; the reappointment was annulled in 1589.

60 *English Martyrs*, 141; McCoog, *Our Way of Proceeding*, 242

61 *CSP Spanish*, IV, 156

62 Ibid., IV, 180; H. Chadwick, SJ, 'Father William Crichton S.I., And a Recently Discovered Letter (1589), *AHSI*, 6 (1937), 259, 279 [Chadwick, Crichton Letter]

63 *CSP Spanish*, IV, 242, 255, 542–4; *Border Papers*, I, 298, 307; on Bothwell see E.J.Cowan, 'The Darker Vision of the Scottish Renaissance: the Devil and Francis Stewart' in *The Renaissance and Reformation in Scotland: Essays in honour of Gordon Donaldson*, edd. I.B.Cowan and D.Shaw (Edinburgh, 1983), 125–40 [*Renaissance and Reformation*] and on Maitland see Lee, *Maitland*

64 McCoog, *Our Way of Proceeding*, 243

65 Murphy, Robert Abercromby, 65

66 *BUK*, II, 702, 716–7

67 *Miscellaneous Papers Mary and James*, 42–56

68 *CSP Spanish*, IV, 260–1; the knight, Amadis of Gaul, was the hero of a medieval French chivalric romance of of the same name.

69 Spottiswoode, *History*, II, 378

70 *CSP Spanish*, IV, 224–5

71 Pollen, *Papal Negotiations*, lxxn.; *CSP Spanish*, IV, 224–5

72 *CSP Spanish*, IV, 227–8

73 Ibid., IV, 287; W. Fraser, *The Book of Carlaverock* (Edinburgh, 1873), I, 276–80; Forbes-Leith; *Narratives*, 369; Sempill, the illegitimate son of Robert 3rd Lord Sempill, was also responsible for the foundation of the Scots College in Madrid in 1627. In a letter to Mendoza, Philip expressed his concern about Sempill: 'He seems a zealous man, although doubtless, a thorough Scot, and you will consequently govern yourselves towards him with the caution you always display', *CSP Spanish*, IV, 171

74 On the Armada see G. Mattingly, *The Defeat of the Spanish Armada* (Harmondsworth, 1962); on the effect on Scotland in particular see C. Bingham, *James VI of Scotland* (London, 1979), 101ff and J.D.Mackie, 'Scotland and the Spanish Armada', *SHR*, XII (1914), 1–23; Mackie claims that everywhere the average man 'felt the unseen presence of the agents of the League, the Jesuits especially', 2; James Melville also described the public reaction to the threat of the Armada: 'Terrible was the feir, persing war the pretchings, ernest, zealus, and fervent war the prayers, sounding war the siches and sobbes, and abounding was the tears and that Fast and General Assemblie keipit at Edinbruche, when the newes was crediblie tauld, sum tymes of thair landing at Dumbar, sum tymes at St Andros, and in Tay, and now and then at

Aberdein and Cromertie first; And in verie deid, as we knew certeanlie soone efter, the Lord of Armies, wha ryddes upon the wings of the wounds, the Keipar of his awin Israell, was in the mean tyme convoying that monstruus navie aboutes our costes, and directing thair hulkes and galiates to the ylands, rokkes, and sandes wharupon he haid destinat thair wrak and destruction', Melville, *Diary*, 174

75 Chadwick, Crichton Letter, 260

76 A number of Spanish sailors came ashore at Anstruther, 'for the maist part young berdles men, sillie, trauchled and houngered', Melville, *Diary*, 176; The provost and baillies of Edinburgh showed great charity towards a party of Spaniards who arrived in Edinburgh after being shipwrecked off Ireland, *CSP Scot.*, IX, no.532; though not all those who came ashore in Scotland were treated well. Francisco de Cuellar, a Spanish captain, who arrived in Scotland also via Ireland was scathing of James: 'It was said that the King of Scotland protected all the Spaniards who reached his kingdom, clothed them and gave them passage to Spain, but all was in reverse, for he did no good to anyone, nor did he bestow one real in charity', *The Great Enterprise: The History of the Spanish Armada*, ed. S. Usherwood (London, 1978), 191

77 *CSP Scot,* IX, nos. 532, 589

Chapter 7: Brig O'Dee and the Affair of the Spanish Blanks

1 *CSP Scot.*, IX, no.589; Chadwick, Crichton Letter, 275–6; Foreign supporters were often wary of paying out subsidies to the Scottish Catholic nobles as they had no control over how they were spent. There are a number of examples of them being mis-spent, though the subsidy paid in the summer of 1594 does appear to have been an exception, R.Grant, 'The Brig o'Dee Affair, the Sixth Earl of Huntly and the Politics of the Counter-Reformation', in Goodare and Lynch *James VI*, 93–109

2 Calderwood, *History*, V, 1, 29

3 Calderwood, *History*, V, 5

4 Ibid., V, 1, 39; *RPC*, IV, 358–9

5 Calderwood, *History*, V, 8–35; *RPC*, IV, 361, 820–1; *CSP Scot.*, IX, no. 589; the Spanish saying 'la vaca no es de donde nace, sino de donde paco' – 'the cow is not from where it is born, but where it grazes' – gives an indication of the level of commitment expected from the Scottish nobles and priests by their Spanish paymasters. It is not surprising that they soon became disenchanted with the Scots' continual demands for financial assistance. Thank you to Conchi Saenz of Edinburgh University for this saying.

6 *CSP Scot.*, IX, no. 589

7 Ibid., IX, no.594; *RPC*, IV, 821–2;

8 *CSP Scot.*, X, no.103; Calderwood, History, V, 36; Goodare and Lynch, *James VI*, 106

9 *CSP Scot.*, IX, nos. 593, 594; Bingham suggests that James's ready acceptance and forgiveness of the earls' treasonable activities smacked of collusion, Bingham, *James VI and I*, 104

10 Goodare and Lynch, *James VI*, 98ff; *CSP Scot.*, X, nos. 51, 52, 53, 113, 123

11 M. M. Meikle, 'A Meddlesome Princess: Anna of Denmark and Scottish Court Politics, 1589–1603', in Goodare and Lynch, *James VI*, 126ff; See also D. Stevenson, *Scotland's Last Royal Wedding: The Marriage of James VI and Anne of Denmark* (Edinburgh, 1997)

12 Calderwood, *History*, V, 112

13 HMC, *Salisbury*, III, 447; Chadwick, Crichton Letter, 278, 284; *CSP Scot.*, X, no. 578

14 F. de Borjia Medina, SJ, 'Intrigues of a Scottish Jesuit at the Spanish Court:

Unpublished Letters of William Crichton to Claudio Acquaviva (Madrid 1590–1592)', in McCoog, *Essays*, 215–245, for Crichton and Robert Bruce see 220–1

15 Ibid., 219–20, 222–3, 228

16 Ibid., 222; Oliver, *Collections*, 9; Foley, *Records*, VII, 347, 1461

17 Edwards, *Robert Persons*, 171

18 McCoog, *Essays*, 223, 231

19 Ibid., 225

20 Urban VII (15–27 Sept. 1590), Gregory XIV (5 Dec. 1590–16 Oct. 1591), Innocent IX (29 Oct.-30 Dec.1591) and Clement VIII (30 Jan.1592–5 Mar.1605); see J.N.D. Kelly, *The Oxford Dictionary of Popes* (Oxford, 1986), 273–6

21 McCoog, *Essays*, 225; Chadwick, Scots College, 580–1; Baldwin was later involved in the Gunpowder Plot

22 see Crichton's 'Apologie and Defence' of James in Law, Documents Illustrating Catholic Policy, 41ff

23 Lee, *Maitland*, 212; Calderwood, *History*, V, 86; *The Letters and Despatches of Richard Verstegan (c.1550–1640)*, ed. A.G. Petti, (CRS, vol. 52, 1959), 75 [*Verstegan*]

24 *CSP Scot.*, XI, no.273; Calderwood, *History*, V, 192ff; *Warrender Papers*, II, 192ff; Law, *Essays*, 244ff; Elder, *Spanish Influences*, 181ff; Shearman, Spanish Blanks, 81ff and 'The Spanish Blanks', *IR*, 4 (1953), 60; see also H.G. Stafford, *James VI of Scotland and the Throne of England* (New York, 1940), 74–123

25 *Warrender Papers*, II, 192n.

26 Ibid., II, 195; *Hist.KJS*, 256–7; Kerr was a kinsman of Crichton, both his grandmothers being Crichtons, *The History of the Kirk of Scotland from the year 1558 to August 1637 by John Row, Minister of Carnock*, ed. D. Laing (Wodrow Society, 1842), 146 [Row, *History*]

27 *Warrender Papers*, II, 194ff

28 HMC, *Salisbury*, IV, 214–6; Shearman, Spanish Blanks, 84.; Willson, *James VI and I*, 111

29 Forbes-Leith, *Narratives*, 228; *Warrender Papers*, II, 195

30 *CSP Scot.*, X, no.765

31 Ibid., X, no.721

32 Simpson was himself a student of Pont-à-Mousson and a monk at Ratisbon. He also had connections with George Kerr and a number of leading Catholic families, Dilworth, *Scots in Franconia*, 158–9, 274; *Records of the Scots Colleges*, I, 4; McCrie, *Melville*, app. II, 522–3

33 *CSP Scot.*, X, no.775

34 Ibid., X, no. 776

35 *CSP Scot.*, X, no. 1 at p.13; Calderwood, *History*, V, 197–8

36 *Hist.KJS*, 256ff; Calderwood, *History*, V, 192–3

37 *CSP Scot*,. X, nos. 773, 778, 785

38 *RPC*, V, 5; *CSP Scot.*, X, no. 785; XI, no. 1

39 *RPC*, V, 33–4

40 Details of the Blanks and the other correspondence can be found in Calderwood, *History*, V, 192ff; *CSP Scot.*, X, nos. 783, 785; XI, no.1; *Warrender Papers*, II, 192–202

41 *CSP Scot.*, XI, nos. 1, 18; *RPC*, V, 521; *Memoirs of the Affairs of Scotland by David Moysie from 1577 to 1603*, ed. J. Dennistoun (Bannatyne Club, 1830), 99–100 [Moysie, *Memoirs*]

42 *Hist.KJS*, 267–8; Calderwood, *History*, V, 223

43 Calderwood, *History*, V, 254; *CSP Scot.*, XI, nos. 28, 132; despite his capture and imprisonment Kerr continued to act as a messenger for the Catholic earls, *CSP Scot.*, XII, no. 181

44 *Letters of Queen Elizabeth to King James VI of Scotland*, ed. J. Bruce (Camden Society, 1849), 88 [*Letters Elizabeth and James*]

Chapter 8: Glenlivet and the Gowk's Storm

1 Calderwood, *History*, V, 232–5, 238; *RPC*, V, 44–52

2 E.J. Cowan, 'The Darker Vision of the Scottish Renaissance: the Devil and Francis Stewart', in *Renaissance and Reformation*, 125ff; *Letters Elizabeth and James*, 99–102; For Elizabeth's robust response see Ibid., 103–5

3 Law, *Essays*, 244

4 *Verstegan*, 193, 196; Patterson gives a good summary of James's wider strategy and his reasons for courting the Catholics in Scotland: 'He not only wanted to avoid generating opposition on the part of the Catholic powers abroad; he also wanted their support. Consequently Catholics were, for the most part, admonished and exhorted in Scotland, rather than persecuted, and James managed to stay on good terms with France, Spain, and the Spanish Netherlands, as well as with the Protestant states that were now Scotland's more natural allies', Patterson, *James VI and I*, 19

5 *BUK*, III, 829–30; *RPC*, V, 103–5, 108; Melville, *Diary*, 209; Moysie, *Memoirs*, 108–9; Calderwood, *History*, V, 262, 271–80; *APS*, IV, 46–8; *Hist.KJS*, 294

6 *APS*, IV, 52–3, 99; Calderwood, *History*, V, 332–6

7 For a list of Scottish Jesuits in 1593 see Foley, *Records*, VII, 879. Oliver also mentions a Thomas Becam, though he appears never to have worked on the Scottish Mission, Oliver, *Collections*, 3

8 *English Martyrs*, 242; Anstruther, *Seminary Priests*, 182–4

9 *CSP Scot.*, XI, no. 60; *DNB*, XXXIII, 314; Forbes-Leith, *Narratives*, 353

10 Anstruther, *Seminary Priests*, 183; Ingram was imprisoned in Berwick, York and London. While in the Tower awaiting execution he carved a large number of epigrams on his cell wall using a blunt knife, including the following lines:

> 'In early spring I sought the realm of the Scots, but these limbs
> Which that land had given me, she took from me in early spring....
> Scotland loved me, Scotland succoured me in my need....'

For these and other epigrams see *English Martyrs*, 270ff

11 Anstruther, *Seminary Priests*, 63–8; Calderwood, *History*, V, 193–4

12 *English Martyrs*, 198–201

13 Foley, *Records*, VI, 112, 142, 164; *English Martyrs*, 259

14 *CSP Domestic Elizabeth*, 1595–1597, 145

15 *CSP Scot.*, XI, nos. 257, 261; HMC, *Salisbury*, IV, 548; *RPC*, V, 145

16 In 1594 Cecil was with Maxwell at Carlaverock and then with Hew Barclay of Ladyland, Anstruther, *Seminary Priests*, 66–7

17 Forbes-Leith, *Narratives*, 222; HMC, *Salisbury*, IV, 536, 553–4

18 HMC, *Salisbury*, IV, 554: In early 1592 Murdoch was in jail in Aberdeen. He was banished but returned sometime prior to February 1594 when he was a teacher at the grammar school in Edinburgh, Durkan, Early Jesuit Missions, 3–4

19 Bellesheim, *History*, III, 499

20 Forbes-Leith, *Narratives*, 356

21 Moysie, *Memoirs*, 118; Calderwood, *History*, V, 340–1; *Extracts from the Council Register of the Burgh of Aberdeen 1570–1625*, ed. J. Stuart (Spalding Club, 1848), II, 91–3; Forbes-Leith, *Narratives*, 222–3

22 *RPC*, V, 155

23 HMC, *Salisbury*, V, 73;

24 P. Marren, *Grampian Battlefields* (Aberdeen, 1990), 128 [Marren, *Battlefields*]; Calderwood, *History*, V, 348–53; Bingham underestimates the significance of the battle when she describes it as 'a skirmish dignified by the name of 'the battle of Glenlivet'', Bingham, *James VI and I*, 136

25 Mullan, *Episcopacy*, 74ff

26 *Letters Elizabeth and James*, 108–10
27 Alexander McQuhirrie's Account of the Battle of Glenlivet, NLS MS 33.2.36; Account of the Battle of Balrinnes 3rd October 1594, *The Spottiswoode Miscellany*, ed. J Maidment (Spottiswoode Society, 1844–5), I, 259ff [Balrinnes]; *Scottish Poems of the Sixteenth Century*, ed. J.G. Dalyell (Edinburgh, 1801), I, 136–52 [Dalyell, *Scottish Poems*]; Tytler, *History*, IX, 146ff; *CSP Scot.*, XI, nos.378, 379; *Hist.KJS*, 338–42; Moysie, *Memoirs*, 120; Calderwood, *History*, V, 348–53; for modern accounts see Marren, *Battlefields*, 128ff and N. Maclean-Bristol, *Murder under Trust: The Crimes and Death of Sir Lachlan Mor Maclean of Duart 1558–1598* (East Linton, 1999), 125ff
28 *CSP Scot*, XII, no. 287; Forbes-Leith, *Narratives*, 246, 248
29 Forbes-Leith, *Narratives*, 225
30 Dalyell, *Scottish Poems*, 137, 143
31 Ibid., 146ff; Balrinnes, 261ff; *CSP Scot.*, XI, nos. 378, 379
32 *CSP Scot.*, XII, No. 98
33 Marren, *Battlefields*, 135
34 Tytler, *History*, IX, 165–7
35 The earls' estates were protected from spoilation on the orders of James, *The Miscellany of the Spalding Club*, ed. J.Stuart (Spalding Club, 1841), I, 9; On Jane Gordon, the widow of the Earl of Sutherland and James Gordon's sister see M.H.B. Sanderson, *Mary Stewart's People* (Edinburgh, 1987), 34–54
36 *CSP Domestic Elizabeth*, 1595–97, 46, 55
37 *CSP Scot.*, XI, no.565
38 'SUMMARY of the MEMORIALS that JOHN OGILVY, Scottish baron, sent by the King of Scotland, gave to his Catholic Majesty in favour of a League bewteen the two Kings; and what JOHN CECILL, priest, an Englishman, on the part of the Earls and other Catholic Lords of Scotland, set forth to the contrary in the city of Toledo, in the months of May and June 1596', Law, Documents Illustrating Catholic Policy, 32ff
39 *RPC*, V, 172; HMC, *Hatfield*, IV, 216; Elder, *Spanish Influences*, 242ff; A.O. Meyer, 'Clemens VIII. und Jakob I. von England', *Quellen und Forschungen aus italienischen Archiven und Bibliotheken*, 7, 2, (1904), 271–3
40 Law, Documents Illustrating Catholic Policy, 36–7
41 Elder, *Spanish Influences*, 247; Law, Documents Illustrating Catholic Policy, 6; *CSP Scot*, XII, no.193
42 Bellesheim, *History*, III, 462–3
43 Law, Documents Illustrating Catholic Policy, 7; *CSP Scot.*, XII, 192
44 Pritchard, *Catholic Loyalism*, 18–27
45 Knox, *Cardinal Allen*, 384; Law, Documents Illustrating Catholic Policy, 63–4
46 *CSP Scot.*, XIII, nos. 622, 631, 635 and Appendix A no. 2; Law, Documents Illustrating Catholic Policy, 9
47 'AN APOLOGIE and DEFENCE of the K. of Scotlande against the infamous libell forged by JOHN CECILL, English Priest, Intelligencer to treasurer CECILL of England', in Law, Documents Illustrating Catholic Policy, 41ff; 'A DISCOVERYE of the Errors Committed and Inuyres don to his Ma: of Scotlande and Nobilitye off the same realme and John Cecyll Prest and D. of divinitye by a malitious Mythologie titled an Apologie, and compiled by William Criton, Pryest and professed Jesuite, whose habite and behavioure, whose cote and conditions, are as sutable as Esau his handes and Jacob his voice. Addressed to Criton by his unworthyly abused brother and servaunte In oure Lorde, John Cecyll Pryest', in Elder, *Spanish Influences*, 293ff
48 Law, Documents Illustrating Catholic Policy, 42, 46; Elder, *Spanish Influences*, 294ff; Gaius Maecenas c.70–8BC was a Roman statesman and advisor to Emperor Augustus. He was also a patron of the arts, including the poets, Virgil and Horace
49 *Dodd's Church History*, IV, 53

50 On the Archpriest Controversy and the Wisbech Stirs see T.G.Law, *A Historical Sketch of the Conflicts between Jesuits and Seculars in the Reign of Elizabeth* (London, 1889); J.H.Pollen, SJ, *The Institution of the Archpriest Blackwell* (London, 1916); Hay, *Blairs Papers*, 71–3; Bellesheim, *History*, III, 469ff; Anderson, Narratives II, 117–20

51 *CSP Scot.*, XII, nos. 20, 22, 153, 181

52 Shearman, McQuhirrie, 29, 34

53 Row, *History*, 165

54 *CSP Scot.*, XII, no.216; Shearman, McQuhirrie, 34

55 See M.Lee, Jr., 'King James's Popish Chancellor', in *Renaissance and Reformation*, 170ff; *CSP Scot.*, XII, no.98

56 Calderwood, *History*, V, 548. Seton was also referred to by the same writer as a 'good justicier, courteous, and humane both to strangers and to his owne countrie people', Ibid., VII, 549; The other members of the committee were Walter Stewart, Commendator of Blantyre, David Carnegie of Colluthie, Sir John Skene of Curriehill, Sir Thomas Hamilton of Drumcairn and Sir Peter Young.

57 Forbes-Leith, *Narratives*, 231; Tytler, *History*, IX, 232

58 Forbes-Leith, *Narratives*, 232–3

59 Ibid., 235; Spottiswoode, *History*, III, 61; Although Huntly remained a Catholic his conformity marked the end of militant Catholicism in Scotland and his own political decline: 'The first rush of the Counter-Reformation was then receeding with a hissing sound as of a broken wave on the shingle', MacLean, *Counter-Reformation*, 77

60 Forbes-Leith, *Narratives*, 236–42

61 *New Catholic Encyclopedia* (Washington, 1967), vol. 14, 356; 'The Memoirs of Father Robert Persons, Memoir IV: An Observation of Certayne Aparent Iudgments', ed. J.H.Pollen, SJ, in *Miscellanea II* (CRS, 2, 1906)

62 Forbes-Leith, *Narratives*, 243ff; *RPC*, V, 503–4; Bellesheim, *History*, III, 369; Shearman, McQuhirrie, 35

Chapter 9: Fresh Tumults and Severer Persecution

1 *CSP Domestic Elizabeth*, 1598–1601, 418–19. The persistent belief that James was a Catholic at heart was described by Maurice Lee as a 'curious delusion [which] flew in the face of all the facts', Lee, *Maitland*, 39

2 Forbes-Leith, *Narratives*, 268ff; Shearman, McQuhirrie, 36, 37; Murphy, Robert Abercromby, 66n.; D. McRoberts, 'George Strachan of the Mearns, an early Scottish Orientalist', *IR*, 3 (1952), 114 [McRoberts, George Strachan]

3 Bellesheim, *History*, III, 346ff; David Willson's description of Anne is no more complimentary than most of his comments about her husband: 'She had a quick temper, high words came easily, and in her childish tantrums she could be violent, spiteful, indiscreet and quite ingenious in her efforts to annoy... Very likely she adopted Catholicism in the half trifling way in which idle persons sometimes occupy themselves with a new faith. Her conversion did not make her serious or devout, nor did it strengthen her character... Alas! The King had married a stupid wife', Willson, *James VI and I*, 95; For a modern reassessments of Anne see M. M. Meikle, 'A Meddlesome Princess: Anna of Denmark and Scottish Court Politics 1589–1603', in Goodare and Lynch, *James VI*, 126ff and S. Murdoch, *Britain, Denmark-Norway and the House of Stuart 1603–1660* (East Linton, 2000) [Murdoch, *Britain, Denmark-Norway and the House of Stuart*]

4 Edwards, *Robert Persons*, 287

5 M. Barrett, *Sidelights on Scottish History* (London, 1918), 180; Forbes-Leith, *Narratives*, 272–3; Bellesheim, *History*, III, 347; Anne's chief maid was Barbara Abercrombie, perhaps a relative of the Jesuit, Robert Abercrombie, Murdoch, *Britain,*

Denmark-Norway and the House of Stuart, 3

6 Forbes-Leith, *Narratives*, 263–5

7 In an interview with William Watson, an eccentric and untrustworthy Appellant priest, James apparently told him: 'Na, na, we'll nae need the Papists now', quoted in P.Hughes, *Rome and the Counter-Reformation in England* (London, 1942), 273; on Watson see Anstruther, *Seminary Priests*, 372–4

8 On the Hampton Court Conferences of 1604 and 1606 see *Calderwood* History, VII, 241ff; Mullan, *Episcopacy in Scotland*, 90, 93–4, 98–102; Patterson, *James VI and I*, 43–8; Willson, *James VI and I*, 202–9

9 Forbes-Leith, *Narratives*, 281

10 Bellesheim, *History*, III, 344; *Ancient Criminal Trials in Scotland from 1488 to 1624*, ed. R. Pitcairn (Bannatyne Club, 1833), II, 348 [Pitcairn, *Criminal Trials*]

11 Calderwood, *History*, VI, 102–3, 104–5; Pitcairn, *Criminal* Trials, 347; RPC, VI, 233, 235n.; F. Shearman, 'James Wood of Boniton', *IR*, 5 (1954), 28–32

12 Forbes-Leith, *Narratives*, 269, 273

13 Shearman, McQuhirrie, 37; McRoberts, George Strachan, 110ff. McRoberts describes the *Album Amicorum* as a type of autograph book 'intended to receive the autograph encomia of fellow students, professors and friends. The autographs are generally accompanied by verses in Latin or Greek, heraldic devices, pictorial illustrations or some other embellishment'. Strachan, a former student of Pont-à-Mousson, where he met William Crichton, spent an amazing career as an academic, traveller, merchant and doctor in Europe, the Middle East and India.

14 H. Chadwick, SJ, 'The Arm of St. Ninian', *Transactions of the Dumfries and Galloway Natural History and Antiquarian Society*, Third Series, XXIII, 30–5; Bellesheim, *History*, I, 14; *Records of the Scots Colleges*, I, 8, 10

15 P. Caraman, SJ, *Henry Garnet 1555–1606 and the Gunpowder Plot* (London, 1964), 312

16 Forbes-Leith, *Narratives*, 276–7; Shearman, McQuhirrie, 38

17 Forbes-Leith, *Narratives*, 276–7; Shearman, McQuhirrie, 34–5, 38.; Murphy, Robert Abercromby, 65, 67; McCoog, *Our Way of Proceeding*, 241–2. On the theories of religious resistance and political obedience see Holmes, *Resistance and Compromise*, 2, where Holmes expresses well the Catholics' dilemma: 'exile or martyrdom, stealth or discovery; a measured degree of conformity or extirpation'; 'The Notebook of John Southcote, D.D. from 1623 to 1637', ed. J. H. Pollen, SJ, in *Miscellanea I*, (CRS, vol.1, 1905), 111–2. This comment by Southcote is inconsistent with earlier views on Gordon and would suggest that the stance subsequently adopted in Scotland was still too lax for some of the hard-liners south of the border.

18 Forbes-Leith, *Narratives*, 280; Pitcairn, *Criminal Trials*, II, 442

19 Forbes-Leith, *Narratives*, 280, 285

20 For recent studies of the Gunpowder Plot see A. Haynes, *The Gunpowder Plot* (Stroud, 1994) and A. Fraser, *The Gunpowder Plot, Terror & Faith in 1605* (London, 1996); On the aftermath of the plot see J. Wormald, 'Gunpowder, Treason and Scots', *Journal of British Studies*, vol.24 no.2 (1985), 141–168, which analyses the anti-Scottish xenophobia in English society; J.L. La Rocca, SJ, '"Who Can't Pray With Me, Can't Love Me": Toleration and the early Jacobean Recusancy Problem', *Journal of British Studies*, vol.23 no.2 (1984), 22–36; Willson, *James VI and I*, 227ff; For a comprehensive modern study of the Oath of Allegiance and James's attempts to provide an international solution to the religious polarisation of the period see Patterson, *James VI and I*, 75–123; For a study of confessional compromise elsewhere in Europe see Louthan, *The quest for compromise*, which looks at irenicism at the Imperial Court and the peaceful attempts to reconcile the theological differences between the various confessional groups in Austria.

21 *RPC*, XIV, 487–9

22 Shearman, McQuhirrie, 39
23 *Original Letters Relating to the Ecclesiastical Affairs of Scotland, 1603–25*, ed. D Laing (Bannatyne Club, 1851), I, 85–6 [*OLS*]
24 *RPC*, XIV, 478–80, 486–90; *OLS*, I, 95
25 Pitcairn, *Criminal Trials*, II, 530–1; Calderwood, *History*, VI, 679
26 Shearman, McQuhirrie, 42–5
27 More information on the later careers of the Scottish fathers is given in McCoog, Jesuit Missions to Scotland, 159–88
28 Bellesheim, *History*, III, 351–2, 455–7; In the charge against him Abercrombie was described as 'an old Jesuite of Brunsberg, who sundrie tymes hath entyced young gentleman scholers from Scotland and ar now broght up in his scoole', Murphy, Robert Abercromby, 58; Foley, *Records*, VII, 2
29 Foley, *Records*, VII, 533; Oliver, *Collections*, 19
30 Bellesheim, *History*, III, 407–8; Foley, *Records*, VII, 181; Oliver, *Collections*, 4
31 Foley, *Records*, VII, 309; Oliver, *Collections*, 7–8; Durkan, Sidelights, 40
32 Durkan, Early Jesuit Mission, 10
33 Forbes-Leith, *Narratives*, 314–5; *Spain and the Jacobean Catholics, volume 1: 1603–1612*, ed. A.J. Loomie, SJ (CRS, vol. 64, 1973), 127–8, 129n.
34 Bellesheim, *History*, III, 414ff; Forbes-Leith, *Narratives*, 297ff; Chadwick, Scots College, 571; J. Durkan, 'Two Jesuits: Patrick Anderson and John Ogilvie', *IR*, 21 (1970), 157–61; Calderwood, *History*, VII, 193, 196; *OLS*, II, 400
35 J. Burton, *History of Scotland* (Edinburgh, 1905), VI, 12; Durkan, Sidelights, 39–45
36 Forbes-Leith, *Narratives*, 290–6, 314–7, 347–8; W.V. Bangert, SJ, *A History of the Society of Jesus* (St Louis, 1972), 236

Chapter 10: Leaders of a Forlorn Hope

1 The title of this chapter is taken from a book of the same name, F.A. Forbes, *Leaders of a Forlorn Hope: A Study of the Reformation in Scotland* (London, 1922). The book is a study of the main figures in the Scottish Catholic Reformation, but makes no mention of the role of the Society. With the benefit of hindsight Forbes concluded that 'Those who were struggling against such desperate odds to uphold the Catholic Church in Scotland were indeed leading a forlorn hope, and the end was a foregone conclusion', 37; Lynch, *Oxford Companion to Scottish History*, 501
2 The comments regarding Scotland and Poland are from a discussion with Father Mark Dilworth, formerly the archivist at the Scottish Catholic Archive, Edinburgh. In 1570 there were 12 Scottish Jesuits. By 1602 this figure had risen to 27. In contrast there were 140 English and Welsh Jesuits between 1555 and 1585.
3 Durkan, Sidelights, 34
4 W.J. Anderson, 'Rome and Scotland, 1513–1625', in McRoberts, *Essays*, 480; for an analysis of various phases in the decline and reorganisation of the Catholic church in Scotland in the post-Reformation period see M.Dilworth, 'Roman Catholic Worship', in Forrester and Murray, *Worship in Scotland*, 127

Bibliography

Manuscripts

British Museum (BM), London

BM PS 318 013 – Popish Plots and Treasons from the Beginning of the Reign of Queen Elizabeth by Cornelius Danckerts

Archive of the British Province of the Society of Jesus (ABSI), London

46/4/7/68–77 – Beginning of H. Chadwick's History of the Society of Jesus in Scotland 1542 –

Archivum Romanum Societatis Iesu (ARSI), Rome

Angliae 42 ff 5v–6r – Father Crichton's Map of Scotland 1595

National Library of Scotland (NLS), Edinburgh

MS 17.1.3 fos.367, 369 – Reorganisation of Dunkeld Chapter

MS 33.2.36 – Alexander McQuhirrie's Account of the Battle of Glenlivet

Scottish Record Office (SRO), Edinburgh

RH6/8/1654 – Calendar of Charters

RH9/2/180 & 284 – Correspondence re William Murdoch

Printed Primary Sources

Monumenta Historica Societatis Iesu (MHSI)

Epistolae et Acta patris Iacobi Lainii secundi praepositi generalis Societatis Iesu, ed. E. Astudillo, SJ, 8 vols., 44, 45, 47, 49, 50, 51, 53, 55 (Madrid, 1912–16)

Epistolae P.P. Paschasii Broëti, Claudii Jayi, Joannis Codurii et Simonis Rodericii, ed. F. Cervós, SJ, vol. 24 (Madrid, 1903)

Epistolae P. Alphonsi Salmeronis Societatis Iesu, edd. R. Vidaurre, SJ and F. Cervós, SJ, 2 vols., 30, 32 (Madrid 1906–7)

Monumenta Angliae, edd. T. M. McCoog, SJ, and L. Lukács, SJ, 3 vols., 142, 143, 151 (Rome, 1992–2000)

Other Printed Primary Works

Anderson, J., *The Winter Night,* (Glasgow, 1713)

Anderson, J.M. ed., *Early Records of the University of St. Andrews* (SHS, 1926)

Bain, J., ed., *Calendar of Letters and Papers relating to the Affairs of the Borders of England and Scotland* (Edinburgh 1894–6)

Bain, J. and others, edd., *Calendar of State Papers relating to Scotland and Mary, Queen of Scots 1547–1603* (Edinburgh, 1898–1969)

Bain, J., ed., *The Hamilton Papers* (Edinburgh, 1890–2)

Braunsberger, O., SJ, ed., *Beati Petri Canisii Epistulae et Acta* (Freiburg, 1896–1923)

Bruce, J., ed., *Letters of Queen Elizabeth to King James VI of Scotland* (Camden Society, 1849)

Burton, J.H., and others, edd., *The Register of the Privy Council of Scotland* (Edinburgh, 1877–)

Cameron, A.I., ed., *Warrender Papers* (SHS, 1931–2)

Caraman, P., SJ, trans., *John Gerard: The Autobiography of an Elizabethan* (London, 1951)

Cody, E.G., and Murison, W., edd., *The Historie of Scotland wrytten First in Latin by the most reverend and worthy Jhone Leslie, Bishop of Rosse* (STS, 1888, 1895)

Cranstoun, J., ed., *Satirical Poems of the Time of the Reformation* (STS, 1891–3)

Dalyell, J.G., ed., *Scottish Poems of the Sixteenth Century* (Edinburgh, 1801)

Dennistoun, J., ed., *Memoirs of the Affairs of Scotland by David Moysie from 1577 to 1603* (Bannatyne Club, 1830)

Dickinson, W. C., ed., *John Knox's History of the Reformation in Scotland,* (Edinburgh, 1949)

Dickson, T., and Paul, Sir J.B., edd., *Accounts of the Lord High Treasurer of Scotland* (Edinburgh, 1877–1916)

Donaldson, G., ed., *Accounts of the Collectors of Thirds of Benefices 1561–1572* (SHS, 1949)

Duncan, W.J., ed., *Miscellaneous Papers principally illustrative of events in the Reigns of Queen Mary and King James* (Maitland Club, 1834)

Dunlop, A.I., ed., *Acta Facultatis Artium Universitatis Sanctiandree, 1413–1588* (SHS, 1964)

Easson, D.E., and Macdonald, A., edd., *Charters of the Abbey of Inchcolm* (SHS, 1938)

Edwards, F., SJ, ed., *The Elizabethan Jesuits. Historia Missionis Anglicanae Societatis Jesu (1660) of Henry More* (London, 1981)

Fleming, D.H., ed., *Register of Ministers, Elders and Deacons of the Christian Congregation of St. Andrews* (SHS, 1889)

Forbes-Leith, W., SJ, ed., *Narratives of Scottish Catholics under Mary Stuart and James VI* (London, 1889)

Ganss, G.E., SJ, trans., *The Constitutions of the Society of Jesus* (St Louis, 1970)

Goodier, A., SJ, ed., *Letters and Instructions of St. Ignatius Loyola* (London, 1914)

Hannay, R.K, ed., *Rentale Dunkeldense* (SHS, 1915)

Hannay, R.K., and Hay, D., edd., *The Letters of James V* (Edinburgh, 1954)

Hansen, J., ed., *Rheinische Akten zur Geschichte des Jesuitenordens 1542–82* (Bonn, 1896)

Harrison, G.B. ed., *Anthony Munday: The English Romayne Lyfe 1582* (London, 1925)

Hewison, J.K., ed., *Certane Tractatis for Reformatioun of Doctryne and Maneris in Scotland by Niniane Winzet* (Maitland Club, 1835)

Hicks, L., SJ, ed., *Letters and Memorials of Father Robert Persons, S.J., vol. 1 1578 to 1588* (CRS, vol. 39, 1942)

Hume, A.S.M., ed., *Calendar of Letters and Papers preserved principally in the Archives of Simancas* (London, 1892–9)

Irving, D., ed., *Thomae Dempsteri Historia Ecclesiastica Gentis Scotorum: sive De Scriptoribus Scotis* (Bannatyne Club, 1829)

Kinloch, G.R., ed., *The Diary of Mr James Melvill, 1556–1601* (Bannatyne Club, 1829)

Knox, T.F., ed., *The First and Second Diaries of the English College, Douay* (London, 1878)

Knox, T.F., ed., *The Letters and Memorials of William Cardinal Allen (1532–1594)* (London, 1882)

Kretzschmar, J., *Die Invasionsprojekte der katolischen Mächte gegen England zur Zeits*

Elisabeths (Leipzig, 1892)

Laing, D., ed., *The History of the Kirk of Scotland from the year 1558 to August 1637 by John Row, Minister of Carnock* (Wodrow Society, 1842)

Laing, D., ed., *The Works of John Knox,* (Wodrow Society, 1846–64)

Laing, D., ed., *Original Letters Relating to the Ecclesiastical Affairs of Scotland 1603–25* (Bannatyne Club, 1851)

Law, H.D.G., ed., 'The Antiquity of the Christian Religion of the Scots', in *Miscellany of the Scottish History Society Second volume* (SHS, 1904)

Law, T.G., ed., *Catholic Tractates of the Sixteenth Century 1573–1600* (STS, 1901)

Law, T.G., ed., 'Documents illustrating Catholic Policy in the Reign of James VI, 1596–1598', in *Miscellany of the Scottish History Society First volume* (SHS, 1893)

Lemon, R., and others, edd., *Calendar of State Papers, Domestic Series of the Reigns of Edward VI, Mary and Elizabeth* (London, 1856–72)

Livingstone, M., and others, edd., *Registrum Secreti Sigilli Regum Scotorum* (Edinburgh, 1908–)

Loomie, A.J., SJ, ed., *Spain and the Jacobean Catholics, volume 1: 1603–1612* (CRS, vol. 64, 1973)

MacDonald, A., ed., *History of Mary Queen of Scots, A Fragment, translated from the original French of Adam Blackwood* (Maitland Club, 1834)

Maidment, J., ed., *The Spottiswoode Miscellany,* (Spottiswoode Society, 1844–5)

Murdin, W., ed., *The Burghley State Papers* (London, 1759)

Padberg, J., SJ, ed., *Documents of the Thirty First and Thirty Second Congregations of the Society of Jesus* (St Louis, 1977)

Parks, G.B., ed., *Gregory Martin, Roma Sancta 1581* (Rome, 1969)

Patrick, D., ed., *Statutes of the Scottish Church 1225–1559* (SHS, 1907)

Petti, A.G., ed., *The Letters and Despatches of Richard Verstegan (c.1550–1640)* (CRS, vol. 52, 1959)

Pitcairn, R., ed., *Ancient Criminal Trials in Scotland from 1488 to 1624* (Bannatyne Club, 1833)

Pollen, J.H., SJ, ed., *Mary Queen of Scots and the Babington Plot* (SHS, 1922)

Pollen, J.H., SJ, ed., 'The Memoirs of Father Robert Persons' in *Miscellanea II* and *Miscellanea IV* (CRS, vol. 2 and 4, 1906,1907)

Pollen, J.H., SJ, ed., 'The Notebook of John Southcote, D.D. from 1623 to 1637' in *Miscellanea I* (CRS, vol.1, 1905)

Pollen, J.H., SJ, ed., 'Official Lists of Catholic Prisoners during the Reign of Queen Elizabeth 1581–1602' in *Miscellanea II* (CRS, vol. 2, 1906)

Pollen, J.H., SJ, ed., *Papal Negotiations with Mary Queen of Scots during her Reign in Scotland, 1561–67* (SHS, 1901)

Pollen, J.H., SJ, ed., 'Tower Bills 1575–1589' in *Miscellanea III* (CRS, vol.3, 1906)

Pollen, J.H., SJ, ed., *Unpublished Documents relating to the English Martyrs, vol. 1, 1584–1603* (CRS, vol. 5, 1908)

Pollen, J.H., SJ, & McMahon, W., SJ, edd., *The Ven. Philip Howard, Earl of Arundel 1557–1595* (CRS, vol. 21, 1919)

Rahner, H., SJ, ed., *Saint Ignatius Loyola: Letters to Women* (Freiburg, 1960)

Ramsay, J. H., ed., *Bamff Charters 1232–1703* (Oxford, 1915)

Records of the Scots Colleges (New Spalding Club, 1906)

Reports of the Royal Commission on Historical Manuscripts (London, 1870–)

Rigg, J.M., ed., *Calendar of State Papers relating to English Affairs, preserved principally at Rome* (London, 1916–26)

Rogers, C., ed., *Estimates of the Scottish Nobility during the Minority of James the Sixth* (Grampian Club, 1873)

Rogers, C., ed., *Rental Book of the Cistercian Abbey of Cupar-Angus* (Grampian Club, 1879–80)

Russell, M.,ed., *The History of the Church of Scotland. By John Spottiswoode, Archbishop of St Andrews* (Bannatyne Club, 1850)

Ryan, P., SJ, ed., 'Some Correspondence of Cardinal Allen, 1579–1585 from the Jesuit Archives' in *Miscellanea VII* (CRS, vol.9, 1911)

Stevenson, J. and others, eds., *Calendar of State Papers, Foreign Series, of the Reign of Elizabeth* (Nendeln, Liechtenstein, 1966)

Stevenson, J., ed., *The Correspondence of Robert Bowes of Aske, Esquire, The Ambassador of Queen Elizabeth in the Court of Scotland* (Surtees Society, 1842)

Stuart, J., ed., *A Breiffe Narration of the Services Done to Three Noble Ladyes by Gilbert Blackhal Preist of the Scots Mission in France, in the Low Countries and in Scotland 1631–1649* (Spalding Club, 1844)

Stuart, J., ed., *Extracts from the Council Register of the Burgh of Aberdeen 1570–1625* (Spalding Club 1848)

Talbot, C., ed., *Miscellanea Recusant Records* (CRS, vol. 53, 1960)

Teulet, A., ed., *Relations politiques de la France et de L'Espagne avec L'Ecosse au XVIème siecle* (Paris, 1862)

Thomson, J.M., and others, edd., *Registrum Magni Sigilii Regum Scotorum* (Edinburgh, 1984)

Thomson, T., ed., *The Historie and Life of King James the Sext* (Bannatyne Club, 1825)

Thomson, T., ed., *A Diurnal of Remarkable Occurrents that have passed within the country of Scotland, since the death of King James the Fourth till the year 1575* (Bannatyne Club, 1833)

Thomson, T., ed., *Acts and Proceedings of the General Assemblies of the Kirk of Scotland from the year M.D.LX* (Bannatyne Club, 1839–45)

Thomson, T., ed., *The History of the Kirk of Scotland by Mr David Calderwood sometime minister of Crailing* (Wodrow Society, 1842–9)

Thomson, T., and Innes, C., edd., *The Acts of the Parliaments of Scotland* (Edinburgh, 1814–75)

Tierney, M.A., ed. *Dodd's Church History of England* (London, 1839–43)

Usherwood, S., ed., *The Great Enterprise: The History of the Spanish Armada* (London, 1978)

Young, W.J., SJ, ed., *Letters of St. Ignatius of Loyola* (Chicago, 1959)

Secondary Works

Anson, P.F., *Underground Catholicism in Scotland 1622–1878* (Montrose, 1970)

Anson, P.F., *The Catholic Church in Modern Scotland 1560–1937* (London, 1937)

Anstruther, G., OP, *The Seminary Priests, A Dictionary of the Secular Clergy of England and Wales 1558–1850, I, Elizabethan* (Gateshead, 1968)

Aveling, J.C.H., *The Jesuits* (New York, 1982)

Bangert, W.V., SJ, *A History of the Society of Jesus* (St Louis, 1972)

Bangert, W.V., SJ, *Claude Jay and Alfonso Salmerón* (Chicago, 1985)

Bangert, W.V., SJ, *Jerome Nadal, S.J. (1507–1580): Tracking the First Generation of Jesuits*, ed. T.M. McCoog, SJ (Chicago, 1992)

Barrett, M., *Sidelights on Scottish History* (Edinburgh, 1918)
Basset, B., SJ, *The English Jesuits* (London, 1967)
Bellesheim, A., *The History of the Catholic Church of Scotland* (Edinburgh, 1887–90)
Bingham, C., *James VI of Scotland* (London,1979)
Bingham, C., *Darnley* (London, 1997)
Bolt, R., *The Mission* (Harmondsworth, 1986)
Bossy, J., *The English Catholic Community, 1570–1850* (London, 1975)
Bossy, J., *Under the Molehill: An Elizabethan Spy Story* (New Haven, 2001)
Brady, W.M., *The Episcopal Succession in England, Scotland and Ireland A.D. 1400–1875* (Rome, 1971)
Brigden, S., *New Worlds, Lost Worlds: The Rule of the Tudors 1485–1603* (London, 2000)
Broadie, A., *The Tradition of Scottish Philosophy* (Edinburgh, 1990)
Brodrick, J., SJ, *The Life and Work of Blessed Robert Francis Cardinal Bellarmine, S.J. 1542–1621* (London, 1928)
Brodrick, J., SJ, *Saint Peter Canisius* (repr. Chicago, 1998)
Brodrick, J., SJ, *The Progress of the Jesuits* (1556–1579) (repr. Chicago, 1986)
Brown, W.E., *John Ogilvie: An Account of his Life and Death* (London, 1925)
Burton, J., *History of Scotland* (Edinburgh, 1905)
Campbell, T.J., SJ, *The Jesuits 1534–1921* (New York, 1921)
Cameron, J., *James V: The Personal Rule 1528–1542* (East Linton, 1998)
Caraman, P., SJ, *Henry Garnet 1555–1606 and the Gunpowder Plot* (London, 1964)
Carrez, L., *Catalogi Sociorum et Officiarum Provincae Companiae Societatis Jesu* (Châlons sur Marne, 1897–1914)
Cockburn, J.H., *The Medieval Bishops of Dunblane and their Church* (Edinburgh,1959)
Collins, T., *Martyr in Scotland, The Life and Times of John Ogilvie* (London, 1955)
Cowan, I.B., *The Enigma of Mary Stuart* (London, 1972)
Cowan, I.B., *The Scottish Reformation* (London, 1982)
Cowan, I.B., and Shaw, D., edd., *The Renaissance and Reformation in Scotland: Essays in honour of Gordon Donaldson* (Edinburgh, 1983)
Davidson, G., *A Dictionary of Angels* (New York, 1967)
Delattre, P., SJ, ed., *Les Establissement des Jésuites en France depuis quatre siècles* (Enghien, 1949–57)
Dictionary of National Biography, edd. L. Stephen and S. Lee (London, 1908–12)
Dictionary of Scottish Church History and Theology, edd. N.M.de S. Cameron and others (Edinburgh, 1993)
Dictionnaire d'Histoire et de Géographie Ecclèstiastique (Paris, 1912–90)
Dilworth, M., *The Scots in Franconia: A Century of Monastic Life* (London, 1974)
Donaldson, G., *All the Queen's Men: Power and politics in Mary Stewart's Scotland* (London, 1983)
Donaldson, G., *Scottish Historical Documents* (Edinburgh, 1974)
Donaldson, G., *The Scottish Reformation* (Cambridge, 1960)
Donohue, J.W., *Jesuit Education: An Essay on the Foundations of its Idea* (New York, 1963)
Dowden, J., *The Bishops of Scotland* (Glasgow, 1912)
Durkan, J., and Kirk, J., *The University of Glasgow 1451–1577* (Glasgow, 1977)
Durkan, J., and Ross, A., *Early Scottish Libraries* (Glasgow, 1961)
Eco, U., *Foucault's Pendulum* (London, 1990)

Edwards. F., SJ, *The Jesuits in England from 1580 to the present day* (Tunbridge Wells, 1985)

Edwards, F., SJ, *Robert Persons: The Biography of an Elizabethan Jesuit 1546–1610* (St Louis, 1995)

Elder, J.R., *Spanish Influences in Scottish History* (Glasgow, 1920)

Evennett, H.O., *The Spirit of the Counter-Reformation*, ed. J. Bossy (Notre Dame, 1970)

Fichter, J.H., SJ, *James Laynez, Jesuit* (St Louis, 1944)

Foley, H., SJ, *Records of the English Province of the Society of Jesus* (Roehampton-London, 1877–84)

Forbes, F.A., *Leaders of a Forlorn Hope: A Study of the Reformation in Scotland* (London, 1922)

Forbes, F.A., and Cahill, M., *A Scottish Knight-Errant: A Sketch of the Life and Times of John Ogilvie, Jesuit* (New York, 1920)

Forbes Leith, W., SJ, *Pre-Reformation Scholars in Scotland in the XVIth Century* (Glasgow, 1915)

Forrester, D., and Murray, D., edd., *Studies in the History of Worship in Scotland* (Edinburgh, 1996)

Fouqueray, H., SJ, *Histoire de la Compagnie de Jésus en France des origins à la suppression (1528–1762)* (Paris, 1910–25)

Fraser, A., *King James VI of Scotland and I of England* (London, 1977)

Fraser, A., *Mary Queen of Scots* (London, 1981)

Fraser, A., *The Gunpowder Plot, Terror & Faith in 1605* (London, 1996)

Fraser, W., *The Book of Carlaverock* (Edinburgh, 1873)

Froude, J.A., *History of England* (London, 1870)

Fülöp-Miller, R., *The Power and* Secret *of the Jesuits* (New York, 1930)

Futrell, J.C., *Makng an Apostolic Community of Love: the Role of the Superior according to St. Ignatius of Loyola* (St Louis, 1970)

Giblin, C. *Irish Franciscan Missions to Scotland 1619–1646* (Dublin, 1964)

Goodare, J., *State and Society in Early Modern Scotland* (Oxford, 1999)

Goodare, J., and Lynch, M., edd., *The Reign of James VI* (East Linton, 2000)

Graham, R., *John Knox: Democrat* (London, 2001)

Guilday, P., *The English Catholic Refugees on the Continent, 1558–1795* (London, 1914)

Gwynn, A., *The Medieval Province of Armagh 1470–1545* (Dundalk, 1946)

Hamilton, D., *The Healers: A history of medicine in Scotland* (Edinburgh, 1987)

Harrison, B. A., *A Tudor Journal: The Diary of a Priest in the Tower 1580–1585* (London, 2000)

Hasler, P.W., *The History of Parliament, The House of Commons, 1558–1603* (London, 1981)

Hay, M. V., *The Blairs Papers (1603–1660)* (London, 1929)

Haynes, A., *The Elizabethan Secret Services* (Stroud, 2000)

Haynes, A., *The Gunpowder Plot* (Stroud, 1994)

Hewitt, G.R., *Scotland under Morton 1572–80* (Edinburgh, 1982)

Hicks, L., SJ, *An Elizabethan Problem: Some Aspects of the Careers of Two Exile Adventurers* (London, 1964)

Hollis, C., *A History of the Jesuits* (London, 1968)

Holmes, P.J., *Resistance and Compromise: The Political Thought of the Elizabethan Catholics* (Cambridge, 1982)

Houston, R.A., and Knox, W.W.J., edd., *The New Penguin History of Scotland from the*

Earliest Times to the Present Day (London, 2001)
Hughes, P., *Rome and the Counter-Reformation in England* (London, 1942)
Hume Brown, P., ed., *Collected Essays and Reviews of Thomas Graves Law, LLD* (Edinburgh, 1904)
Jones, M.D.W., *The Counter-Reformation: Religion and Society in Early Modern Europe* (Cambridge, 1995)
Kelly, J.N.D., *The Oxford Dictionary of Popes* (Oxford, 1986)
Kirk, J., *Patterns of Reform: Continuity and Change in the Reformation Kirk* (Edinburgh, 1989)
Lacouture, J., *Jesuits: A Multibiography* (Washington DC, 1995)
Lang, A., *A History of Scotland* (Edinburgh, 1902)
Law, T.G., *A Historical Sketch of the Conflicts between Jesuits and Seculars in the Reign of Elizabeth* (London, 1889)
Lee, M., *Great Britain's Solomon: James VI and I in His Three Kingdoms* (Urbana, Ill., 1990)
Lee, M., *John Maitland of Thirlestane and the Foundation of Stewart Despotism in Scotland* (Princeton, New Jersey, 1959)
Lennon, C., *An Irish prisoner of conscience of the Tudor era; Archbishop Richard Creagh of Armagh, 1523–1586* (Dublin, 2000)
Lennon, C., *Sixteenth Century Ireland: The Incomplete Conquest* (Dublin, 1994)
Lewis, J.E., *Mary Queen of Scots: Romance and Nation* (London, 1998)
Letson, D., and Higgins, M., *The Jesuit Mystique* (Toronto, 1995)
Loomie, A.J., SJ, *The Spanish Elizabethans: The English Exiles at the Court of Philip II* (London, 1963)
Louthan, H., *The quest for compromise: Peacemakers in Counter-Reformation Vienna* (Cambridge, 1997)
Lynch, M., *Edinburgh and the Reformation* (Edinburgh, 1981)
Lynch, M., ed., *Mary Stewart, Queen in Three Kingdoms, IR*, 38 (Edinburgh, 1987)
Lynch, M., ed., *The Oxford Companion to Scottish History* (Oxford, 2001)
Lynch, M., *Scotland: A New History* (London, 1991)
MacDonald, A.A., and others, edd., *The Renaissance in Scotland: Studies in Literature, Religion, History and Culture* (Leiden, 1994)
Mackay, D., *In My End is My Beginning, A Life of Mary Queen of Scots* (Edinburgh, 2000)
MacLean, D., *The Counter-Reformation in Scotland, 1560–1930* (London, 1931)
Maclean-Bristol, N., *Murder under Trust: The Crimes and Death of Sir Lachlan Mor Maclean of Duart 1558–1598* (East Linton, 1999)
MacPherson, H., *The Jesuits in History* (Edinburgh, 1914)
McCluskey, R., ed., *The Scots College Rome 1600–2000* (Edinburgh, 2000)
McCoog, T.M., SJ, ed., *English and Welsh Jesuits 1555–1650, Part II: G-Z* (CRS, 1995)
McCoog, T.M., SJ, ed., *The Reckoned Expense: Edmund Campion and the Early English Jesuits. Essays in Celebration of the First Centenary of Campion Hall, Oxford (1896–1996)* (Woodbridge, 1996)
McCoog, T.M., SJ, *The Society of Jesus in Ireland, Scotland and England, 1541–1588: 'Our Way of Proceeding?'* (Leiden, 1996)
McCrie, T., *Life of Andrew Melville* (Edinburgh, 1824)
McRoberts, D., ed., *Essays on the Scottish Reformation, 1513–1625* (Glasgow, 1962)
Marren, P., *Grampian Battlefields* (Aberdeen, 1990)

Marshall, R. K., *John Knox* (Edinburgh, 2000)
Martin, A. L., *Henry III and the Jesuit Politicians* (Geneva, 1973)
Martin, A. L., *The Jesuit Mind: The Mentality of an Elite in Early Modern France* (Ithaca, New York, 1988)
Mattingly, G., *The Defeat of the Spanish Armada* (Harmondsworth, 1962)
Meyer, A.O., *England and the Catholic Church under Queen Elizabeth* (London, 1916)
Moore, B., *Black Robe* (London, 1994)
Mullan, G.D., *Episcopacy in Scotland: The History of an Idea 1560–1638* (Edinburgh, 1986)
Mullett, M.A., *The Catholic Reformation* (London, 1999)
Murdoch, S., *Britain, Denmark-Norway and the House of Stuart 1603–1660* (East Linton, 2000)
New Catholic Encyclopedia (Washington, 1967)
Oliver, G., *Collections Illustrating the Biographies of the Scotch, English and Irish Members S.J.* (Exeter, 1838)
O'Malley, J.W., SJ, *The First Jesuits* (Cambridge, Massachusetts, 1995)
O'Malley, J.W., SJ, and others, edd., *The Jesuits: Culture, Sciences and the Arts, 1540–1773* (Toronto, 1999)
O'Malley, J.W., SJ, *Trent and all That: Renaming Catholicism in the early modern era* (Cambridge, Massachusetts, 2000)
Patterson, W.B., *King James VI and I and the Reunion of Christendom* (Cambridge, 2000)
Paul, Sir J. B., ed., *The Scots Peerage* (Edinburgh, 1904–14)
Philippson, M., *Histoire du règne de Marie Stuart* (Paris, 1891)
Piaget, E., *Histoire de l'establissement des Jesuites en France (1540–1640)* (Leiden, 1893)
Plowden, A., *Danger to Elizabeth: The Catholics under Elizabeth I* (London, 1974)
Plowden, A., *The Elizabethan Secret Service* (Hemel Hempstead, 1991)
Pollen, J.H., SJ, *The Counter-Reformation in Scotland* (London, 1921)
Pollen, J.H., SJ, *The English Catholics in the Reign of Queen Elizabeth: A Study of Their Politics, Civil Life and Government* (London, 1920)
Pollen, J.H., SJ, *The Institution of the Archpriest Blackwell* (London, 1916)
Pritchard, A., *Catholic Loyalism in Elizabethan England* (London, 1979)
Ronan, M.V., *The Reformation in Dublin 1536–1558* (London, 1926)
Sanderson, M.H.B., *Mary Stewart's People* (Edinburgh, 1987)
Schurhammer, G., SJ, *Francis Xavier: His Life, His Times* (Rome, 1973–82)
Scott, H., ed., *Fasti Ecclesiae Scoticanae* (Edinburgh, 1915–50)
Scott-Moncrieff, G., *The Mirror and the Cross, Scotland and the Catholic Faith* (London, 1960)
Shaw, D., *The General Assemblies of the Church of Scotland 1560–1600* (Edinburgh, 1964)
Simpson, R., *Edmund Campion* (London, 1896)
Smout, T.C., ed., *Scotland and Europe 1200–1850* (Edinburgh, 1986)
Sommervogel, C., and de Backer, A., *Bibliothèque de la Compagnie de Jésus* (Paris and Louvain, 1890–1960)
Spottiswoode, J., *An Account of all the Religious Houses that were in Scotland at the time of the Reformation* (Edinburgh, 1824)
Stafford, H.G., *James VI of Scotland and the Throne of England* (New York, 1940)
Starkey, D., *Elizabeth: Apprenticeship* (London, 2000)

Stevenson, D., *Scotland's Last Royal Wedding: The Marriage of James VI and Anne of Denmark* (Edinburgh, 1997)

Thompson, F., *Saint Ignatius Loyola* (repr. London, 1962)

Torrance, T.F., *Scottish Theology from John Knox to John McLeod Campbell* (Edinburgh, 1996)

Tyrie, A., *The Tyries of Drumkilbo, Dunnideer and Lunan* (Glasgow, 1893)

Tytler, P.F., *History of Scotland* (Edinburgh, 1841–3)

Warden, A.J., *Angus or Forfarshire, the Land and People* (Dundee, 1882)

Watt, D.E.R., ed., *Fasti Ecclesiae Scoticanae Medii Aevi ad annum 1638* (Edinburgh, 1969)

Watt, D.E.R., and N.F. Shead., edd., *The Heads of Religious Houses in Scotland from Twelfth to Sixteenth Centuries* (Edinburgh, 2001)

Waugh, E., *Saint Edmund Campion, Priest and Martyr* (repr. Manchester, 1996)

Webster, Rev. J.M., *Dunfermline Abbey* (Dunfermline, 1948)

Willson, D.H., *James VI and I* (New York, 1967)

Wodrow, A., *The Jesuits: A Story of Power* (London, 1995)

Wolfe, M., *The Conversion of Henri IV: Politics, Power and Religious Belief in Early Modern France* (Cambridge, Massachusetts, 1993)

Wormald, J., *Court, Kirk and Community, Scotland 1470–1625* (Edinburgh, 1981)

Wormald, J., *Mary, Queen of Scots: Politics, Passion and a Kingdom Lost* (London, 2001)

Articles

Anderson, W.J., 'Abbe Paul MacPherson's History of the Scots College Rome', *IR* , 12 (1961) 3–172

Anderson, W.J., 'Narratives of the Scottish Reformation, I. Report of Father Robert Abercrombie, S.J. in the year 1580', *IR*, 7 (1956), 27–59

Anderson, W.J., 'Narratives of the Scottish Reformation, II: Thomas Innes on Catholicism in Scotland, 1560–1653', *IR*, 7 (1956), 112–21

Begheyn, P.J., SJ, 'Nik Goudanus en het Godsdienstgesprek van Worms in 1557', *Archief voor de Geschiedenis van de Katholieke Kerk in Nederland,* XI (1969), 12–53

Brown K.M., 'The Making of a *Politique*: The Counter Reformation and the Regional Politics of John, Eighth Lord Maxwell', *SHR*, LXVI (1987), 152–75

Burns, J.H., 'Nicol Burne: plane disputation bayth at libertie and in persone', *IR*, 50 (1999), 102–26

Chadwick, H., SJ, 'The Arm of St. Ninian', *Transactions of the Dumfries and Galloway Natural History and Antiquarian Society,* Third Series XXIII, 30–5

Chadwick, H., SJ, 'Father William Creichton, S.I., and a Recently Discovered Letter (1589)', *AHSI*, 6 (1937), 259–86

Chadwick, H., SJ, 'A Memoir of Fr Edmund Hay S.I.', *ASHI*, 8 (1939), 66–85

Chadwick, H., SJ, 'The Scots College, Douai, 1580–1613', *English Historical Review*, 56 (1941), 571–85

Clancy, T.H., SJ, 'The First Generation of English Jesuits 1555–1585', *AHSI,* 57 (1988), 137–62

Darowski, R., 'John Hay, S.J., and the origins of philosophy in Lithuania', *IR*, 31 (1980), 7–15

Davidson, P., 'Saint Mary, Queen and Martyr: An Alternative History of Mary Stuart', *History Scotland*, vol. 2 no. 1 (Jan./Feb. 2002), 32–7

Dilworth, M., 'Abbot Gilbert Brown, a sketch of his career', *IR*, 40 (1989), 153–8

Durkan, J., 'The identity of George Thomson, Catholic controversialist', *IR*, 31 (1980), 45–6

Durkan, J., 'Robert Wauchope, Archbishop of Armagh', *IR*, 1 (1950), 48–65

Durkan, J., 'Sidelights on the Early Jesuit Mission in Scotland', *Scottish Tradition*, XIII (1984–5), 34–45

Durkan, J., 'Two Jesuits: Patrick Anderson and John Ogilvie', *IR*, 21 (1970), 157–61

Durkan, J., 'William Murdoch and the Early Jesuit Mission in Scotland' *IR*, 35 (1984), 3–11

Hicks, L., SJ, 'The Strange Case of Dr William Parry', *Studies* (1948), 343–62

Mackie, J.D., 'Scotland and the Spanish Armada', *SHR*, XII (1914), 1–23

MacRoberts, D., 'George Strachan of the Mearns, an early Scottish Orientalist', *IR*, 3 (1952), 110–28

McCoog, T.M., SJ, '"Pray to the Lord of the Harvest": Jesuit Missions to Scotland in the Sixteenth Century', *IR*, 53 (2002), 127–88

McNeill, W.A., 'Scottish Entries in the *Acta Rectoria Universitatis Parisensis* 1519 to c. 1633', *SHR*, 43 (1964), 70–83

Meyer, A.O., 'Clemens VIII. und Jakob I. von England', *Quellen und Forschungen aus italienischen Archiven und Bibliotheken*, 7, 2 (1904), 268–306

Murphy, M., 'Robert Abercromby, S.J. (1536–1613) and the Baltic Counter-Reformation', *IR*, 50 (1999), 58–75

Rocca, J.L. La, SJ, ' "Who Can't Pray With Me, Can't Love Me": Toleration and the Early Jacobean Recusancy Problem', *Journal of British Studies*, vol. 23 no.2 (1984), 22–36

Sanderson, M.H.B., 'Catholic recusancy in Scotland in the sixteenth century', *IR*, 21 (1970), 87–107

Shearman, F., 'James Wood of Boniton', *IR*, 5 (1954), 28–32

Shearman, F., 'The Spanish Blanks', *IR*, 3 (1952), 81–103; 4 (1953), 60

Shearman, P.J., 'Father Alexander McQuihirrie S.J.', *IR*, 6 (1955), 22–45

Stevenson, A.W.K., 'Notice of an early sixteenth-century Scottish colony at Bergen-Op-Zoom and an altar there once dedicated to St. Ninian', *IR*, 26 (1975), 50–2

Verschuur, M.B., 'The Perth Charterhouse in the sixteenth century', *IR*, 39 (1988), 1–15

Wormald, J. 'Gunpowder, Treason and Scots', *Journal of British Studies*, vol. 24 no.2 (1985), 141–68

Yellowlees, M.J., 'Dunkeld and Nicholas de Gouda's Mission to Scotland, 1562', *IR*, 44 (1993), 48–57

Yellowlees, M.J., 'The Ecclesiastical Establishment of the Diocese of Dunkeld at the Reformation', *IR*, 36 (1985), 74–85

Zapico, D.F., SJ, 'La Province d'Aquitaine de la Compagnie de Jésus d'après son plus ancien catalogue (1566)', *ASHI*, 5 (1936), 268–92

Unpublished Theses

O'Donoghue, F.M., SJ, 'The Jesuit Mission in Ireland 1598–1651' (Catholic University of America, Washington, 1981)

Yellowlees, M.J., 'Dunkeld and the Reformation' (Edinburgh, 1990)

Index